Hanging Off the Edge —

Hanging Off the Edge —

✦

Revelations of a Modern Troubadour

Priscilla McLean

iUniverse, Inc.
New York Lincoln Shanghai

Hanging Off the Edge —
Revelations of a
Modern Troubadour

Copyright © 2006 by Priscilla McLean

iUniverse books may be ordered through booksellers or by contacting:

iUniverse
2021 Pine Lake Road, Suite 100
Lincoln, NE 68512
www.iuniverse.com
1-800-Authors (1-800-288-4677)

ISBN-13: 978-0-595-37548-6 (pbk)
ISBN-13: 978-0-595-67527-2 (cloth)
ISBN-13: 978-0-595-81942-3 (ebk)
ISBN-10: 0-595-37548-0 (pbk)
ISBN-10: 0-595-67527-1 (cloth)
ISBN-10: 0-595-81942-7 (ebk)

Printed in the United States of America

This book is dedicated to my husband Bart—
the other half of my soul

Contents

Preface xiii

Prologue 1

CHAPTER 1 Beginnings and Endings 3

- *1. "Perhaps I can begin…"* *3*
- *Saturday, Feb. 20, 1993* *8*
- *2. "My mother used to tell me…"* *11*
- *Monday, Feb. 23, 1993* *16*
- *3. "I remember my birth…."* *20*
- *Friday, Feb. 27, 1993* *29*
- *4. "Today a flower bloomed,…"* *40*
- *Wednesday, March 10, 1993* *50*
- *5. "About this time we moved again,…"* *53*
- *March 17&18, 1993* *57*
- *6. "To close this Section,…."* *67*

CHAPTER 2 Becoming 70

- *1. "In Old Wachusett's Shadow…"* *70*
- *Thursday, April 16, 1981* *75*
- *2. "End of 'observations on a winter's day'.* *81*
- *Monday, May 4* *87*
- *3. "In June 1965 I graduated…"* *96*
- *Thursday, May 14, 1981* *105*
- *4. "Indiana University offered…"* *113*

CHAPTER 3   The Composing Life 135

- *Credo*. *135*
- *1. "Variations & Mozaics On a Theme of Stravinsky"* *137*
- *2. "Interplanes for Two Pianos"*. *143*
- *3. "Dance of Dawn"*. *149*
- *4. "Beneath The Horizon I and III"* *159*
- *5. "The Inner Universe"*. *164*
- *6. "In Wilderness is the Preservation of the World"* *170*
- *7. "A Magic Dwells"*. *179*
- *8. "The Dance of Shiva"*. *184*
- *9. "Rainforest Images"*. *191*
- *10. "In The Beginning"* *198*
- *11. "Jambori Rimba"* *203*
- *12. "The Ultimate Symphonius 2000" and "MILLing in the ENNIUM"* *210*
- *13. "Symphony of Seasons" and The Future...* *213*

CHAPTER 4   Dangling Thoughts 223

- *1. Inside the mind of a (woman) composer* *223*
- *2. Studio and Touring Axioms* *229*
- *3. Dropping (famous) Names* *233*
  - 1. John Cage 233
  - 2. Henry Brant. 235
  - 3. Henry Cowell 237
  - 4. Pauline Oliveros. 238
  - 5. Vladimir Ussachevsky 240
  - 6. Morton Subotnick 242
  - 7. Vivian Fine 245
  - 8. Carter Harman 247
  - 9. Oliver Daniel. 250
  - 10. Moses Asch 252
- *4. To Borneo, with Love* *254*
- *5. Conclusion: On Being a Woman Composer* *259*

Listed Works of Priscilla McLean 263

Recordings and Music Publishers 267

Major Articles, Books, and Biographical Descriptions: 269

Musical Excerpts for Section THREE available free on the Web 273

Endnotes 275

Acknowledgments

I began writing this book twelve years ago, fitting in time between my duties as a troubadour, and my busy life as an American married woman in the 20th and 21st Centuries. At the end of 2002, after years of flagging uncertainty, I spent a month working on the third section of the book at The MacDowell Colony, Peterborough, New Hampshire, and the enthusiasm and confidence the writers had toward my readings fired me up to finish this book. Bless the MacDowell Colony—again!

Many thanks must go out to the several readers who red-penciled their way through my drafts, from first to last, making this book immeasurably better: Cynthia Peterson, Carol Hovland, Larry Austin, Lesley Wright, and lastly, my most vocal critic, Barton McLean. Thanks also go to my first cousin Dick Taylor for his interest in genealogy and his correcting and adding to the section about my ancestral history. And to his sister Helen Taylor Branch, who has become a close friend in the last few years, and who fleshed out some of my memories of my grandmother's life.

Because the focus of this book is on my composing/performing life, my extended family is mentioned only briefly at the beginning. I have not forgotten you all and extend thanks for your being there to keep me sane and connected to the world. I thank also my small village of Petersburgh with its spirited group of artists and nature lovers, and the Petersburgh Public Library for its total support towards all creative efforts, making this town in the mountains a wonderful place to reside and grow new music and artworks, along with the beautiful views.

Perhaps my biggest appreciation goes to all those friends and strangers who, over the decades, have believed in *The McLean Mix* and have hired us to perform, sometimes as many as seven engagements in any one venue over the years—this, in spite of very tight arts budgets and restrictions. And last, thank you, our Audience, who have allowed us to keep "humming our tunes" and kept us alive all these years. Without you, there would be no book!

Preface

Several years ago when I was a guest professor of music at the University of Hawaii, I taught a survey course about women in music. Specifically, it was about women composers, and when I reached the 300-year period from 1300 to 1600 A.D., I could find no information or examples of music by women (this has changed slightly). This Dark Ages period of history, along with the church composers, saw many troubadours, all male composer/performers who traveled from castle to castle. Women composer/performers lived in the castles as royalty and played their music on the premises, which was basically not preserved.

I began to realize that, echoing that Medieval period, very few books about today's classical women composers have been written, and virtually no notable autobiographies. It began to haunt me that, although many new books are gradually emerging containing biographical excerpts and short biographies, the women composers themselves are not enlightening the world about their own lives, which are surely different, sometimes quite so, than the lives of male composers.

I now feel that I may be able to contribute to filling this gap a little, as my life as a contemporary troubadour—composing, performing, traveling over the world from "castle" to "castle"—can not only enlighten but has also been full of adventures, some very strange indeed. I hope I can inspire other women to come forth with their own stories. If we do not speak, how is anyone to know?

Unlike those women composer/performers of royalty in the past, this book is an attempt to illustrate the struggles of a 21st Century woman to overcome probably one of the worst cultural and educational backgrounds of any classical composer, to pull herself up by her "bootstraps" while hoping to retain the joyeouse de vive of the early years of her life: to become two persons—one, the classical Artist—and two, the "down-to-earth" woman who can relate to world under the Ivory Tower, because she was born far underneath.

Prologue

Two roads diverge
in a yellow wood,
A branch stems from
the lesser-traveled one...
A twig snakes out
from the tiny branch,
And hanging off the edge
Dangle..., I—
(Apologies to Robert Frost)

A terrifying wolf howl splits the air in the Alpena, Michigan, high school auditorium. "Oh, Hell!" a man's voice yells out, followed by suppressed giggling. On stage, I stare into the blackness menacingly, hissing the words of Carl Sandburg: "There is a wolf in me. Fangs pointed for tearing gashes, a red tongue for raw meat, and the hot lapping of blood..." On tape, the growl and frenetic buzz of honeybees plays along with synthesized instruments and strange musical sounds. More audience giggling is heard, and a palpable tension...

An old memory comes to mind as I dramatize and intone the next line of the graphic Sandburg poem called *"Wilderness"*—an image of a snowy night in a white-spired New England church—the lit sanctuary bestrewn with Christmas decorations and a tree covered with childrens' paper strings and balls, the pews full of heavy-coated festive people watching a trembling young school girl attempting to sing *"O Holy Night"* while standing in the choir loft—my first vocal solo, my pre-adolescent voice struggling for the high notes, whispery, feathery, the patient sanctuary of parents and children smiling up benevolently, tolerantly, safely...

The next morning in Alpena, lying exhausted in bed in yet another strange (but oh so familiar) motel room, I think about my life—our lives, Bart's and mine. Touring from town to town—no health insurance, no steady jobs, no children, no insurance of any kind against the dark forces in the world...two middle-aged Babes in Toyland, playing our own musical toys, dependent upon the goodwill of the world to hire us, to be interested in our strange, exotic music and message…I wonder, "How did I ever arrive at this point, from that safe choir girl of long ago, the comfortable American Dream future I had planned for myself—schoolteacher, mother, Pillar of the Community, owner of a nice suburban ranch house in New Hampshire—none of which ever came to pass?"

It is hard, when actively creating music and art and touring full-time, to find time to examine one's life. But perhaps the history of Alzheimer's disease that runs through my mother's side of my family has spurred me on to remember as much as I can while I still am able! Lao Tsu, the great Chinese philosopher who wrote The Tao te-Ching once said, "Sanity is a haircloth sheath/With a jewel underneath…", and that is one's core, including all those unique happenings played out in one's life. And I am discovering that it is wonderful fun to visit these thoughts and old memories, because all of one's moments on this earth, which includes also the pain and agony, are precious jewels that fit only our own personal belt wrapped around us, and are our gifts from life.

1

Beginnings and Endings

1.

Perhaps I can begin by trying to connect with the dark fog-bound hazy horizon that is my little-known ancestral past. Perhaps the common ground of creative influence is the flair for the dramatic that ran through both branches of my family. Back in Liverpool, England, my mother's maternal grandfather, Frank Maude, was related to Cecil Maude, the famous English actor. And on my father's side, his paternal grandfather, also English in origin, was married to Anna Custer, a close relative of General George Custer. One would be led to believe that all this related "fame" would have rubbed off on these grandfathers, but in truth, Frank Maude emigrated to Massachusetts to work in a paper mill, while Carrington Taylor, a devout Mason, was a bookkeeper in the millinery business in Philadelphia.

The Taylor side of Dad's family arrived in America on the ship with William Penn, and settled in the Philadelphia area. Dad's mother's ancestors, also from England, settled near Pittsburgh and were Quaker farmers. Mary Jones, my grandmother (who always called herself Marie), when she was twenty-five, while working on the Quaker family farm, now outside of Philadelphia, alternating with an office job in the city, became attracted to a young traveling candy salesman. Conrad Taylor was charming, devilish, free-wheeling, womanizing, and dangerous, and she loved it—for awhile. They eloped in 1902, committing two sins in the Quaker religion—eloping and marrying outside the faith—which caused an unhealable breach in her family. Living in Collingdale with his father Carrington, Conrad Taylor delivered candy to local stores by day and was a pharmacist at night, while Marie began a family. In 1905 my father, Conrad Jones Taylor was born, and three years later his brother Richard (Dick).

1905 was a placid time in the U.S., but baby Conrad was born with a deadly disease called in those days "cholera infantum", a foggy title for something that resembled Lou Gehrig's Disease in reverse. Too weak to move and predicted dead within weeks, Conrad was carried around in a basket for two years, crying in pain constantly, then spent his time on the floor, unable to walk, resentfully watching others' lives go by. Life was hard, as his mother and father increasingly were uncomfortable with each other. Smoking and drinking were forbidden in the Taylor house; his father spent more and more time away.

Conrad Sr.'s philosophy of wives being "in the kitchen and pregnant" was intolerable to Marie. Not allowed to work now that she was married, she was expected to stay at home and raise a large family. But with a live-in (unfriendly) father-in-law, two growing boys—one severely crippled, and with no money for extra help, she was unwilling to bring yet another child into the world. With no family support or religion, now that she was ostracized from the Quaker church, and afraid to turn to the unhelpful medical world, Marie secretly aborted herself with a hatpin each time she became definitely pregnant, a situation never revealed to her husband (or to me until I was an adult). There were no "women's rights" in those days, only the will of the individual, which has run as a steel wire throughout my family line.

Finally, at the age of eight, my father had developed enough strength to lift himself off the floor and walk, and to attend school. Watching everyone rushing around while towering above a person, who has been suffering a lifetime of fragile weakness, can mold a rather strange personality—perhaps one would sense that the world is a hostile place, that one's weakness is permanent (perhaps if not physically, then psychologically), that somehow one is guilty of great sin to have had this fate, that if one ever did get off the floor, he would yell, run, rip and tear the world to shreds, laughing in a high, defiant wild voice! That just about sums up my father, who was always a mixture of great affection and love, powerful anger and resentment, wild drunken gaiety, barroom jokes, lonely sad reflection, dogged determination, and impatient rebellion.

Having been deprived of normal peer relationships for so long, he almost immediately turned to alcohol, a remedy already well established by his father. Dad told me many times of an incident when he crawled out of the schoolroom window with a chum, and the two of them, jaunty "Our Gang" caps perched on their heads, downed a fifth of whiskey while leaning against their classroom wall. He was about eleven years old.

At twelve years of age, another calamity happened: Conrad came down with "Bright's Disease", which landed him, having gone blind, in the hospital, fighting for his life for six months. Gradually the disease wore off, but his eyes were damaged for life. This was 1917, the year before the worst influenza epidemic in U.S.

history, when over a half million people died (twenty million worldwide), during World War I, and his father became frantically busy filling (and inventing) prescriptions, his pharmacy job—which was his night job after selling candy on the road all day—consuming every free minute. Absolutely exhausted from his efforts, Conrad Sr. took ill after the epidemic was over, and died of colon cancer at the age of thirty-nine, in 1920. Conrad Jr. was pulled out of school (having been there only for a few years) to become the man of the family at the age of 14, working for several years at John Wanamaker's Department Store in Philadelphia.

Dad loved music, and taught himself the bagpipes to play in the Wanamaker Band, which marched on Saturdays, and later he joined an ad hoc Dixieland band to play drums. He had grown into a tall, curly black-haired fair-skinned man, very slender, with dark bushy eyebrows and cunning dark but smiling eyes—very attractive to women. He supported his mother, who now ran a boardinghouse in Philadelphia. Wanting to be on his own, Conrad joined the Army, and in 1925, after basic training at Fort Drum, NY, was sent to aid in the opening of the Panama Canal. My yellowed brittle photographs show a thin Cary Grant-like scowling man on a horse, desultorily aiming a rifle. His photos always were without the eyeglasses he would have to wear for the rest of his life. With glasses he resembled a young professor, and indeed put himself through night extension courses at the University of Pennsylvania, studying draftsmanship, after he was pulled out of the Army on a hardship discharge filed by his mother—to continue supporting her and his brother—after only six months of service.

I learned in more detail about those six months without his mother, expounded by Dad who rarely talked about his early life. He used to love to tell about the tropical nights scratching in the hot army cots while lying on straw mattresses, of nightly squashing of bedbugs, of drowning table cockroaches in beer, of digging endless latrines (which seemed to be his principal job in the army), of the dark and heavy hot jungle the corps cut its way through, which was everywhere, all pervading, all stifling, crawling and seething with insects, snakes, and abundant wildlife in this virgin territory. I think my fascination with rainforests began in those summer nights in the late 1940's, sitting out on our backyard porch for a breath of cool air while listening to Dad make us squirm with his tales of the Panama jungle in 1925.

◆   ◆   ◆

There is a large photograph in my house of my mother's family, who are all sitting, formal and uncomfortable in front of their 22-room house on South Street in Fitchburg, Massachusetts. In the midst of this extended group of relatives sits a big woman with a very commanding face—Great Grandmother Dickinson, the matriarch. She had emigrated up from the South after the Civil War, and while working in the paper mills married Cecil Maude, giving him eleven children and living to be ninety-nine years old. My mother, her grandchild, is also in the photo sitting cross-legged beside her twin sister Alice, both about twelve years old. My grandmother Cora Maude was fascinated by family genealogy, and managed to trace back seven generations, which ended in England for all her relatives. Her husband, my grandfather Frank Lesure, also from English stock had come from Canada. Frank eventually owned a laundry in Fitchburg, ran for mayor, and became a local VIP.

I marvel now at this restricted English heritage. It was no accident that these ancestors married only other English like themselves. Even in my youth, the message was clear in our house: you *must* continue the lineage. After all, the English (at the turn of the century) practically ran the whole world, and must be the *superior* nationality! My father's brother Dick Taylor married (eloped—again, to escape the stultifying mores of the era) an eighteen-year-old girl of Irish heritage, causing a giant rift in the Taylor family, which has been left to my generation to change (which it has been doing with a vengeance). I look in the mirror and see an Englishwoman staring back, but my youngest relatives are now Polish, Egyptian, part-Jewish, Irish, and oh-yes, some English as well!

One bright May morning in 1907 two baby girls were born to Cora and Frank Lesure, fraternal twins, one blond and the other dark, each with the characteristic English "Bob Hope"-style nose. The Lesure family lived for decades in the stately gothic house just described, overlooking the small but bustling city of mills and seven steep hills, and scores of semi-segregated ethnic communities: Finnish, French, Italian, Irish, Greek, Italian, and the older English community who largely made up the upper echelons of Fitchburg society. Cora was an imperious lady of leisure, who acted the role of mayor's wife, despite Frank's one failed attempt at securing the office.

The twins Grace and Alice were best friends to each other, except Alice was born weak, and struggled through myriad childhood diseases of the day, including rheumatic fever which ultimately damaged her heart. By high school, Alice was a year behind, and was sent to the Cushing Academy for private schooling. In her class was the actress Bette Davis, who was protected and guarded from ordinary student life, and whisked away for acting purposes, and Miss Davis was only known vaguely by her classmates. By this time, ten years' older sister Etheline had graduated from college, spent a year in Paris, and was teaching French in high school in Wilmington, Delaware. She was also an accomplished organist.

By 1924 Grace was the youngest graduate in her Fitchburg High School class, a tallish willowy, pale blond thin-lipped girl of sixteen, having skipped two grades, not out of natural genius but from overcrowded class conditions. This made her shy and awkward socially for many years, and she spent her time mainly with her sister and one or two girlfriends. Grace had been trained to do the housework her mother hated, and had come to the idea that she was not overly talented in anything, but could serve people and make them happy.

Grace had read to and tended her sister Alice, and decided to devote her life to teaching children. She entered Fitchburg Normal School never having had a date or a "beau", never having uttered, or hardly encountered, a swear word, and waiting for life to become more than a daydream. Always an energetic person, Grace became editor of the college newspaper, and performed in the Glee Club, Debating Club, Drama Club, and several other organizations as well. By her third year, the normal school began a new four-year program, to come into line with the private college requirements. She was one of the two four-year graduates of that first class of 1928, and at the age of twenty, she took the boldest step yet of her young life. Grace who had never been away from her family, walking daily to high school and college for eight years, applied for a teaching job out of state-in Orient Point, Long Island—a dangerous and unheard of disloyalty to the Commonwealth of Massachusetts (which was suffering from a severe teaching job shortage at the time). Thus she was dressed down and chastised by the horrified college president in his office. She fled the room in tears. How could she by so ungrateful, so disrespectful? Her mother responded to the news of the teaching position in Long Island by taking to her bed in total despair (more of losing a maid, perhaps, than a daughter).

I always felt proud of my mother when I heard this story—her courage to pursue her dreams, even when chastised by family and community. Ahead for Grace lay the most exciting adventure yet—a tiny two-room schoolhouse at the tip of Long Island, a many day's journey from Fitchburg, all children handled by two young green school marms, who had sworn an oath of allegiance to teaching: to remain unmarried and uncorrupted, and to give their lives to the noble mission of molding young minds and character.

SATURDAY, FEB. 20, 1993

We have set up our basic concert equipment in our electronic studio, which resides in an ancient bedroom at the street front of our 1790 rented farmhouse, and is furnished with tables, tape recorders, synthesizers, sound equipment, mixers, and computer, plus miles of wires covering three walls from floor to ceiling. The third and fourth walls, varying in their state of decrepitude, have 170-year-old hand stenciling on them—fanciful cornucopias, fruit, and in orange, brown, yellow, blue, and red hues, painted as early "wallpaper" by two maiden ladies whose ancestor built this house. Our stark modern black and white rectangular electronic paraphernalia forms a jolting contrast of centuries and opposing ways of life with these delicate unctuous hand-drawn stencils so carefully and decorously created centuries ago. Composing something new in this room is always a philosophical experience, with the ghosts of bygone creation ever reminding one of the end result of all human endeavor—art, life, or long thoughts.

Puffs of snow splatter against the small distorted farm windows, slightly moving the fragile red and white speckled gingham curtains, the wind somehow filtering in through the thin uninsulated walls. The room, always unheatable in spite of a large basement oil furnace and woodstove sitting in the nearby dark living room, is an immutable 60 degrees, and I shiver, as I lay out an array of million-year-old glacial rocks collected a few summers ago in Alberta, Canada, discovered while hiking near a glacier in the mountains above Hamilton Lake one evening in 1987. As we walked over a giant bed of prehistoric shale deposits, we heard musical tinkles with each step. Fascinated, we knelt down and had a "jam session" playing our knuckles against several different rocks, all sounding different clear tones. Somehow the 500 million-year old shale layers produced air pockets, which allowed the rocks to ring, producing hauntingly beautiful pungent percussive sounds. Enchanted, we immediately filled up our day packs, and carrying the heaviest ones in our arms, climbed the long many-miles trek back to our Honda and campsite, all the while dreaming up a way to perform these as soon as they were safely back in New York State. Now I carefully place about fourteen of the clearest ringing rocks on a music stand topped with foam-covered wood strips, to aid their ringing voices.

Bart stands walled in by keyboards and digital music processors, and he warms up on a weird-looking Dr. Seuss-like instrument that I developed and he perfected—a clariflute, which has a clarinet mouthpiece fastened to a wooden recorder body by a small section of green garden hose and black duct tape. It squawks as he coaxes vibrating tones out of it, the sound resembling a cross between an Australian black swan (the impetus for its invention) and an unhappy oboe. I shiver once more and smile. Today we will rehearse for the final time our "Gods, Demons, and the Earth" concert, the cornerstone piece being Bart's *"Earth Music"*, which is a tour de force of my singing and dramatic narrating and use of almost my whole vocal range—using extended vocal techniques, plus playing small native round ceramic Ethiopian flutes called ocarinas, and striking the glacial rocks as Bart performs on the keyboard and clariflute, and manipulates twenty electronic switches going between the processors and the synths. It is a "solidified" improvisation, performed by us so often that it has congealed into a classical piece almost as determinate as one completely written down. Yet our "scores" have only words—no music notes at all. The words I dramatize are from Cecil Wright, a turn-of-the-century photographer and nature-lover, and begin:

"A tree retains a deep serenity. It establishes on the earth not only its root system but also those roots of its beauty and its unknown consciousness. Sometimes one may sense a glisten of that consciousness, and with such perspective feel that (hu)man(kind) is not necessarily the highest form of life...Music arrives in the deep hum of river and wind through the forest, swelling the chorus joining its universal breath."[1]

As we rehearse I am equally thrilled and saddened, caught up in the joy of the music and yet knowing that only we and no one else will ever perform this piece...Perhaps we know *"Earth Music"* as well as any music in the classical literature, and have presented it to thousands of people worldwide, yet in twenty years it will rest as dry and forgotten as a buffalo skull on a lonely Arizona hillscape. It is a startling concept that everything we create in this ancient (American) farmhouse bedroom will never be as "immortal" as this early 19th Century wall stenciling we stare at daily, yet it too is cracked and crumbling, soon to disappear...

Sunday, Feb. 21, 1993

A wall of snow and wind obliterates the winding narrow dirt road leading from Petersburgh, a 200-year old ancestral Dutch village laid along two main highways, which converge on a weather-beaten out-of-business general store housed in a gray asphalt-shingled, flat roofed round two-story building, which sits daringly in the middle of the road and has been crashed into by several large trucks careening down the steep hill towards Williamstown, Massachusetts, just over the Taconic Mountains to the east of town. Turning left from the store is a small street with leaning ancient narrow houses resembling Yorkshire, England except for their wooden rather than stone exteriors. The road winds over a small stone bridge overhanging a boulder-strewn rushing mountain stream, and continues left up a long steep Hill Hollow Road, which at the present moment looks more like a lost cattle path in Alaska, the surrounding wall of mountains whitely glaring down on the cold huddling New England farmhouses and their centuries-old red barns.

After two miles the unfortunate traveler will come to a strange sight—two parka clad grim people carrying a parade of gray metal boxes, suitcases, and weirdly shaped objects covered in plastic, and stuffing them into a ridiculously small gray Honda wagon, which sits like a vulture, all wings extended, gathering for flight. The Nor'easter whaps another blinding swirl of zero-degree snow against the carnival, as the two figures frantically scramble to fill the car from floor to ceiling, the seats in the back removed for more space. Words as blue as their faces are ejected as they sweep out the intruding snow, which cares not a whit about electronics, autos, or silly people who dare to plan cross-country tours from this God-forsaken piece of earth deep in the bowels of New York State! The neighbors, who are stoking their wood stoves at this minute and wondering why they have not yet moved to Florida, have given up commiserating about this sad nomadic band, and have long-since congratulated themselves on never having had to feel the poisonous urge to create music and to drag it annually all over the place, sometimes even further into the evil grasp of Winter's fingers...

◆　　　◆　　　◆

I have wondered for years why a non-commercial artist does what (s)he does, that is, create a work that does not function in the practical world, and not only entertains but also stirs something in the soul as well as intellect. A composer is even a greater mystery—why compose black dots or wiggles on paper (or on a computer), to be translated into sound by either an acoustic or an electronic instrument (if the composer is fortunate enough to cajole a performer to give up his (her) scarce time to commit such an act), and then listened to. Often there is a solid reason, such as a residency with an orchestra or as musical director with a dance troupe, which involves a salary or commission and has a definite performance as the end result, with paying audience attending. But what about the composer who writes with only a faint hope of a future performance, with no commission or obvious external stimulus? This extends also to the creator of electronic sound, who may have no opportunities for it to be heard past a few friends, quietly-suffering family, and colleagues, and then to have the piece sit unperformed and unheard for several years or forever after? This is not a rare occurrence. Every composer I know has written music like this. But why?

Several years ago at a music conference, some composers were asked by Ev Grimes, radio announcer at the University of Kansas, why they composed. Karl Korte of Austin, Texas, said, "It seems ridiculous in this mercantile society, but somebody has to do it." The most interesting answer was by Canadian composer Murray Schafer. He stated, "Because if I didn't compose, I would—die." How astounding that is—why die over something that isn't wanted, has no use, gains little money, and is actually shunned by most of society? Why *do* we compose?

Answering for myself, I compose to visit a sacred space inside me that opens into a special enchantment, that shares for a few flawed moments the feeling of the original Creation, of something beautiful culled from diffuseness. Carl Sandburg reached his "archangels" through his "invisible chariots", the poems that ride him up to the "tall sky" as he wrote: "I have seen these chariots. So have you, or you have missed something...We are riders of chosen chariots..."

His poem *"The Isle of Patmos"*,[2] from which I just quoted, inspired my second large electronic work *"Invisible Chariots"*, as I rode my inner musical ideas, flying in the sky, not knowing where they were going next, but holding on for dear life and relishing the ride! A composer must deeply trust her(his) own inner unexpressed direction, helped along by the intensive training and musical discipline of her lifetime.

If I did not compose, I would live, but sadly and with little vigor, and eventually I would end my grieving and would be intensely into creating something else—art, poetry, photography, video—because I am a chameleon at heart. The soul can be accessed in many ways, by many mirrors, but my clearest and happiest mirror right now is music.

◆   ◆   ◆

2.

My mother used to tell me how she was standing in her classroom teaching in Orient Point, Long Island, when the fire inspector arrived, and upon seeing all ages of children crowded together on benches and chairs, filling the entire room, including the aisle areas (there were sixty children), he asked, "Is this an assembly?" "No," she replied, "just my ordinary class!"

The long ensuing silence was a tinkling of a very large bell which clamored for consolidating the overpopulated pioneer one-and two-room schoolhouses of the tiny communities into the now common regional schools, ending forever a unique era of many grades of children learning together, stoking the room's wood stove, reciting the Lord's Prayer, and with the older children tutoring the younger in the few basic subjects while the teacher, hardly paid and female, tried to hold order and not run out the door screaming. Grace's first teaching job lasted for two seasons of extremely long hard hours, with nights spent sleepily correcting papers or card playing with girlfriends in a wind-blown quaint village that only came alive for tourists in summers, but was as quiet as a sea corpse during the school year.

Not regretfully, Grace was forced to find another teaching position after that year of the fire inspection, as the two-room schoolhouse was shut down. She chose a total opposite—a new junior high school just opening its doors on the edge of the exciting, booming city of Philadelphia. Her mother had hoped that this folly of her daughter's working so far away from her family would be rectified with the closure of the school, and that Grace would return home to again shoulder the household's responsibilities as she *should* and not only during summer vacations, which were spent in Fitchburg.

Cora was horrified by this latest move, and again took to her bed ill, venting her miseries on the care-taking oldest daughter Ethel, who also returned each summer to the ancestral home from her Delaware teaching job. Only Alice had not returned, having found a full-time position in the New York City Public Library. So at the end of the summer of 1930, full of renewed guilt, fear, and secretly joyful anticipation, Grace Lesure took the train to Philadelphia.

The year is 1933. A young blond woman, sweaty from after-school tennis, bounds into the local news store for a newspaper and a few candies. She smiles and chats familiarly with the tall young man with black curly hair and bushy eyebrows behind the counter, who is speechless with a fluttering joy at her innocent, cheerful, fresh beauty. His life has been far from innocent…Stone drunk at one of the many wild Prohibition parties he had attended, he had eloped with a drunken flapper girl several years before. He had been but twenty-two, and six months later his pretty but bored young wife, sharing unhappily the "love-nest" apartment with his disapproving mother, ran off with the mailman, and the ill-fated marriage was annulled. His life has been dark indeed, with little education, poor jobs and Depression lines and an ever silently chastising mother, and has left him defenseless against this sunny woman.

Grace is attracted to this handsome fellow who seems too bright to be selling newspapers, and who has passed her many times carrying groceries to his probable wife in the apartment just above hers. This day, however, he turns pink, summoning his inner courage, and fumblingly asks her to go to a movie, as his meager paycheck allows. The revelation of mother instead of wife in his apartment sends clouds of laughter and relief from Grace, and the courtship that lasted 57 years has begun.

1933 in Philadelphia was the height of the depression, and many men were reduced to selling apples on street corners and standing in long relief lines for food. Conrad and Grace's courtship had the contour of a Utah mountain—very quickly did they become acquainted through long walks, movie dates, and sitting together in the evenings, and almost immediately they fell in love, each personality complementing the other's, but then a long hiatus occurred before the next step could be reached: Conrad could not find a decent job. The work available was either menial or part-time, and he had had several unsatisfactory jobs in the past. Grace, on the other hand, had taken a teacher's vow of chastity, would lose her job if she married, and would not be allowed to take another teaching position in the whole U.S.! So they continued to be suspended in a dating position while he lived with his mother and spent evenings with Grace. In the summer of 1934, Grace went home to Fitchburg and had many earnest discussions with her father, who agreed to take Conrad into his laundry business following several weeks of intensive training at laundry school, to be financed by the generous father.

I have my mother's diaries of this period, and her passion and joy at this time explodes from every page. "I love him, I love him, I love him!!!" she would squeal, and the wait of two years to marry must have seemed unending. I was never told whether the long wait until marriage ended twenty eight years of virginity or not, but despite their mutual passion (and Conrad's previous history), I would think only that the opportunities were not very frequent, with her fiancée's apartment guarded by Mother on one side, and her apartment by two school teacher housemates on the other. After Conrad attended the preparatory school and was accepted into the family business, Grace reluctantly resigned from her teaching. On July 20, 1935 they were wed in a quiet ceremony in Grace's Fitchburg home, her twin sister Alice as bridesmaid, and Alice's husband of one year, Gordon Tripp, acting as best man. Although Conrad was quakingly nervous but sober at the ceremony, Gordon had to be trundled out of the attic, stone-drunk, and deeply involved in a poker game. He managed to stand up during the proceedings, but the ring had to be pried out of his clutched hand.

So Conrad and Grace Taylor with mother Marie moved to Fitchburg, Massachusetts into a small apartment, and a difficult peace ensued. I would love to say they lived "happily ever after", but life is unfortunately much more complicated than that, of course. For three years they were a three-way team of sorts. Conrad was groomed for eventual taking over of the laundry business. Grace, escaping her mother-in-law's complete domination of the apartment and missing her beloved school children, became bookkeeper in her father's office in the laundry. Marie, as she had done for so many years, acted as housekeeper and cook for the small family. Marie kept a one-year diary also of this time, and hers reveals a very bitter and unhappy woman, envying the new marriage, and resenting any time her son and wife spent without her. She cleaned and cooked ferociously. She opened their mail. She read Mom's diaries. She accused Grace of hiding the negative statements she assumed had been written about her. Conrad had unfortunately become the husband Marie always wanted, but not to her! Grace's diary becomes more guarded and formal at this point, aware of prying eyes.

But the three-way pull had not manifested itself yet in palpitant dissatisfaction, and this was relieved, after years of hope and frustration, by the birth of a boy on March 7, 1938. Even the long-awaited joy of birth proved almost to be a disaster, as the nine-pound baby was a breach birth, and at one point the doctors told Conrad that either mother or son would not live. When both survived, a chilling day came when the medical establishment tried to force Grace's body, exhausted and without milk, to breast feed, almost starving the baby to death. This torture was finally stopped by Conrad, who was irate and grieving over so much misery and pain.

The baby turned out to be a wonderful tonic for all. For over a year my brother Conrad Jr., an incredibly beautiful child, with curly carrot-red locks and gentle happy manner, charmed and united the family. Grace quit her bookkeeping job to tend the baby. Frank Lesure felt it was time to retire and hand over the business to his son-in-law, of whom he was very fond, as they not only worked together but played golf together on Saturdays. It was the stepping-stone up to gentility for Conrad who was proving to be bright, aggressive, and reliable in the business.

But if there is such a phenomenon as a malevolent guardian angel, then it had chosen this family to persecute. In order to qualify to take over the laundry and be properly certified, in 1940 a state examination had to be passed. What it involved, I will never know, but it must have called upon some kind of advanced formal school training, and study as he might, Conrad, who had had only five years of basic schooling and a night course in draftsmanship, could not pass the exam. This was a disastrous blow to his whole future plans and his fragile self-esteem. Everything fell apart. Heartbroken and crushed, losing his sure key to affluence and prosperity, Conrad took to drinking heavily, spending his evenings in bars to avoid the sad, angry faces of wife and mother. Grace, equally distraught and incredulous, was left alone with Mother Taylor and infant Conrad Jr.. In a desperate attempt at renewal of spirit, the family rented a run-down house, and with Conrad still mostly absent, the two women inexhaustibly repaired, cleaned, painted, and moved in, while the fiery-haired toddler played among the paint cans and boxes.

Grace, not completely recovered from the birth, gradually became thin and wan, literally working herself into collapse. Her parents became extremely alarmed, and an ultimatum was given from Frank Lesure to Conrad: Frank would finance Grace's removal to a tuberculosis sanitarium for a complete rest, and Conrad would give up the nightly bingeing, or Conrad would lose his job, wife, and child. This was the wake-up call needed, and a skeletal trembling Grace was sent to the Burbank Hospital tubercular sanitarium unit for six weeks. During this time of absence, my brother Conrad Jr. grew very close to his grand-mother, a friendship which remained between them and which I envied later. Grace's healthy return was to a briefly harmonius household and a meek, chastised (sober) husband.

By the summer of 1941, the tenuous peace of the small Taylor family was again evaporating. Grace had grown so tired of her mother-in-law's constant accusations, self-pity, and dominating ways that she begged Conrad to find a separate apartment for Marie. An opportunity came when they decided to rent a cottage at a local lake for two weeks. Conrad surreptitiously found a very pleasant three-room apartment, and on pretext of looking after the laundry business, he gradually moved all of his mother's personal belongings there during the two weeks everyone was at the lake cabin. When vacation time was over, and the family drove back to Fitchburg, he drove Marie to the new flat and said, "This is your new home now. All of your things have been moved here. It is time for Grace and my son and I to be by ourselves, and for you to have your own place. We'll all be happier."

Marie was utterly incredulous and shocked. Hadn't she *saved* the family, bringing up the child when Grace had weakly succumbed to such exhaustion that she had to be institutionalized for six weeks? Wasn't Marie the Rock that sustained the three of them, as she had been all her adult life to her husband, and then after his death, to her two children? Furious and grieving, she went into her new apartment, and taking a razor blade from the bathroom cabinet, sliced both wrists. She then called Conrad and told him that she was in the act of killing herself. Conrad and Grace raced back to the apartment in terrified trepidation, to find the mother-in-law lying unconscious in a pool of blood, and then quickly binding up the wrists, called an ambulance. Later in her hospital room wrapped in large white mitts, Marie heard the unwelcome news from Grace. "You know, as soon as you recover, you are going back in that apartment. You are not living with us anymore, so give that idea up."

My mother's voice was hard and cold when she related this to me. That woman, she said, would try anything to get what she wanted! How unhappy and desperate Marie must have felt, how abandoned, losing her bond with the grandson and her lifetime companion in her son. Hatpins and razors defined the sick shadow of death hovering over Marie's adult life, as she fought to control her unwanted destiny.

After that episode, she reluctantly accepted her new circumstances, and a great joy and relief came into the young Taylor family. They had given up hoping for another child, as it had been six years since marriage, and three since their only son was born. But that autumn's happy relief worked its magic, and Grace became pregnant again. My grandmother never quite forgave me for being the proof of their happiness away from her, and from my first memories a simmering hostility shaped my relationship with her until she was in her late eighties in a nursing home and grateful for my visits.

Monday, Feb. 23, 1993

7 a.m.: Bart is shoveling our driveway from the foot of new snow while I finish packing the suitcases. By 9:30 a.m. we are on the road to California, heading yet again over the New York and snowy mountainous Pennsylvania roads, this stretch of highway having earned the distinction of being labeled "the worst highway in America" by the American Automobile Association. We drive on potholed and rutted roads between endless long dirty trucks sporadically vomiting mudslush on our windshield, along with the continuing snowstorm, up over the top of the ridge, and past the town of Lord's Valley, an alarmingly bleak and barren frozen plateau. Near the summit of the mountain range, I begin to repeat the 23rd Psalm, distractedly wondering if this is how the town earned its name. My rising panic hangs suspended through Scranton, and not until the wall of darkness descends at 7 p.m., near Clarion, when a very bad snow squall strikes, do I resort to alternating between The Lord's Prayer and hysterically screaming (my

usual reaction to total whiteouts in heavy traffic on major highways at night), punctuated by Bart's frustrated cursing at my outbursts. We can go no further tonight and pull into a small motel in Clarion. After unpacking we eat at a deserted Rax restaurant, where we and a harried policeman are the only customers. None of the local people are outside tonight.

Tuesday, Feb. 24

Sitting behind a jack-knifed truck on Rte. 80 for an hour while it is removed, I reroute our trip away from the Cleveland area. The snow has lessened to squalls, and we crawl to Cincinnati. Tonight we gratefully stay at the home of Tim and Lisa Kloth. Tim is a young composer, good friend, and has arranged our performance tomorrow at the Seven Hills private high school where he teaches music. As we and Tim are gathered laughing and reminiscing around the hors d'oeuvres and beer, Lisa, not expected, rushes in, announcing that her overnight business trip to Cleveland has been canceled due to the eighteen-inch blizzard now happening there! I close my eyes and see snow blowing over the windshield, Honda overturned in a ditch by Cleveland...

Wednesday, Feb. 25

Our first performance of the tour finds us nervously connecting wires and readying for a high school assembly, not a common experience for us, as our music is not considered to have "mass appeal". But this is not an ordinary high school. During the assembly we talk about our music, about being living classical music composers and life on the road, and play tapes. I sing "Wilderness" to an enthralled group of teenagers, who flock to the stage to buy records and tapes afterwards. We are stunned and pleased by their enthusiasm, and feel again the conviction that our music, labeled "complex, contemporary, electronic, etc." is capable of being enjoyed by a much vaster audience than we are generally allowed. I have always wondered where the missing "wire" is which would connect our music to all those who would love it, and if we will ever find it...

After the assembly we hurriedly pack up, canceling plans to spend a second delightful evening with Tim and Lisa, and hustle away in the cold sunny afternoon to outrun the next snowstorm rolling in. Around 11p.m. we pull in tiredly to a Budget Host Inn with kitchenette in Greenville, Illinois. One hour later we hear pelting snow, lift the motel curtain, and see a second blizzard arriving. I silently wonder if this is the ill-fated beginning of our last tour, and today's high schoolers will be the last group to have seen us alive...

Thursday, Feb. 26

Lying in our snowed-in motel room, I awake to a strange tingling in my jaw and neck, on the right side of my face, with my right ear aching. Instantly I bolt upright, fully alert and terrified, remembering the month-long agony of facial shingles I had in 1988, which left much of the right side of my face superficially numb, with underlying pain sensitivity, and both right eye and ear permanently damaged. The shingles virus, born from earlier chicken pox, sits and waits for its human victim to become weakened by illness or stress. When I asked my eye doctor if I could ever have another attack, Jim Fitzgerald only smiled and stated, "You'll never have any trouble again if you go to bed at eight o'clock every night and live a placid, unemotional life. Then I guarantee you'll be fine." So this morning in 1993, lying here in the midst of the second blizzard of our just-begun tour, watching the piling snow rattle against the cold motel room window, I gently touch my aching face and wonder…

Waiting until noon for the storm to diminish, I stretch my legs, weaving along the highway edge and briefly into a snowy field, sinking to my thighs in the wet snow. After twenty minutes of falling down and freezing, I return to the motel room and pack, pushing worries about my face away. Continuing our journey, our Honda bumps and grinds, finally stalling in the middle of a busy intersection one mile from the motel. Not a good omen! One service station and some dry gas later, and we have recovered enough to nose out to Rte. 74 and the ensuing blizzard…A few miles later the bridge to Rte. 70 is closed, so we drive a three-times longer route around St. Louis at 35-40 mph., amid "dead bodies" of trucks, cars in snow drifts, giant snow piles…The exit lanes are all impassable, so we find ourselves circling round St. Louis like an excruciatingly slow airplane, wondering if we will ever leave the St. Louis area or if this a circle of Dante's *"Inferno",* where we will wander, round and round, lost composers never reaching their concert hall until Time itself slows…

Finally an exit onto Rte. 70 is clear, and we cheer, that is, until we actually *see* the road we are now on. The ride on Rte. 70, before they close the highway, is…eventful. I am driving now, reciting The Lord's Prayer and alternately the 23rd Psalm again, my favorites during times of total insane panic. At one point heavy fog, blowing snow, and lines of trucks make visibility zero, and I begin hyperventilating. There is no extra time allotted for bad weather in our schedule, so on this 3,000 mile trip to California, we must drive ten hours a day at 60 mph. to make our installation next Tuesday. We've been averaging one state a day, and are now, it seems, down to one city a day! Bart begs to take over, but my hands are death-gripping the steering wheel, and I will never let go. If I am going to die, I want to be responsible for the final flip over the edge! Finally at 5 p.m. we reach Columbia, Missouri, and exhausted, with great relief pull off, just before they close down the highway. Now we are 120 miles short of our calculated driving mileage.

We find a nice motel, and to relieve the built-up tension I romp in the drifts, kicking and screeching, with an obsessive desire to have fun and gaiety. Bart is catching up on all the weather news on the cable TV. After a nice restaurant meal we rent a video—"Sister Act" with Whoopi Goldberg, eat junkfood, and relax. I have decided to live every minute away from the highway in a blissful state, in case there is no future existence after this tour. I block any uneasy questions about a career that demands, for so little financial reward, this kind of dangerous driving—have been blocking it for twelve years, much like the overly optimistic little boy who digs joyously in a giant pile of horse manure, exclaiming, "There must be a pony in here somewhere!"

◆   ◆   ◆

Where do Art and Life separate? An ingredient necessary for all Art is Time. Time to think, ruminate, wonder, to reach inside and chance the formlessness residing there that boils with all of the good ideas, time to trust that one can make a good work of art, worth the sacrifice to family and community, time to be alone. For most of this country's population, struggling through the Depression and world wars, all their psychic energy went into building a better world for their families, and Art seemed only justified as relief from the real business of work or as pleasant entertainment during the church service. They could not conceive of spending selfish time creating art works that were not immediately serviceable, and passed these judgments on to their children.

Today, the beginning of the twenty-first century, there again is a separation in value judgments toward Art, as the children and grandchildren of the Depression-age families work overtime to achieve a frenzy of consumerism, to fill all the ghost-needs of the early generations with multiple automobiles, TVs, computers, and thousands of material items inconceivable to their ancestors. Things we consider necessities now were not given even a passing thought then, such as the incredible, sophisticated medical advances changing daily, a four-year college for the children, trips abroad for high school children as well as whole families, video games that alone would have paid for a whole week's family food. The gap between my parents' civilization and mine takes on mythical dimensions, and their struggle has become part of our collective unconsciousness, perhaps fueling our endless desire to own and obtain, and to deaden the inevitable pain that arises from pillaging our natural resources, inside and outside of ourselves.

The consumer list goes on and on, and has added a new web of complexity to our lives today, all of which must be financed, which was not a consideration in past history. Where is there any time for Art in this new world? How can a man or woman, after working two-three jobs and trying to unveil the computer's mysteries on weekends after taking the children to their many lessons and activities, even care to listen to a thoughtful, riveting piece of classical music, let alone a new work which seems incomprehensible to tired ears, and especially, to find the energy and confidence to compose such a work oneself?

Is it any wonder that the classic arts are in crisis in this country, with the crisis spreading throughout affluent parts of the world today? Is there any mystery as to why granting agencies and arts patrons are disappearing, and governments are cutting back on the pitifully small music fellowships only recently funded in this U.S.? Why do the people need more aggravation in the form of High Culture when one can daily rent or borrow an infinite number of videos of all movies, past and present—enough entertainment for several lifetimes—or tune to the endlessly playing popular culture which pervades every part of our lives? When do we have time to think? We create a wall of constant sound or video action to deaden any tranquility that must arise before any expansion to creative thought can be attained. To create the empty spaces that will allow for a blossoming of spirit, the artist must simplify, simplify, and quiet down both the cluttered life and yammering voices. And when that is accomplished (a difficult task!) how can we point the way for a (steadily shrinking) audience to do the same?

◆   ◆   ◆

3.

I remember my birth. This may be hard to believe, but I remember being suspended in an infinitely calm, peaceful grayness, and then suddenly exploding out into startlingly bright lights and several happy sets of eyes looking down and cheering. The sound seemed deafening, as loud cheers and unintelligible speech roared from their faces. My first audience, and I was a standing ovation! I remember thinking the equivalent of "Wow!" Perhaps that successful performance began a small seed in my mind for the future, who is to say not?

I was born at 1 a.m. on May 27, 1942, in the Lucy Helen Hospital, actually a birthing center, in Fitchburg, Massachusetts. Contrary to the traumatic birth of my brother, I, as my mother said, "just slipped out" after only a few minutes in the delivery room. After all, it was time. My mother had had a ten-month pregnancy, and I was to establish another lifetime characteristic of mine—taking my time about the really important things. I was very tiny, at 5 1/2 pounds. My mother said that I could fit in the palm of her hand! My father was not in the delivery room, nor in the waiting room. He had had a State Guard meeting that night, which always ended with revelry in bars, and my mother called her own taxi, prepared her suitcase, and walked unaided into the hospital.

I believe character traits and lifelong interests are formed in very early baby-and-childhood. When my mother and I came home from the hospital, my brother told me much later, "You were the worst thing that had ever happened to me. I hated you!" Grace's diary writing ends shortly after this. She was dismayed but not surprised at her son's hostility, as he had been Child King of the Taylor family for four years. My earliest memory of him is complete adoration, as when at the age of one-and-a-half years I toddled after him around the wide lawn, calling "Brubby! Brubby!" while he whined, "Mom, can you get rid of her?" I was born a fireball, never resting, always running and getting into everything, causing grief on all sides.

From the beginning I was an insomniac. When I was six months old and placed in my crib upstairs in my room at night, I would joyously ride the crib around the wood floor, propelled by banging my head against the back of the crib, and squealing delightedly at the loud squawks the crib wheels gave off as it lurched in all directions. This must have been my earliest musical influence, as I have held a lifelong love of bubbly, squealy, bright sounds, as anyone could guess who has listened to my electronic music!

My parents were at wit's end, as these squealing, thumping episodes would occur for hours every night when they were trying to relax by the radio, and even into their own sleep times. Finally, after months, they confronted the doctor and asked for sleeping pills to quiet me down, Dr. Simmons wisely refused to give medication, and suggested putting a thick rug under the crib. "She won't hurt her head banging it. No baby will do that," he reassured. So my pre-electronic "performances" were suddenly curtailed, and I took to screaming for several nights until I gave it up. There is a valuable lesson in discovering when a performance has gone on too long…

Another fascination I had was with climbing to high places. Before I could walk, I was found clinging to the top rod of the living room drapes, and another time my mother found me sitting on top of the upright piano, laughing and waving. Once when I was two we were picnicking at Caugshall Park in Fitchburg, and my parents turned around to find me gone. After much frantic searching through a large dense area of pine woods, they spotted me sitting atop a large granite boulder up a steep hill, again waving and shouting, "Hi! Hi!"

I alternated climbing heights with running away. This was not done out of any desire to rid myself of my family, but from an intense curiosity about what lay beyond my immediate eyesight. My mother would invent ever more sophisticated knots in the rope she had tied around my waist, which was attached to the backyard fence. Then as she would run to answer the phone I would avidly untie myself, and by the time she returned I would be gone. A born wanderer. I remember one occasion, upon just moving to Buffalo, New York, while the family was coping with cartons and piles of furniture, when I, at the age of three, decided to explore the neighborhood. I walked down the sidewalk, and on and on, finally crossing a busy four-lane highway and hiking to the other side of town several miles away, when I started to become apprehensive. Not only was I lost, but I had no idea where I lived or what the address was—similar to one of those common nightmares.

So I did the best thing I could envision. I spotted a woman resting on her front stoop, and went to her, crying. At this time I was very small, had curly platinum blond hair and big hazel eyes, and she melted instantly. She took me into her kitchen and fed me chocolate ice cream, and in a half hour or so my parents arrived with the police, wringing their hands. It was my first solo adventure, and I loved it!

My first memorable accident came when I was a year old. Sitting in a high chair in our kitchen in Leominster, the town next to Fitchburg, I leaned too far forward and tipped the whole thing over, falling on my head. I can still hear my mother's agonized voice crying, "Priscilla!" and can remember wishing that she didn't sound so terrified. That flash "photocopied" the whole kitchen scene in my memory, with the family gathered round the white table at breakfast, and the red and white gingham curtains fluttering by the open windows. I wasn't hurt, although I screamed long and heartily.

Into that same kitchen at night came a tall elderly man I was very fond of. He would open the door, crow with delight in seeing me, always there at the door for him, and throw me high into the air. I loved the flying motion, and I loved this kind, affectionate man. Sadly, by the time I was less than two years old, my grandfather Lesure had died from cancer, and these few times at the door in the kitchen are the only experiences I ever remember with a grandfather.

I have two more very early memories, which shaped my life. One came on my third birthday, with Grandmother Taylor—I have no early memories of Grandmother Lesure, and assume she never visited us, although they lived only a few miles away. The two grandmothers disliked each other intensely, and Mom's mother also did not like Dad. On my birthday we were in a sunny room with colorful wrapped presents, perhaps a dining room. My grandmother presented me with a large rubbery baby doll with bright blue glass eyes. The doll interested me not at all, but I wanted to pluck those eyes out and roll them around on the floor. Also, I was very curious as to how they were held on to the doll's face, so I began trying to pull the eyes off the doll. Grandmother Taylor (Nana, as we called her) was horrified, and snatched the doll away from me, and I felt the first of innumerable clouds of disapproval descend around me from her and my mother. I busied myself with a colored dots game instead, as the two women fussed about how malformed I was to be more interested in colored cardboard dots than an expensive lifelike baby doll! I remember feeling distinctly different from my family even at this young age, somehow harboring a different and wicked view of what was interesting and important in life, a view that would set me apart from my family and early friends forever.

All my attempts at satisfying a technical curiosity about how things were put together and functioned were crushed. I was continuously given baby dolls, doll clothes and doll houses, and firmly instructed to play with them. No radios or watches to dissect, no Lego toys or building blocks, no small workshop or lab to try experiments in or put things together. This training was of course the norm for the age–1945 to 1955–and I settled in on teaching my dolls in an imaginary classroom, as that was acceptable play.

Finally, when I was seven years old I begged my mother to make me a boy doll—there were none in the stores—so I could have more variety. I vividly remember her sitting by me, sewing the rag doll every night after work, while I painted on the face. I loved that doll, and he became my ticket to all those adventures locked away from a girl. His name was Jim Brown, he was twenty-five years old and a detective, and "Jim" and I concocted an endless series of adventures and travels together for years. Our house had no television set at that time, so the adventures were more in the line of fairy tale stories and radio dramas. I kept my beloved Jim doll until he disintegrated back into rags just a few years ago.

In my third year I became very ill with swollen tonsils and adenoids, and could hardly breathe or talk. I was placed in the hospital and operated on, and can remember being very alone and terrified, screaming for my mother all night. She was not allowed to stay overnight in the hospital room with me. At home the night after the operation, I became direly ill from a throat infection, as I had been released too soon from the hospital, and my temperature shot up to 106 degrees. I vividly remember my mother holding and rocking me in her arms as I cried in the small bedroom with the crib. Suddenly I was outside the second story room looking in on a small blond child, red-faced and crying, being held and comforted by her very worried mother. I thought, "Poor little girl—she's going to die." I remember the window, the dark winter night, the warm lit up scene with mother and child. This is as far as the memory goes, and it took me over forty years to realize that I had experienced an out-of-body episode. The memory seemed so natural, I had thought nothing of it. However, I have never doubted the continuation of the "I" behind the self, or as it is called, the immortal soul, and this early experience may be the reason why.

In 1944 Frank Lesure, my beloved grandfather, died. As soon as she could, Cora sold everything and accompanied by her oldest daughter Ethel, newly widowed and acting as caretaker, moved permanently to Florida, a distance so great in those days that no family member could visit them. Cora and Ethel lived a quiet monastic existence of genteel poverty until my grandmother died, about ten years later.

When Grandmother Lesure sold the family laundry business, it was bought by a company who sought to hire all new managers, but retained the workers. Conrad, my father, found himself out of a job, and his brother Dick, who had been recently hired as a worker, was soon promoted to almost the same managerial position as Conrad. This was ringing irony to Conrad, who had worked so hard to attain this position, almost becoming the new owner. A hard Diaspora of several years followed, as Dad, now with strong skills as a laundry manager, sought new positions wherever he could. He quickly discovered that these were all family-run businesses, inherited from father to son, and the only available openings were temporary fill-ins for the absent sons who were abroad, fighting the long, drawn out World War II.

So our family became semi-nomadic, following Dad across the country, living for a year or two or a few months in quick rental houses, which were readily available everywhere. Dad would go ahead, working for a few weeks, then send for us, who would hurriedly pack, be taxied to the nearest railroad station, and with all our worldly belongings be glided, often overnight, to the next town with the job. I have memories of being very ill with diarrhea when I was three and riding the train to Buffalo. The Lone Ranger was at the train station signing autographs, and my brother ecstatically ran over to him amid a huge crowd of youngsters while I tearfully and bitterly was forced to remain lying on the seat, near the toilet room.

Dad's heart was with the workers, even as a manager, and once he was fired for organizing a worker's revolt against the unfair management—not a wise idea in his position! As the owners' sons returned, he would have to seek new laundries, which unfortunately were beginning to be challenged by the advent of the home washing machine, and were just starting to downsize, until by the late '40s, the old all-encompassing laundry was gone, and only the dry cleaning and self service that we have today remained.

Now all this was hard enough, with all this chasing after the temporary position, and Grace not being allowed to teach, when a new malevolent twist of fate occurred. When I was three, Dad, after consuming a large quantity of liquor, was unsteadily driving home alone late on a very black night, and perhaps falling asleep, careened off the road and into a telephone pole. There were no seat belts in those days, but he seemed to emerge unhurt, with only a demolished car. But a few weeks after this incident, he began to have ominous problems with his spine. His feet went numb; he had trouble walking. A saga of trips to various doctors ensued, but they could find nothing wrong. Meanwhile he kept working, as always.

We moved from Buffalo to Williamsville, NY, to Council Bluffs, Iowa. Conrad and I would walk to school each day, a distance of two miles, he in the third grade and I in kindergarten, and I would come home alone after class. A dramatic occurrence happened at this time, and was the first of several dangerous situations I would encounter throughout my life of being a female. There was a disturbed, very beautiful blond boy of the same age as I who also attended kindergarten. The school had grown so that two sessions of classes met in the same room, one in the morning, and one after lunch. Mine was the morning class, and this boy would wait, hidden in a clump of bushes by the sidewalk, and pounce on any small girl walking by. All of the girls were terribly afraid of him, as he would grab and choke them, inflicting misery if not a lot of pain. It was my turn one morning, when I found myself walking alone. First he lunged out of the bushes and made hand gestures, finally grabbing me, but I fought and ran away sobbing. Unlike the other girls, I reported him to my mother, who decided that immediate action was necessary.

She insisted on a meeting of the school board, and brought me along to describe what had happened, in order to have this child taken out of the kindergarten and given some psychiatric help. But I took one look at the long table of elderly male eyes staring at me and couldn't speak. My mother pleaded with me:

Please speak up for yourself! My throat was paralyzed, but I finally managed to describe the choking gestures the boy made, but forgot to mention the actual choking…They decided I was over-dramatizing, and it was resolved to place me in the afternoon session, but to do nothing about the offending child. Mom was sad and angry, and she taught me a lesson I have never forgotten: "Always speak up for yourself and demand justice. Only *you* are in charge of your life. Without courage you will always be a victim. Do not sit on the sidelines, and do not be afraid of speaking the truth!" I often wonder what crimes that boy has committed since. Is he a serial killer, never stopped by anyone? A child molester? Ah but for my shy childish silence he could have been helped, maybe saved…But perhaps, I will hope, he was.

In the summer after my episode with the boy molester our family moved to Ypsilanti, Michigan. I remember the summer we arrived, with the country in the middle of a severe drought. We had rented a small, mostly unpainted house across from a gas station, on the edge of town. Mom would hang out clothes on the clothesline in back of the house, next to a dirt road, and the dust would blow over the clothes from the autos on the road. One day there were giant brown "grasshoppers" all over the clothes, and I ran in to Mom. She came running out, and shouted, "Oh! These are locusts! We are having a locust attack!" So we hurried inside as they pelted the windows and crawled all over everything for a while, then flew away. Mom was standing by her filthy clothes in tears, saying, "I hate this place! When are we ever going home?!?"

In the autumn I attended the first grade, and a miracle happened. We children were shown a giant poster with a drawing of two children on it and words underneath: Dick and Jane. We all recited the words together, after the teacher. Then the next page: "Look! See Dick run!" with the picture of the boy running. This went on, with Jane running, then Spot the dog playing, etc. Halfway through the first day's group rote recitation, having mastered several days of drill on the alphabet and phonemes, my mind had a huge flash—I *knew* how to read! Now I didn't need the teacher to say the words, I could read them myself! When she handed out the first readers that autumn day, I sat there and read the whole book, more excited than I had ever been in my whole life.

That afternoon I ran home from school. I remember crashing in the kitchen, and asking Mom if we had any easy books I could read. She led me to the attic, and there in a dusty bin was her first old reader, with antiquated stern-looking children and longer words. I sat there in the dim room, with my mother's help, and read the short book, which I refused to put down. Then I ran down the stairs and out onto the back porch, where Dad was reading the evening paper. "I can read!" I yelled excitedly. "Can I have part of the paper?" He looked at Mom, smiling derisively, and said, "Sure! Have the front page!" So I sat there on the porch, with the late afternoon sun streaming hotly in, and read, very slowly and with many missed words, the headlines and a few of the columns, sounding out all the words. I looked over to Dad's face, and he was almost in tears. "My God," he said, "She really *can* read!" I was never so proud as that shining day the words opened up to me.

It would be nice to say that I went on to higher and higher reading abilities, and combed libraries for all those books with magical words in them, but that never came to pass. Very soon after that day, we were notified that Conrad and I had been going to the wrong school, that our house was on the "wrong" side of the railroad tracks, and that we were to transfer immediately to the school on the poor side of town. My first day at this school was an education in reverse. The children were from deprived families, and the teacher, very young, had not the faintest idea on how to teach.

Reading was a disaster. They were just starting the Dick and Jane first posters, and I, in the other school, had gone through three readers already. I told the teacher that I had already read all the books, and she looked at me in disgust and said, "Well, I guess you'll just have to read them over again!" So for the next three months I stared dejectedly at the same readers, and my interest in reading slowly evaporated. I began to learn a lifelong lesson: never be too advanced or smart, because the world will resent you, and you will be punished by having to stand in place while the others are catching up. Better to stay back and slow down. My reading became picky, as I dawdled over the words to pass the time. And now, while I read extensively, it is still very slow and tedious.

I will not blame my parents for this, because at this time, their lives were in complete turmoil. I did not know that at this time my father was in frantic pain with his spine problems, and he had been advised to seek help from an experimental medical clinic at the University of Michigan. At this point he had given up working, and Mom found a job as a typist in an office in Ann Arbor. This must have been the lowest point in their lives, but I was, at the age of six, hardly aware.

The next months were a turning point in the family. Just before the operation, the doctors warned Conrad that the procedure was brand new, and that he may never walk again, and if he did, it would be with a cane and a limp. He had a slipped disk in his lower spine, a condition that had come as a result of the automobile accident, and that in the past meant an operation to fuse the two vertebrae together, resulting in a partially stiff spine and often paralysis. This time the university interns did not fuse the bones together, but I do not recall the procedure that was used, only that it was a total success. This was in 1947, when many new medical techniques had been learned because of the war casualties. Dad came home in a back brace, which he was supposed to wear for the next six months. Within a week he had stopped wearing it, and within two weeks he was carefully walking around the house. Mom wept for joy, and my admiration for Dad was immensely increased. For all his problems, he had more grit than anyone I have ever known.

With Dad home all the time and Mom working, I got to know him better, and to my amazement I discovered a gentle, shy man who had a tremendous sense of humor and liveliness, who was wonderfully affectionate, and who had decided to learn to cook by studying the cookbooks while Mom was working. Dad always related to people best when one-on-one, and often with my brother away on childhood pursuits and just myself at home, he became my friend. I helped him around the kitchen and became his assistant. One day I learned to tell time by asking every five minutes whether Mom would be home soon (she came home at 5 p.m.), as I watched the minute hand move around the numbers, thinking that each minute was an hour! When he laughed and explained the hour hand vs. minute hand, I instantly understood, with a kind of flash, and could tell time from then on.

At times I think back to this period and wonder what it would have been like to have books around the house, or a children's library to go to. The only music I ever heard came from the radio on the popular stations. The days of our owning a piano were long gone and we also did not go to church. These years were the bleakest of my life, but I was too young to know or to be disturbed by it. Meanwhile, the euphoria of Dad's successful operation was barely subsiding when we were evicted from our house. The owner had decided to sell, and we were handed an eviction notice and given thirty days to move out.

This was a devastating blow. With the war over and the population increasing, rental houses were unavailable. Money had run out, and my parents decided to cut their losses and return to Fitchburg, jobless. We boarded an overnight train, and arrived in Fitchburg just before Christmas 1948. The only affordable place was the four-room apartment of Nana, Grandmother Taylor. I was too young to be aware of the irony of the move back with the hated mother-in-law, but I must admit that Nana took this return very graciously. Although this meant snug crowding for her, I believe she enjoyed having her family around her, as we had been gone for four years.

I had just gotten into the new school's first grade and was enjoying the better learning situation when I awoke one morning to red spots all over my chest, a raging headache, and high fever. Scarlet fever. A medical van came and nailed on the front door a big red Quarantine sign, which meant that no one was allowed to leave the house, except for emergencies, or to let anyone in. Dad had found a job as salesman for Bolduc Fuel Oil Co., and had to sneak in and out of the house for his work, while the rest of us, including my brother, were trapped in the small apartment for the duration of this very contagious, potentially deadly illness, about a three-week span. Fortunately, no one else caught the disease, and the quarantine was lifted, finally.

A tradition was started during this confinement. My mother would come to the bed and read to me every day, often at night. She had read to me before, fairy tales and the like, but now she started reading real literature. She had acted in several dramatic monologues when teaching in Philadelphia, to entertain the teachers, and had a real flair for dramatic reading. She would act out all the characters' lines, and make the books come to life. My favorite was "Alice in Wonderland", which I asked to hear again and again.

My mother related to me that when she was a child of six in 1913, people regularly caught such diseases as rheumatic fever, whooping cough, diphtheria, tuberculosis, small pox, and fatal influenza, along with all the familiar diseases my brother and I caught: measles, mumps, chicken pox, and others, and a child's future in 1913 was a perilous adventure that often ended in death. Later, when I began composing, she told me of her very talented cousin Barbara, who was the first woman to be accepted into the New England Conservatory of Music as a double piano and composition major, around 1925. The pride of her family, she endured cold and hunger while living in an unheated student apartment, with little money, and in the winter of her first year caught diphtheria and died in three days! I often wonder if cousin Barbara has been my guardian angel throughout my career, having finally found someone else in the family to carry on her choked-off ambition...

FRIDAY, FEB. 27, 1993

Goal: to drive over 500 miles, to the border of Colorado. Blessedly, it is a sunny day. Highway 70 begins nice and cleared off, but deteriorates to drifts and a muddy dangerous crawl around snow-clogged Kansas City. The world is thickly fluffy-white today, picture-postcard trees and farms rolling by. We argue around

Kansas City, crawling at 35-40 mph. More time lost. I have long ago stopped caring when we arrive at Chico, Cal. Bart defensively has become obsessive about it. That tends to be a pattern in our marriage—as a problem magnifies, one of us stops caring and the other absorbs it all and pushes twice as hard. Not good for marital relations! After leaving the surreal white lumpiness of the Kansas and Colorado prairies, walled in by huge snow banks by the highway, the Rockies appear as giant white gumdrops! The rest stations on the highway over the mountains are completely iglooed by snow and stopping there is akin to entering a lit cave. The driving continues to be good, and we gain hours, arriving in a small western Colorado town by local time of 6:30 p.m., staggering with fatigue.

The motel room is thin-walled and across from a bar, which makes for some noise, but we are too comatose to care. Deciding to avoid any social interactivity, we cook dried noodle soup on our hot plate in our room plus having bread and chocolate pudding. Venturing out in the dark for some exercise, I walk down the small business road to a beautiful little town, which has been newly rebuilt from a devastating tornado, and revel in the all-glass walled city hall, diamond-shaped, at the end of the road. In the back of the town hall where a railroad used to run is now a park. This is one of the joys of touring—discovering that part of America which we would never experience any other way, and which at times offers delightful treats like this town, the name of which in my advanced state of sleepiness I never registered in my memory. The experience of seeing the beautiful results of this town's climbing back from disaster and creating a much nicer downtown stays with me, and soothes the memory of the last few days.

Saturday, Feb. 28

We are now into a period of sunny days, and driving through Wyoming is a pleasure. We avoid Rte. 70 over the mountains, because of the news of many bad avalanches spilling onto the highway this year. The state, like all the others, is completely buried in snow. I have driven and flown through the western states over a dozen times in my life, and have never seen it like this! It is obvious that prairie states such as eastern Wyoming harbor very many road warriors, because the motels have become huge and sprawling and much more elegant. Along a strip of dozens of new lavish motels we choose the Prairie Inn in Evanston, Wyoming, which has sumptuously large rooms, and an inner corridor between the double line of motel rooms which sports skylights, tropical plants, and colored mood lighting. Eating at a forgettable bistro engulfed in cutesy "tombstones" with messages on the walls, I walk back to the inn, basking in the brilliant starlit night with crescent moon and below-zero temperatures. Bart has been avoiding exercise so far on this trip, but I am not afraid to be alone at night on these rural roads, and fortunately have never had any problems. I am a wanderer by nature, and there is an aura of buoyancy about me when I walk, perhaps shielding me from evil.

Sunday, Mar. 1

On through Utah. Normally we would perform our way across the country, but this year's tour has been set around the Chico, Cal. residency, and all other performances are after that one. Even the bleak bleached desert in Utah has been transformed into magic. A most amazing view greets us at the Bonneville Salt Flats outside of Salt Lake City, Utah, which normally are salty-white, utterly flat and desolately dryly dead. This time it resembles the Arctic, with a glassy "lake" as far as the eye can see, with gorgeous snow-capped purple mountains in the distance—a postcard to send home to friends! Suddenly I feel that the blizzard-crippling drive has been worth it, to see the whole country transformed into a winter fairyland, breaking all records for snowfall.

We drive to Winnemucca, Nevada, arriving at five p.m. at an off-highway very nice, cozy local motel. This evening before dinner Bart and I walk together through the neat, new suburbs towards the mountains for about three miles, until we are separated from civilization and into sagebrush. The sunset is western-broad and colorful, and for the first time we feel a vacation-like enjoyment.

The evening ripens into clear stars and moon as we enter our first casino of the trip for a $5.99 roast beef dinner, with coupons from the motel for drinks and playing a few slots. The casino, one of many nearby, is just about deserted, with just a few hollow-eyed men and women glued to slot machines and hunched over the gaming tables. One man seems to be losing a large amount of money, but is apparently caught in the net of trying to gain back his losses, and looks grimly trapped. The dealers have a world-weary silent coldness about them, which adds to the dark atmosphere with all its overly bright colorful lights. This is my happy time off from the road, however, and I intend to use my coupons. Bart refuses to gamble at all, and watches as I am lucky enough at a 5-cent poker slot machine to play for an hour and win $2! This is tremendous fun, but I am tiring. My whole life is a gamble, so I am not very avid for more thrills from unnecessary risks. If I had lost my coupon-worth of coins, I would have stopped, but decide to try something more daring now with a blackjack game at the tables, which lasts about thirty seconds and eats up my $2 winnings. We soothe ourselves with the free drinks at the bar, and go "home" singing—an evening of delicious food, drink, and entertainment for $5.99 apiece! (this time, "but Beware the Jabberwock, my son!"[3]—the monster people-eater covered with colored lights, bells, and coins for eyes...)

Monday, March 2

Our last leg. We drive through the Sierras, the snowdrifts twenty feet high—so high we can hardly see over them. This is the longest driving trip without a long stopover we have ever accomplished, but the snow has made the last two-thirds of it fascinating. At one point in the mountains we drive off the highway to a small road to see the houses, all of which are buried in snow-tunnels which lead to them, like a picture I once saw in a Grimm's fairytale book. I can't imagine living with total darkness, except for the one dugout hole to look through all winter, and indeed these houses are all deserted, being summer homes. I muse on how fortified they must be, to keep the snow from caving them in, and how the owners must grieve and worry all winter about them...This is a record snowfall year, and perhaps it is not always like what we see today. We walk down Highway 20 a bit before driving on to Chico, our final destination.

After leaving the mountains, we witness a dramatic change of climate, and drive up the green California valley bursting with fruit tree blossoms. When we drive into warm, green Chico I cannot believe we have actually made it, plus arriving at a decent time—5 p.m.. We are able to secure the same nice motel room we lived in in 1988–EconoLodge, room #209, a corner second story room with birch tree and blooming magnolia growing in front of the window by the balcony walkway. Chico has seen The McLean Mix several times since we first performed there when it was Chico State College in 1982, and we think of it as an extension of home.

Chico has grown since 1976, when we first visited David and Margery Mallory (David is violinist in the California State University (CSU), Chico University Music Department and a dear old friend) on our first trip west on a summer vacation, from a hot dusty small town surrounded by fruit tree growers in the central California hills, to a toney upscale wealthy small city brimming with tourists, students, young professionals, and realtors ready to exploit any available land for a good market, including many of the old orchards. I know my friends are wary of the changes, but to us, having toiled through endless snowy miles of deserted landscape, we rejoice at this little pearl of flowery civilization, a town surrounding a large park of giant old trees and inviting walkways. We head for a Thai restaurant, the first one we have seen in three thousand miles, and certainly not found in our rural New York area, either. The food is incredibly hot—so hot that the people at the next table cannot eat their meal and have to reorder—and very delicious, and I thank California for its immigrants so that they do not have to water down their menus for the bland New England (and Midwestern) palette. Of course my Massachusetts eyes are watering as I think this. Our desserts are fried banana balls with peanut sauce around coconut ice cream with honey, and I wonder again how inventive is the human race to figure out these incredible flavors which I never tasted until a few years ago.

March 2nd–3ʳᵈ

Today is set-up in the Taylor (no relation) Art Building on the Chico, California campus, in their main gallery, a cozy windowless room with white wall available on which to project our slides. We are to perform *"Rainforest"* for two days. *"Rainforest"* is a very unusual, probably unique combination of composed as well as improvised music and photography that focuses on rainforests around the world, and allows the walk-in audience to create their own ideas on our musical instruments. The "piece" can last as short as an hour or as long as the whole day. With classes, it usually lasts fifty minutes, but with individuals walking in, people sometimes stay for four-five hours at a stretch, and then come back the next day! It appeals to all ages, which has its drawbacks as well as its positive aspects.

We project on a white wall or screen 160 slides set in two projectors, which through a fade & dissolve unit alternate slowly at different, previously programmed speeds. The whole program lasts forty-five minutes, but recycles at slightly different places, so the overlapping slides are always different. The slides are photos we have personally taken from our travels, usually on tour, to Hawaii, Puerto Rico, Australia, New Zealand, Peru, the northwest coast of the U.S., Florida, and the Adirondacks in New York State. Arranged and programmed very carefully by Bart, we are very proud of the slide show, and in this video and computer age, people continuously are fascinated with them, their movement, and their brilliant clarity. The downside is the utter manual hands-on of the equipment, dealing with burnt out (expensive) bulbs, heavy slide projectors that may or may not work, slide screens which are too small, too high, or rear projecting backstage, and the very bulk of these items: boxes, special table with extension, suitcases. We, *The McLean Mix*, are notorious for never being easy on ourselves. Our Honda Wagon is jammed to the very rooftop with our equipment, with our clothes in the "Big Mac" car carrier on top.

Along with the slides, we set up five performing stations: two microphones for the audience to sing or make sounds into, and digital processing that changes these sounds by delaying them or changing the pitch, a sampling synthesizer with Peruvian birds recorded in it, so that a person can play the keyboard and have birdcalls that change with the key, a digital synth that has been programmed with imaginative "rainforest"-like digital sounds,[4] and a zither, or autoharp found in the rubbish one day when I was still teaching in elementary school, which we removed the chord bars and untuned, put a contact microphone on, and put through two of the processors. So now a touch on the strings will create weird and wonderful notes that may repeat, change, or slide around. These are all set up in a row, with the slides projected in front in a giant arc on the wall. A composed stereo tape of synthesized drones and real birdcalls, plus many musical sounds that are timeless and static, plays throughout, creating the "floor" to put the other music on top. Mood lighting using bed lamps with green bulbs and heavy black aluminum foil shades create the right ambiance, with the room lights turned off.

The "installation", as we call it, is designed to be an ear-opening creative experience as well as fun and often art, and the reaction of both adults and younger people is similar—first they are all shy and afraid to touch anything or to make a sound. Then they go through a period of experimentation, going from one instrument to another. This is often the most delightful time, as I watch their faces light up with joy and discovery—ninety year old ladies as well as five year old boys, even one-year olds!—and this often leads to wild cacophony and hoots of laughter (we usually have to turn the volume levels down, especially in classes, at this point). Then the third step is when they tire of this and actually become interested in what sound they are producing, and how it interacts with others they are hearing. This is when they notice the slides, and become aware of the whole concept of the nature music idiom. Large classes rarely arrive at this point, because the students don't have a long enough time to play. After this step, the group thins out to the people who are really interested in creating and listening to new music with the rainforest, and these are the people who stay for hours, if they can.

We have been performing *"Rainforest"* since 1989, when it was premiered at the University of Wyoming Art Gallery, with intense participation by the music department. The piece keeps evolving, and at this point thousands of people have participated in it, to our great pleasure. The installation goes well here in Chico, with many music faculty performing on their instruments, to the delight of the students. I notice that the Chicano students take to the music naturally, in a group, and create a lively, rhythmic, very musically exciting *"Rainforest"*. People who have experienced the real rainforest are more advanced towards this kind of music, and it's always a delight to hear them. Dave Mallory brings his violin and plays for hours in the evening. It is always a great joy to play in California, where people seem to be more open-minded and daring!

Tonight I meet with the Chico Symphony, a metropolitan orchestra that performs on campus but is made up of professional musicians, some coming from as far away as San Francisco. Part of our residency here is to perform a concert of our works with the Symphony, and tonight they rehearse my piece for orchestra and stereo tape called *"A Magic Dwells"*, which I wrote from 1982-84, and won the Fargo-Moorhead National Sigvald Thompson Orchestral Composition Competition in 1986. Alfred Loeffler, the conductor, is a composer himself, and a courageous soul who hired us just a few years ago to premiere *"Voices of the Wild"*—he is one of the handful of conductors in this country who will dare to play this music, and for whom I have great love and respect, and gratitude. I haven't heard the piece played live except for the dress rehearsal in Fargo, North Dakota in January 1988. Unfortunately, that concert was postponed due to a blizzard, and performed later without the composer present. They had sent me a good tape of the performance, so I had at least experienced it on vinyl.

The first rehearsal that I hear is heartening. The gist of the music is there, and only needs a little tightening up. Composers who write "dangerous" music never or rarely experience the Chicago Symphony performing it, and are very happy to have at least an opportunity to hear it played by earnest musicians and a good conductor. I have heard the Chicago Symphony play new music of (famous) Hungarian composer Gyorgi Ligeti horribly and retreat happily to a Mozart piano concerto afterwards, which is such a dismal experience for a composer, and quickly cures one of desiring the "ultimate" orchestral premiere.

Wednesday, March 4

Today, the installation over, we break down our equipment and move it all to the orchestra hall across the street. This afternoon and tonight we rehearse with soloists and tomorrow with the Chico Symphony. The big difficult piece is the premiere of Bart's *"Rainforest Reflections"*, which involves two soprano soloists improvising, a soprano saxophonist and oboist also improvising, stereo tape, and full orchestra, whose music is written down. The other soprano is a black student named Jeanette Blakeney, who has a beautiful, powerful voice. Jim Kapphahn, a Masters student, is the saxophonist. Rehearsing this piece is like trying to capture an image on the video screen, and we butt our heads together and struggle. Our efforts help solidify Bart's ideas of what he wants to hear, but we are all frustrated by the end of the evening.

Tuesday, March 2, as Bart and I entered the office of the Music Department to introduce ourselves, the secretary related an ominous message: the head of the Highlands Nursing Home in Fitchburg had called a few days ago to notify me that my father was gravely ill. He had been in the nursing home for three years—eighty-seven years old and weakened by several strokes. Just before I left for our tour, I told him to "be a good boy and not get sick", and he smiled wanly from his wheelchair and said, "I'll try." But influenza had gone through the home, and he had caught it, with disastrous results. His temperature of 104 degrees for a whole week triggered a massive stroke. The doctor had expected him to die last week, but he was still holding on. Meanwhile, they had called the Chico number, which was the only place we could be reached, a week later.

I am stunned but not surprised. Back in our motel room, I call my brother Conrad and give him the details for the funeral, which has been arranged, and which I had anticipated missing, if on tour. Dad's last years have been lonely and friendless, with Mom gone since 1990, and the funeral will be very small. This tour is our livelihood for the year, and it is not possible to cancel concerts at this time. There seems to be a malevolent dark cloud over us this tour, and I am hoping that we survive…

Saturday, March 6

After a good rehearsal last night, the evening concert with the orchestra goes very well, and the small but attentive audience of older people is very appreciative. "*A Magic Dwells*" is quite an unusual piece, perhaps my best orchestral work, with the tape "singing" messages about Creation, such as "the tree of life", "the breath of life", etc.—quotes from native American mythology, Christian religion, and the Tao of Lao Tsu. The title *A Magic Dwells* comes from a quotation from Hermann Hesse's book *"Magister Ludi"*, which states in part: "A magic dwells at each beginning, and teaches us how to live". Hesse was a Swiss mystic who wrote many fascinating books. I love Creation myths, and mysterious sounds in composing, and enjoyed creating this piece very much. My only sorrow is that it is never performed, but this is a common cry of many a composer today.

The premiere of Bart's *"Rainforest Reflections"* is rocky. The oboist forgets to show up, and we three have to make up for his loss, which makes the other singer nervous. Perhaps it will go better tomorrow. I can never understand why all groups want to play premieres rather than second or third performances. These are *always* the worst performances, and by the second performance the bugs will have been worked out, the piece made better. But at the reception afterwards, several people rush up to Bart and me saying, "Thank you for coming! We are so lucky to have you!!" Dave Mallory's son Rod astutely hears influences of Bartok and Takemitsu (probably actually Xenakis) in my piece. Perhaps tomorrow the oboist will show up!

Sunday, March 7

The balmy sunny, warm weather keeps the students away in droves, and only a disappointing one hundred people are in the audience. The performance is better today, especially Bart's *"Rainforest Reflections"*, as the oboist finally arrives. He had not forgotten, but he must travel in from San Francisco, and was unavailable yesterday. Enthusiastically we singers over-sing our improvisations, and the two woodwind performers overplay, effectively drowning out the serene music on tape. This piece needs more notes written down, or more direction from the—ahem! composer, but parts of it are really beautiful. Afterwards we enjoy dinner with Al and Nancy Loeffler at their lovely home, and discuss everything from Paul Hindemith's humorous music to the works of famous nature writers and hiking in the Sierras. Al is retiring next year, which means that our residencies here will probably vanish, but nothing lasts forever. The California university system is trying to entice the faculty to take early retirement before the system goes bankrupt, and our friends all seem to be taking them up on it. We will miss this place! This is our fourth residency here since 1982.

Monday, March 8

I awake feeling very badly. The ominous tingling and burning that feels like the shingles in my neck and right side of throat has returned, and on the day of our big *"Gods, Demons, and the Earth"* concert…The re-attack is very mild, but very faint red blotches can be seen. The whole journey westward I could not hear much out of my right ear, one of the hardest hit areas during the first shingles attack I had in 1988. The whole right side of my face is slightly swollen, burning, and aching. Oh Virus—will you never let me go? I guess I was meant to stay home, knit doilies, and go to bed every night at 8 p.m.…

After this outburst, I am running out of time, and have to pretend to ignore the trouble. I take some Advil, which has always helped a little, and soon we are at the university and setting up our equipment on the same stage as yesterday, only sans orchestra. By 11:30 a.m. I am adjusting the slide projectors, when an overwhelming feeling of coming down with the flu overtakes me–nausea, head ache, dizziness–and alarmed, I stagger into the green room dressing area back-stage and lie down on the couch. Never has an attack of flu come on so quickly, and I am thinking we may have to call off the concert, that I could never sing like this! I lie there for an hour or so, and miraculously, all the symptoms disappear! The blotches on my neck and throat are still tingling and now itching, but that is all. Bewildered, I rise and go next door to the cafeteria for lunch, and continue to feel good.

Our rehearsal goes well, and we have only one mild problem during the concert when one of the slide projector light bulbs blows at the beginning of *"The Dance of Shiva"*, the last work on the program, at which point I stop the piece, apologize to the audience, and replace the bulb in one minute. It is an annoyance, but fortunately it happens rarely, and this time at the beginning of the piece, so I can minimize the impact. The small but attentive audience of around fifty does not seem unduly upset. They have been listening to one of our most successful concerts, which features our rousing *"Earth Music"* for the first piece, composed by Bart, then Bart's *"Demons of the Night"*, a digital electronic work on stereo tape that rattles the rafters while the audience sits huddling in the dark, Bart's *"Fireflies"* in which he plays a Sparkling Light Console he co-invented with Mike Rose from RPI (Rensselaer Polytechnic Institute), featuring a Windows PC with keyboard that controls a 6x6-foot panel of blinking tiny colored lights—"fireflies" set up with many motion patterns to a stereo tape of his electronic music, from a set of pieces called *"Visions of a Summer Night"*.

The second half of the concert has me singing and dramatizing *"Wilderness"*, the poem by Carl Sandburg, with stereo tape richly endowed with synth sounds, sampled sounds of live instruments, punctuated by bird and a large assortment of animal sounds, as I sing through the seven verses of this long and fascinating poem. The concert closes with *"The Dance of Shiva"* on stereo tape, a panorama of electronic and instrumental sampled sounds, beginning with a real Buddhist chant (The God Shiva is the Hindu god/goddess of Destruction and Creation, his/her home is in the Himalayas, and he/she is also Lord of the Beasts and Lord of the Dance (the dance of the cycles of life and death). Accompanying this is fade and dissolve slides, and as the piece draws to a close with music by 12th Century composer and abbess Hildeguard von Bingen with underlying Buddhist chant, the Madonna is seen on screen merging into the golden statues of Shiva and Parvati, his female counterpart, as they melt into the Himalayan Mountains, from whence they came.

The concert is a very powerful one, creating a strong feeling of the holiness of life, the earth, and nature, even the so-called "demons" that are the magic of our night imaginations. Perhaps we the performers are the most affected by our concerts, but Dave Mallory and the Loefflers shower us with praise, which we lap up like puppy dogs. Dave raves about the Shiva piece, saying that the philosophy, art, and music all culminate in a breathtaking work. I glow happily, as all composers, including even the most modest who are self-effacing about their work, are bottomless sponges for compliments!

Tuesday, March 9

When I am partially awake, flush with artistic victory from the concert the night before, Bart gently tells me that Dad has died, that he actually passed away yesterday, at 3 p.m. Eastern Standard Time, and that the office had notified Bart about it. Bart had postponed telling me until after the concert, as he thought correctly that I would have been too upset to perform. However, he said, "A really eerie thing happened. Just as your father died, you became terribly ill and went to lie down in the green room. It's as if you knew what had happened." Definitely my conscious self did not, but Dad and I have had psychic connection before, with my body imitating his disease, as it did with the "flu" yesterday, and I know from long personal experience that "there is more in heaven and earth than meets the eye". Chills go through my body as I realize what has happened. I am always with Dad, even separated by distance, and now by life itself.

We have a day off, and we head for a large park on the outskirts of Chico. The day is cool and cloudy, and as we scramble down a slope, I scratch my bare legs on what appears to be poison oak bushes, which keep me scratching for the rest of the trip. So now I can alternate between my legs and my neck, and who says that our lives are not stimulating!?! Tonight we hold a private ceremony for Dad in our motel room, #209 EconoLodge, as I know I will not be able to go home for the funeral. We imbed a circle of birthday candles on a plastic plate, surround it with camellias from bushes near the motel, and turn Dad's checkbook with his handwriting in it sideways towards the candles, which symbolizes his presence, as we have no photograph with us. As we light the candles, Bart recites the 23rd Psalm from the motel's Bible and I tearfully read some lines from "Song of Solomon". Holding hands we sing "When the Saints Go Marching In", Dad's favorite song, and I haltingly sing "You'll Never Walk Alone" after a short time where we talked about all of the best qualities Dad had and how much we love and miss him. Somehow I feel he would have liked this ceremony, perhaps more than the formal one in the funeral home in a few days.

◆   ◆   ◆

4.

"Today a flower bloomed,
    And far away I saw a wing
Fluttering amidst the air,
    So light and fresh and fair.
Today the sun is white,
    And many walk with smiling eyes.
Children's voices fill the day
    With laughter, high and gay.
Today my thoughts renew,
    And soon within sing wide and free
The melody of day and dawn
    Until the day is gone."

—text from *"Four Songs in Season: Song to the Spring"*
SATB Chorus and Piano by Priscilla Taylor (1963.)

With the advent of spring, our family had to move again. The confinement with Nana was wearing us all down, and in May, without waiting for the end of school, we all piled in the car and headed for The Farm, the home of Mom's twin sister Alice and her husband Gordon Tripp, seven miles outside of Binghamton, New York, in the small town of Conklin. My description to follow may seem superfluous to the life of a composer, but I give it because so much of my future life, creative thinking, and indeed, hiking the world's wildernesses originated from these trips to my aunt and uncle's home over the years.

After many hours of driving, when we finally reached Conklin Forks, New York, the excitement would mount. Just past a small cement bridge was a general store with gas station in the town square. We children would explode out of the car and run to the long, sprawling candy counter inside while the grown-ups serviced the car and bought some groceries. And what a candy counter! Every kind of penny candy one could think of—red and black licorice strips, caramel rounds with creme filling spiraled inside, candy corns, tiny wax bottles with syrupy juice inside, chocolate covered malted milk balls, and a host of other delectables for a penny apiece—a dime would net you a whole little white bag full of ten different kinds of candy!

The next wave of excitement would come after we drove past Conklin and began to recognize The Farm in the distance, atop one of the many cultivated rolling hills, the small colonial house sitting whitely alone, with a red barn nearby. Then the road would dip down again, and finally, off the main road, came a small dirt road to the right, with a wooden hand-painted old sign on the left stating: "Tripp's Pigs". Down we would descend to the dirt road, and for the next mile we would crane our necks, trying to see the farmhouse rising up on the left, over the trees. All the way from Binghamton were farmhouses and barns of every shape and condition, some large and well-kept, with large red barns trimmed in white, some almost unpainted houses with barns a mere unsteady pile of rotten gray boards, with hardly any other buildings not devoted to farming. My uncle's house was somewhere in-between the two extremes, and we would finally come to the mailbox next to the old garage at the bottom of the driveway.

The driveway was an adventure all in itself. A better description would be "mountain hiking trail", but I have rarely seen hiking trails as bad as this one, and the only road that equaled it was to a hunting camp Bart and I lived in during the summer of 1977 in the Medicine Bow National Forest area of Wyoming. Boulders and pointed rocks filled the quarter-mile roadway, which snaked up to the half-painted white house, and had been the final insult for many an old automobile. My father would curse and yell, and often I would climb out and walk, rather than bang my bouncing head on the ceiling three or four times!

Upon reaching the house and parking our car among the old rusted skeletons of farm machinery and ancient automobile carcasses strewn around, with another crumbling but barely functioning car which was my uncle's, we would gingerly get out, leap the small stream (which never had a bridge) running around the house, maneuver through the tall grass and rocks and usually mud to the side door—the front door stood inaccessibly high in tall grass with no steps leading up to it. There we would be assaulted with a flurry of chickens and roosters, and up to twenty-two cats (no exaggeration!) feeding on milk pans laid out in front of the door for them, plus a few dogs and hundreds of flies that somehow had escaped the house. Now when I visit native tribes in different parts of the world, I realize that I am only one generation from their lifestyle, and a warm nostalgia akin to love floats over me toward the tribal people. We are all closer than we know.

My parents would bemoan the condition of the house and yard while I gazed wonderingly in all directions, for it was truly one of the beautiful settings in America. Rolling farmland and forest stretched out on three sides for miles in the distance, and the backyard of the house lay on the edge of an almost impenetrable hemlock forest, which rose steeply to a plateau that was the Pennsylvania line.

All this commotion brought Aunt Alice to the door to shoo the creatures away, and we entered a small anteroom which held the large metal separator for the cows' milk, which once a day my uncle would operate by grabbing the large wood-knobbed handle and cranking it round and round while the pails of raw milk changed into milk and cream, the rich aroma which I will never forget filling the air and clinging even now as we walked into the room, with no milk in sight. The house was only ten years old, but many an animal had lodged there during a hard blizzard, and the pretty, small house had a decided lived-in look.

That spring and summer of 1949 was spent becoming a part of The Farm, and began with a finishing up of school for the year. I felt like I had been going to the first grade for four years now, but it was just my fourth school in the first grade, and the strangest yet. At five a.m. Uncle Gordon would yell, "Everybody up! The day is wasting!" in his hoarse gravel voice. He would then hand-milk all the cows, sometimes taking me with him. A tall, strongly built middle-aged man with a ring of straight gray hair around his ears and a few wisps on top, he looked like a college professor, even decked in farm overalls and blue cap. Small rimless spectacles sat in front of mild intelligent eyes, and when not working, he would sit in the big rocking chair in the living room and tell endless stories of his past, which was a cross between *"Treasure Island"* and *"The Adventures of Marco Polo"*, although he had a college degree in engineering and had served in the Merchant Marines. Unfortunately, he would tell these stories in the quietest, fuzziest voice I have ever heard, so none of us ever quite understood what he was saying, thus adding a continual mystery to his life and adventures.

Although not the best narrator, Uncle Gordon could milk cows, with his bulky hairy hands steadily gripping the long rubbery teats while he cooed, "There, there. Steady, girl." I don't believe I ever got a drop of milk out of any of those cows, although I tried mightily, and my admiration for Uncle Gordon increased with every failed attempt I made. Then we would hustle in to a pancake breakfast with raw milk straight from the pail and sour butter, and bacon grease sauce for the pancakes along with the maple syrup. Then in the deep chill of early morning we were driven to the nearest neighbor's, a mile away, and Mr. Gow would put me in the cab of his pick up truck and Conrad with his sons in the open back, as we rode several miles down out of the hills to meet the school bus by seven o-clock in Conklin. Conrad and the other boys would be blue with cold by the time the bus came and we all settled in for the ten-mile ride to the large brick Binghamton schoolhouse. Every day took about four hours to go to and from school! There we read out loud in class, everyone with the same textbook, one at a time while the teacher stood at the front with a ruler and thundered "That will do!" if one read correctly, and if not, the agonized pupil would have to read it again and again, while the rest of us rotted with boredom. We never acted up, however, because she wielded the ruler like a whip, especially during our enforced rest periods after lunch, when I earned many a welt on my arms.

I remember the summer as being glorious, with riding in the horse-drawn wagon filled with bales of hay, next to Conrad and toddler cousin Richard, while Uncle Gordon's old father drove—a thin papery man who had orange teeth from chewing tobacco and parchment hands that fascinated me. Sometimes I "helped" Aunt Alice weed the endless rows of vegetables growing in the hot sun, or I would frolic in the hayloft in the red barn, with the animals all grazing outside in the far-flung meadows, and Conrad and I would take small hikes along the rocky stream beds or in the woods while he would continue his job of scaring me with tales of black widow spiders lurking on every branch or poisonous snakes hiding in the waters just waiting for me to come by. I was terrified yet fascinated by all this country. The surrounding land of ninety acres had been in the Tripp family since the American Revolution, given to the soldiers for their long-ago valor.

West of the house lay a series of ponds which were linked by a river-like water-way, built by my uncle and his neighbor Austin Cline, and over the years I learned to spend countless hours catching blue gills and sunfish while day-dreaming whole days away, and swimming in its muddy waters with fish nibbling my unseen toes. Uncle Gordon was a "gentleman farmer" who spent most of the week working in the employment agency in Binghamton, and the rest of his life trying to keep the farm alive. He would have a pen full of pigs for several years, until a fatal disease would carry them off, and then he would try cows or horses. He never was able to make the business pay, but I don't think he cared. He just loved it all—the land, farm, animals, open air—and I grew to love it as much as he did. He came to think of me as his daughter, and I was to model my future husband after him in many ways. My family's visits to this beloved Farm were always only a few days a year, and I knew that my direction did not lie towards this kind of life. It has torn me to this day, loving the country and having to be a composer tied to cities and dense populations, where Art survives.

As I played and dreamed in the south-central New York hills, another young person just a few miles away in Cincinnatus was doing the same. He was the same age as my brother and had a dog named Rusty, the same name as Conrad's dog who romped around that summer with us. This unknown handsome boy in the near-by town built little bridges and dams across a small stream running through his parents' rural property, and he roamed all the fields and woods while humming tunes he had made up, same as I. We were not to meet for another seventeen years, however, and we never met in central New York.

◆   ◆   ◆

One day in the middle of August 1949, my father, who had been staying for the most part in Fitchburg and working while we were at The Farm, announced happily that he had found Mom a job, and we were all going to move into a furnished apartment he had just rented. What wasn't discussed was the furniture, books in boxes, photograph albums, and pictures that they had stored in a warehouse before we left Michigan, all of which we would never see again. There had been a flood, the warehouse had been near the river, and all except a few pictures were ruined beyond recognition. The pictorial history of my mother's family was gone, except for the one water-stained formal group picture of everyone standing in front of her old house in Fitchburg, previously described. This was a tragedy my mother never talked about, and I was unaware until I was older. Her interest in preserving old family heirlooms vanished after that. Only the silver pieces and a few special glasses followed us down through the years, mutely crying that there had been more, much more than I would ever see of this lost family.

Before my mother went to work full-time, we all went for a visit to her cousin Charlotte's home in Pawtucket, Rhode Island. We stayed just a few days, but what was so memorable about this trip was the large upright *piano* in the living room. I was drawn to it, and couldn't be coaxed away for hours every day. I couldn't play, of course, but I was fascinated by it and its tones. At night I had a memorable dream of being in a beautiful flower garden with a birdbath and a large grand piano, at which I sat and played real music! My longing for a piano continued long after the visit, and lasted year after fruitless year.

In South Ashburnham, Mass., a small town west of Fitchburg, our new Main Street apartment on the first floor of a two-story house, with the landlords upstairs, had a few problems. There were only two bedrooms, so Conrad and I slept in the same room. The back yard was pretty and wooded, and decked out with a walk-in playhouse and all kinds of toys for the landlord's five-year-old son, but also had a cesspool, due to a malfunctioning septic system.

With our parents working full-time, I spent after-school hours with a parade of indigent teenage baby sitters, while Rusty the dog often sat tied up in the garage barking continuously. Nevertheless, I have many fond memories of that place, and one memory stands out for its grotesque quality and strange resolution. It was the summer of 1950 and we all went blueberry picking in a field within walking distance of the house. I stepped into a large yellow jackets' nest, and began screaming and waving my arms around. I was stung over a hundred times, which was terribly painful and had profound psychological effects. I would not leave the house for the rest of the summer. I was terrified of all bees, wasps, and hornets—a fear, especially of wasps, that lasted until just a few years ago.

Now I will jump ahead forty years. Imagine someone encountering a wasp on the wall for forty years and running in panic out to the street. Then a miracle happens, and she never again is afraid, can even tolerate it flying around her head inside the room! The Karmic resolution was: Music. The bees, wasps, hornets all *Sing*. With their wings. Beautifully! As soon as I stopped and listened to them, and began to use their songs in my music, I felt a kinship for these tiny musicians that cured my fear forever. And now I learn that bees also dance. Is not the world a marvelous place?! Yes, once in a while I still am stung, and so I live in truce with these musician-stingers and am (mostly) very content.

In South Ashburnham I entered the second grade, and one day the substitute teacher for our class was my mother…This was an awkward situation, and I immediately fell into trouble by calling her "Mom", and at one point I talked back to her and she slapped me right in front of the whole class. She was tougher than I ever remember her being at home! That was an interesting class. There were thirteen of us sharing a room with forty fourth graders. This meant that we spent most of the day reading or writing quietly while the teacher devoted her time to the fourth grade. By the next year, the same situation occurred, this time with our third and the next fourth grade class. I was becoming extremely bored and restless, as I had gone through the scarce supply of children's books on our side of the room, and began creating trouble, talking out and acting up in class, and continually being punished. I formed a gang of three girls who waited after school for the mildest, most timid girl in the class, Eileen. When she came near, we jumped her on the playground and beat her until she cried. I learned curse words from the boys and practiced them on my parents.

Finally my mother went to the principal and asked that I be moved into the next grade level, in the middle of the year. A trial period was set up of three months. This meant that I moved from the left side of the classroom to the right side. Suddenly everything was a challenge. The fourth grade was more than a year ahead of our slow third grade, and Mom tutored me at home to learn the new math concepts of two digit multiplication and long division, while I caught onto the reading immediately. I lost all my friends, though. The day I moved my seat, my "gang" of three evaporated. My friends wouldn't speak to me, and the affronted fourth graders were horrified and intimidated. This was the beginning of my feelings of estrangement from my classmates, which lasted until I entered music study in college. I vividly remember the feeling of intense delight of being moved ahead, mixed with the desolation of suddenly being alone and shunned. Nowadays the education system sustains several levels of achievement in one grade, but in those days, there was only the mainstream, and woe to those too smart or too slow!

Less than three months after my grade skip, my parents decided to move again, to a duplex apartment on the outskirts of Fitchburg, where we would live for almost three years. Because we moved around so much, Conrad and I had difficulty making lasting friends, and we were thrown together much of the time. Conrad was four years older, but was kindly patient with teaching me all of the childhood games, and challenging me, in an imperious way, of course, to beat him. We played chess, Monopoly, and many other favorites for hours, and he played a large part in sharpening my memory and manual skills. Often he would needle me to distraction, so that in losing, I would pick up the cards or pieces and throw them against the wall in great fury. Then he would laugh wickedly and suddenly find a reason to visit his friends outside.

But another diversion was drawing me more and more, and that was the upright piano that Mrs. Parcher, the landlady, had in their living room in the other half of the duplex. Just about every day after school I would beg to "play the piano", and she and Mr. Parcher were always delighted. Mr. Parcher busied himself with a gigantic flower garden in the backyard during the summer, while Mrs. Parcher was always cooking something delicious—they were retired and elderly. As I explored the coveted piano one finger at a time, picking out the tunes I had learned in school, in two-part harmony, she would always offer me sugared grapefruit rind or other homemade candy, and they would sit and listen to my fumblings, just basking in having a child in their home again. Their kindness kept my hopes alive while I at least got a feeling for the keyboard, and immensely enjoyed myself.

The fourth grade in the new Ashburnham Street School was much further advanced than the little country school from which we had just come, and I struggled hard that year, earning the first low grades of my life. But I refused to give up and go back to the lower grade. I liked the challenge. I was a year younger than my classmates, and had virtually no friends, so I took to entertaining them to draw attention to myself. At home I began writing stories, and one, called "The Boy with the Invisible Hand", was read to the class by the teacher, and read to my brownie troupe by the leader. At the age of eight I was becoming very puffed up, convinced that I should become a fiction writer, and had lined up in my imagination all the accolades I would receive from the ungrateful world, when a tragedy occurred. My only manuscript was stolen from the teacher's desk (no copy machines in those days), and was never returned. I was crushed. I hadn't the heart to try and reconstruct the story, and stopped writing for a few years.

—Childhood diary, Sunday, April 6, 1952: "Today I went to Sundy (sic) school. It wasn't bad either. I did my lesson and got a new book. It was fun. About Jesus being crucified. I tried to find some pussy willows but I couldn't find any. I walked down to the park and made a sand house. It started to rain and I came home. We watched television till 9:00 and I went to bed." Friday, May 23, 1952: "Jane couldn't come up today, I asked another one if she could come to my house for my birthday party. Betty doesn't know yet. I finished my hut out in the woods today—it's a nice one, too! But I didn't climb any trees, because I'm lame in the stomach from doing it. We watched television all night to 10:00, and then I went to bed."

Tuesday, March 11, 1952: "I was sick in the middle of night last night. Not sick to my stomach just sick. I had a hundred and one temperature. So I stayed home. So did Mommy. I'm glad I did too. It was horrible out today, raining and warm. Conrad went to his violin lesson today, but I wasn't all alone. No Sirree! Mommy was here. I went to bed at 9:00."

By 1952 several changes had occurred. With both parents working continuously, including most Saturdays, we could afford a television, and in 1951 we got a small black and white set put in the living room. At first we all watched it incessantly, fascinated by the endless playhouse in our living room. Mom and Dad were much more fascinated with it in the long term than Conrad and I were, and my life changed only slightly, as I continued to write, paint, and read, only with a television accompaniment. We had grown up without a TV and had a large arsenal of interests of our own. I began to have a few girl friends and to learn to be a little more sociable. The woods next to our house, which was the last one on the road for about a half mile, and the forest across the street, were my closest friends, and I spent many happy hours dreaming under the trees and musing by the stream, admiring it in mossy summer as well as snow-covered winter.

By November of 1952 we moved again, to 82 Pleasant St., right up the street from Nana's apartment in Fitchburg. This was a much worse apartment, on the second floor, with vertical back and side yards, and no front yard except for a set of steep steps. The house was in a row of other tenement-style houses, and there was no garage. It didn't occur to me then that my father was in the middle of several temporary jobs that were failing to provide much income, but I felt the loss of the landlady's piano and the forested countryside. I was beginning to be socially conscious, and with a dawning sick realization that we were poor. That I may never have a piano of my own to play was becoming a real possibility. I wore clothes from the Thrift Shop and handmade clothes my grandmother made, plus hand-me-downs from the new office at the ABC Trucking Company where my mother worked. That winter I was mortally embarrassed to find myself wearing an ankle-long, blazing red woman's wool coat, with a fake fur collar, horribly out-of-date and old-looking for a girl of almost eleven. I remember standing in the Thrift Shop buying stockings for a dime a pair, wishing to God that I didn't have to be there.

Before I give the impression that I was ill-cared for, I will tell of another simultaneous occurrence. One Saturday in December, with snow coming down, I heard a commotion by the front bedroom window. Coming through the opened window, jacked up from the truck in the street by cranes, was a piano! Oh blessed day!! They had decided to surprise me, and never did an old beat up sprung-notes ancient upright piano ever receive such a warm welcome!

One of the workers in my mother's office knew about our situation, and gave my mother the piano. All that was needed was to pay the mover $10. After the piano came, the mover died of a sudden heart attack, and so we had the piano for free. It was in horrible shape, but was made to play half-decently, except for two sticking notes, by the piano tuner, Mr. Forrest Bunker, down the street, who also became my first piano teacher.

At my first piano lesson, I was handed the Michael Aaron "Very First Book for Beginners", a half-sized book with about twenty exercises, beginning with middle C on the piano, and graduating to simple melodies for each hand separately by the end of the book. Mr. Bunker marked out about three exercises for me to learn, and taught me the first two, telling me to go home and practice, playing as many as I wanted to. At the next lesson a week later, I sat down and played all the exercises in the book flawlessly, as they were very easy. He was a little amazed, then handed me the Book Number One. In two more weeks I had gone through this book, so he switched to the John Thompson series, a much more difficult set, and started me in the middle of the first book. These were mainly watered-down excerpts of famous classical pieces, with a short description of each, and my first-ever experience of hearing classical music. I slowed down for these, as I enjoyed each piece and wanted to learn it well.

After five months I was in the middle of the Thompson Book Two when Mr. Bunker announced he was quitting teaching piano. He said something like, "I am really only a piano tuner. You need a real teacher, who can push you ahead better than I can," and he recommended a teacher who lived several blocks away in the better section of town. I regretted leaving him, because I truly liked him, but he wasn't giving me any of the basic technical skills, and I knew it. The next teacher was a middle-aged gruff pianist from France (whose name I have forgotten) who taught an old school European technique. The half hour lesson consisted of playing a scale from memory, then a few pieces from the Burgmueller book of 25 piano compositions, a piece of sheet music the teacher had picked out and that I would learn and memorize, and then the new material, which the teacher would play flamboyantly, ending with the new scale.

For over two years I happily studied with him, and reveled in the difficult pieces he assigned, but he went too far. I was progressing so fast that he became very excited, even suggesting to my overawed parents that I may be headed for a concert pianist's career. I had started so late that by my third year of piano study I was thirteen, and already halfway through my freshman year in high school. He assigned Beethoven's *"Moonlight Sonata"*, all three movements, to learn and memorize, plus a book of Czerny exercises. I was playing at about the level of someone who had studied seven years, but to do this I had now to practice two hours a day.

I remember, after learning the first two movements, hearing Liberace perform the *"Moonlight Sonata"* on television, and being stunned at the tempo taken of the last movement, thirty pages long, that I was supposed to memorize! I was a young teenager with no history of hard work, of focusing on one area of expertise. Music in our family was a recreation, like playing a game of cards. My brother had stopped his violin lessons after two years, upon reaching high school age. Fitchburg High School's college preparation course was quite taxing, and I had long hours of homework every night. My mother saw the pressure I was under and suggested that I drop the lessons, as I was playing "well enough". Gratefully, I agreed, and my future life suddenly changed, as the concert pianist direction was cut off, to return in a strangely similar but quite new way no one would ever have anticipated...

WEDNESDAY, MARCH 10, 1993

Today we bid our Chico friends good-bye and drive to San Francisco, to the house of Herb and Sondra Bielawa, who are hosting us for the time we are here. They live in a delightful two-story bungalow across the street from Aaron Copland's granddaughter, and we have an enjoyable night together dining at an incredibly elegant restaurant overlooking the Bay Bridge as our treat (uh-oh, I hope the next day's lecture isn't canceled.!), then explore the pier nearby with a tube art installation that magnifies the sounds of the ocean waves. The full moon smiles down upon us all as we duck our heads in and out of the tubes and run around laughing like five-year-olds. Herb, also a composer, has just taken early retirement from San Francisco State University, where he was the head of the music department, and he and Sondra, who is a virtuoso performer on the pipe organ and harpsichord, are planning to do some touring with his music, ala the McLeans.

Thursday, March 11

We are up and over to The Old First Church in San Francisco early, setting up for tomorrow's concert. In late morning Alden Jenks meets us, and we drive to the San Francisco Conservatory to give a lecture to a handful of students from his composition class. I believe Alden is expecting a more cerebral lecture, perhaps with electronic graphs and diagrams, but we instead demonstrate how a (taped) musician wren's song can be wreathed in symbiotic music. We then play the beginning of our *"Rainforest Images"* CD to show how the musical bird fits into the piece. I am not sure he is satisfied, but the students come up enthusiastically and buy CDs anyway. I personally can never remember as a student going up to any guest composer after a class lecture, and asking to buy a record of his music, so we must be doing something interesting.

Sondra and Herb outdo themselves giving us an incredible home-cooked meal tonight, with chicken pan-roasted in artichokes, vinegar and oil, black mushrooms, and wine. During the meal we catch up on the exploits of their very talented adult children, who are involved in alternate music and video, and it is always a pleasure to hear about their latest efforts. We retire early to argue privately about our programming for tomorrow's KPFA broadcast in Berkeley. Our motto: never think too far ahead with programming—life would be too placidly boring! Perhaps my crankiness is due in part to the fact that Dad's funeral is tomorrow in Fitchburg, and I am here, selfishly earning money and enjoying myself. There is an anvil on my heart during this tour.

Friday, March 12

We are up by 6 a.m., and treated to a breakfast of yogurt and fruit by Sondra, who thoughtfully is at the breakfast table to greet us. The drive to Berkeley passes quickly, and we are on the air at KPFA at 9 a.m. for an hour's interview with Russ Jennings, who is the new director. It is always a treat to be on KPFA, because the radio interviewers, both Russ and previously Charles Amirkhanian, are so professional and knowledgeable, and the unseen radio audience actually responds by calling in afterwards. Our show is a potpourri of our music, and we play from tapes and discuss first my short humorous "duet" for my live and taped voice, with Bart on bicycle wheel, accompanied by two mosquitoes and a honeybee on stereo tape called *"On Wings of Song"*. Next is Bart's very funny *"(Too Much) Dandelion Wine"*, a stereo tape work which features the voice of Trevor Wishart plus electronics, followed by half of our newest piece which we are about to put out on a CD called *"Rainforest Images"*. In-between, we discuss and publicize the McLean Mix concert at Old First Church in San Francisco tonight.

Russ, a handsome tall blondish bearded man, has just the right touch for this show—he is casual but exact, and very flattering. After the show is over, we are astounded when the phone begins to ring continuously with listeners requesting tapes and CDs of our music, especially *"Rainforest Images"*. After we leave, Russ, whom we see later at the concert, tells us that the phone continued to light up all the next hour, asking for our music. This is *not* pop music, and this kind of excitement is not common for classical electronic music, but oh, so welcome.

During our rehearsal and setup at Old First Church, I am painfully aware that my throat has become thick and froggy, and I cannot sing the music. At first I wonder if it is because I am grieving for Dad and feeling guilty for not attending his funeral, which is today, when I decide to take a walk to clear my head. Right outside of the front door stands a huge acacia tree in full yellow spring bloom. This means nothing to me until I am told it is the same as the Australian wattle tree, and all is understood—I am extremely allergic to the wattle tree, which I discovered in 1990 when I flew from the autumn misery of New York ragweed and goldenrod directly to Melbourne's early spring bloom of the wattle trees! My lifelong allergies are the main reason that I never planned on a career as a singer decades ago. But I have to sing tonight. I am used to being prepared, however, and I "tank up" all day on antihistamines and nasal spray, which results in my feeling exhausted and deadened.

The hall is the church sanctuary, with wonderful acoustics. We will perform the *"Gods, Demons and the Earth"* concert last performed at Chico. At 5:30 p.m. Jeff Miller, the young director of the concert series who has been assisting us all day, Jeff's young woman assistant, Michael Babcock—our good friend and first instructor in electronic music when we were students at Indiana University—who has come to help us also, Bart, and I all walk to a Chinese restaurant on Polk Street around the corner, and have a wonderful relaxing, hilarious dinner. Our concert at night goes flawlessly, wonderfully. The audience of fifty, with many familiar faces, make up for their small size by being wildly enthusiastic, and we are in heaven. Beforehand, I toyed with dedicating this concert to Dad, but was afraid I would break down and weep in front of the audience, creating unnecessary tension and sorrow in the audience, plus spoiling my voice for the night, so I do a silent dedication backstage before I go on. Dad would have understood.

March 13–19

After bidding good-bye to our California friends, we drive to Ely, Nevada, becoming lost and wasting an hour along the way. We find a quiet motel and the best local sub shop we have ever experienced, and order a sandwich of turkey, artichoke hearts, cranberry sauce, sunflower seeds, beets, and lettuce. This reminds us very much of Australia's famous giant sandwiches, and here in little Ely!

On to Utah, and one of the reasons we tour for a living. Into each tour comes a period of time known as a "break". We have a few days before we have to continue east, and we have planned to visit the desert during springtime. At Moab, a quaint, dusty small town that is growing larger by the day, we find a delightful old motel for $27 a night, flanked by a sandstone cliff on one side, called the Inca Inn. A jolly family has been running the motel for decades, headed by a blond Jewish lady in her seventies. Next door is their very popular Mexican Inca Inn Restaurant. The first hour we are here we settle in our small and gaily Southwestern decorated room, squashing in our room actually, with our equipment taking up all the floor and shelf space except the two beds, along with hiking and cooking gear. Then we literally tear out the door and up the cliff in back, which leads to a plateau of wild sagebrush desert, overrun with deer and elk tracks heading in all directions. The motel and town are below us, and we glory to the blazing sunset and almost-fluorescent glow of the turquoise and gray desert plants, and the bright green junipers sprinkled around.

The more I experience the world, the more I realize that I love all of the different wildernesses, be they rainforests, deserts, swamps, snow-covered prairies, or oceans. Wildernesses remind us, with their stinging cold winds, lack of shade on a hot desert day, blistering wet jungle heat, biting insects, diseases, and ever-present threat of disaster if we become lost or ill that *they* are the strong ones, and we are really only ill-adapted animals who have lost the ability to survive without all of our conveniences and necessities. I think this is the main reason that humankind abuses the unfettered wilderness so much. We don't want any reminders of who we really are. And yet to be humbled is to experience the joy of wonder, of encountering something greater than we, of imaging the ineffable. All nature undisturbed seems to me to be the arms of God enfolding us, and we must look on it with the eyes of a happy child.

◆   ◆   ◆

5.

About this time we moved again, the result of a very happy turn of events for my father. Drowning in debt and desperate, he asked my mother if she could call on a close friend of her late father, who ran the prestigious Fitchburg Gas and Electric Company, and persuade him to give Conrad a sales job. Having his wife intervene this way was mortifying for Dad, who was very proud, but it worked, and he was so successful in selling heating units that after two weeks of trial he was hired full-time, with salary and commission. He continued to work here until he was sixty-nine years old, rising to the level of gas heating sales manager, and he would come home in future years from company parties boasting that he was the only person on the executive staff who hadn't graduated from college, or for that matter, the eighth grade in school!

We moved to a nice neighborhood to the south of town, a tree-lined street of stately old homes owned by the people living in them, wide lawns, porches, sidewalks, large azalea and rhododendron bushes everywhere, and children playing in the quiet street. Hazel Fairbanks, recently widowed and left alone with a three-story house, tremblingly took us in as her first renters, and we had the large first floor apartment with fireplace, wide hallway, and spacious rooms. We were overwhelmed by this elegant change in our lives, and my parents adopted the house as theirs, remodeling it in future more affluent times and living there in quasi-ownership until thirty-five years later when first the landlady, then Mom and Dad, a few years apart, shuffled unbelievingly into a nursing home. This became our first real home, and my life revolved around 26 Atlantic Avenue until just a few years ago, giving me a stability I had never known.

We furnished it with second-hand goods, since all of our former apartments and houses had come furnished. I remember picking out my first bought piano at the used furniture store, a large mahogany-colored upright ancient but working Dennison piano, for the grand sum of $25. This was placed in my large private bedroom, and became the co-inventor of all my first musical works. When I cleaned out the apartment in 1990, I sold the piano back to a used furniture store, and signed in large red ink on its back my name and its role in my life. Parting with that ancient relic of the late 1800s, with its out-of-tune sadly muffled raspy tone of the very old, was a very hard tearful event, akin to a close friend dying.

Fitchburg High School in 1955 was a far better school than it should have been. With the flood of ambitious post-war European immigrants working in the town's many factories and paper mills, many with very intelligent children eager to succeed, and an army of top teachers, the school was equal in rank to the two private Roman Catholic high schools that educated the rest of the town's teenaged children. I owe my entire initial discovery of classical music and great literature to this school and its wonderful teachers, who had a vivid, intense interest in their subjects and a messianic desire to impart this to us. Edward Hanjian opened up the musical world to me, and ecstatically I auditioned and was chosen for his Special Chorus, who performed Handel's *"Messiah"* that year at Christmas, when this oratorio was not yet a household fixture in our culture.

I secretly collected all the choral music we sung over the four years I was there, and played all the parts on the piano in my room, studying and memorizing the different styles of music, from Medieval to Modern, that we sang, the music being equivalent to a good college choir's choice. Just before graduation I presented Mr. Hanjian with a giant pile of scores, about three feet high (because he liked to have us sight-read through much music we never performed, just for the learning experience), and then beat a hasty retreat from his appalled stare!

As I turned fourteen, I took it on as a campaign to discourage my father from drinking so much. So at a restaurant, when he was on his second Manhattan before dinner and already tipsy from drinking at home, I angrily stomped out of the restaurant and took a cab to my best friend Bonnie Jena's house, afraid to go directly home. That was my most blatant act of intimidation, but I nagged at home and was generally obnoxious. At this time my parents decided that a summer-long visit to the Farm was in order for me, without the others in my family.

This was to be my most intimate and last really happy time with Aunt Alice and Uncle Gordon and the Farm. I had never been away from home alone, and was able to capture the last days of sunny tomboy-hood, already fast fading. I brought along an Eb alto mellophone, which has the range and general sound of a French horn, and an instrument often given to young high-schoolers who want to be in the school band and cannot play a band instrument. I had had one lesson, to learn how to blow through the mouthpiece and make a sound, and told to practice all summer, so I took to the fields every day and serenaded all the cows for miles around. Neighbors over the hills several miles away would comment, in rather uncomplimentary terms, about the "horrible moose-like din" emanating from the Tripps' fields.

Nine-year-old cousin Richard fished with me during the early mornings and we explored the pond and fields in the afternoons, sometimes along with a very ardent twelve-year-old handsome blond neighbor boy, Ned Cline, who took it as his mission for the summer to introduce me to the joys of womanhood. On one memorable occasion, Ned and I rode his father's horses up to the farm above the Tripps', resting on the Pennsylvania line, and a small cabin, where a man in his thirties was living with a cot, a table and kitchen area, and an upright piano. Manuscripts were scattered everywhere, and as we entered, the fellow, who seemed to know Ned quite well, sat at the piano and played his classical music in great swathes of Romantic sound, completely overwhelming me. I had never met a composer before, and this one was right out of a textbook! I never saw him again—he was using the farm cabin as a kind of MacDowell Colony for the summer—but the excitement of this kind of life and the sound remains with me still.

After a day of communing with the wide green New York countryside and all the surrounding farm activity, evenings we would all sit in the cozy fireplaced farmhouse living room. Uncle Gordon would read one of his vast collection of history or economic books, Aunt Alice would knit or read, Richard would work puzzles from a children's magazine, and I finally broke my writer's block and finished a science fiction tale about two girls, a spaceship, and multi-dimensional space. What is important here is not the story, but my uncle's avid interest in my work, reading the story and giving me helpful suggestions and grammatical corrections. There were no distractions such as television or radio (played only during the day), and I began to learn about the pregnant contemplative silence that breeds creative ideas. Uncle Gordon and I would stroll around the pond at night, watching for beaver, and look through his telescope at the bright stars in this black countryside sky.

There are a few times in one's life that seem to form the basis of future dreams, that are warm nests of comfort to curl up in during a long serious life, that we covet in our private hearts. This was one of those summers, come and gone a long time ago, but forever alive within me.

My first musical creations were songs. After studying the piano for about two months I made up a song about Ted Williams, my baseball idol, who in 1952 had turned the corner to forty but still played spirited ball. The song, played on the piano with full, sometimes surprisingly sophisticated harmonies, was (fortunately) never written down, although I still remember it, here in the twenty-first century, with complete recall.

I then tried my hand at pop songs, in the style of the new rock & roll that I loved and jived to all over the house, but it was more fun to dance to than to try to create on the piano (I ignored the fact that the real medium of composition for this was the guitar). I was becoming more and more interested in a wide variety of classical music that we performed and sang in the high school, our groups being so good that we regularly traveled all over the state, performing in high schools and contests, staying overnight in students' homes of the schools receiving us. By my senior year I had graduated to playing the baritone horn—the soprano of the tuba family, and performed in the orchestra, band, and chorus. My one public compositional success was the *"1959 Class Song"* (words by Susan Reid), in which I directed the whole senior class in singing for our graduation.

In 1959 Massachusetts started a tradition of All-State concerts, by combining the winning musicians of all the high school ensembles in the state, to play a series of college-quality classical concerts of music by Brahms, Sibelius, Orlando Gibbons, Mozart, etc. along with lighter fare. It was a great honor to be chosen, and I had performed (and won) in the selective regional concerts in all three ensembles. During the first All-State Festival in Hyannis, Mass. I sang second alto in the chorus, surrounded by a powerhouse of wonderful young singers, conducted by James Aliferis. As we sang part of the Brahms' *"Requiem"*, I was so overwhelmed, I cried, right there in front of 800 people.

I had planned all along to become an elementary school teacher, like my mother. In 1955, just after we moved to our final family home, the national ban on married women teachers had dissolved, and my mother returned to her chosen profession, at the Lunenburg Middle School, in the quiet country town next to Fitchburg. A hiatus of thirty years and a complete change in teaching styles created a tremendously difficult obstacle, and Mom became gravely ill from overwork, being hospitalized and almost dying from pneumonia two winters in a row.

Still, she loved teaching, and her contagious enthusiasm filled me with the desire to emulate her, so I applied and was accepted at Fitchburg State College in 1959.

There was another reason for choosing this local college: the tuition was $50 per year! I knew how desperately my parents had struggled their way out of debt, and had no desire to run up more loans attending a more expensive school. My life ambitions were very mild in those days—just to find a nice male teacher, marry and teach together in New Hampshire while skiing and singing happy Alpine songs…perhaps adding a child or two for variety. Just turning seventeen at graduation, I had had little opportunity to earn any money on my own, but we didn't need much in those days. Health insurance was minimal and completely covered by most businesses; semi-private hospital rooms were $22 a day; there were no fancy sneakers or designer clothes to buy. Students walked to school or drove ancient wrecks worth $25; gasoline prices were 25 cents a gallon; there were no computers or the hundred other electronic gadgets we all have today. Skiing was also cheap: $10 battered wooden skis and $4 junior lift tickets at major mountains—also no malls, black and white TVs, 75-cent 45 rpm records, summer vacations at relatives or friends' summer camps, etc..

MARCH 17&18, 1993

"The tall moon gleams silver through knife-thin yucca,
Bleeding stripes on the sand."

"Bird standing on saguaro spike,
Your liquid song fills the dry air with spring!"

"Plick plick tickle tearing tall ocotillo
Spiney sticking stinging starkly winding
Spring pink fingers flaring!"

"Ancient voices are the wind,
Cries and whispers, sending echoes
Calling, circling, calling…"

(Priscilla McLean, *"desert images"* for
whisper station, *"Desert Spring"* installation, 1997)

Today begins an incredible journey, into one of the most beautiful deserts on the planet—Arches National Park, Utah. We of the dark New York forests are awe-struck at the blinding light bouncing off the multitude of sandstone arches throughout the park, framing snow-capped distant mountain peaks against a deep blue sky. The soil is rust-red, often crinkled, housing millions of clumped-together microscopic bacteria, in-between the brilliant green gnarled juniper trees and turquoise sagebrush. Bright yellow flowers pop up nakedly from the red soil, and bouquets of vivid red paintbrush, along with a multitude of other spring flowers.

As we gaze and walk we see the different arches change color throughout the day, from early morning rusk, to bright yellow in midday, to flaming red at sunset. Poems begin to shape themselves in my mind, and I envision people whispering evocative desert image thoughts while others are plucking cactus spikes or juniper cone leaves into a processed microphone, desert birds such as the canyon wren are heard on the keyboard, and on tape is playing synthesizer and wind music with Navajo voices softly speaking about the beauty of it all…This all comes to me as a flash, and I say out loud, "a desert installation—we need to create another installation, about spring in the desert!" Bart looks at me with his characteristic sideways frown, and says, "Oh? How? We didn't bring any cameras on this trip, this is a *vacation* trip, if you'll remember, we tour for a living in the winter and spring, and we happen to live 3,000 miles in the opposite direction…"

But of course we both immediately begin planning to come back, and to bring cameras and tape recorders, and to map out creative ideas in advance. As the day wears on we become more and more excited.

Quote from 1993 Journal: "We are thinking of creating an installation about the desert, similar to our *"Rainforest"*, entitled *"Desert Wildness"* (actually it became *"Desert Spring"*), using slides, high surreal thin long notes, clumps of sounds (bushes, soil), animals: wolves, cats, coyotes, snakes, insects, bird calls, buzzards…Of course the desert is a very quiet place, so there would have to be silences and very quiet times…fun to think about!"

We end the day by hiking to the most spectacular arch of all, Delicate Arch, and find several other hikers, all with large cameras, and discover this is one of the most photographed scenes in the world, as it should be. As the sun sets, the colors change from yellow to orange, burnt sienna, red, and purple, with the snow-capped blue-tinted mountains seen through its arch. Professional photographers line up here with their standing cameras on tripods, trying out different filters and taking hundreds of photographs. My yearning for just one picture becomes acute, and on our way out we buy a few sheets of slides from the National Park Service display room. Of course, these won't do, but will serve as a catalyst to return…

The next day we explore Canyonlands National park, hiking an eight-mile, all-day trek down into the canyons from the sagebrush rim, not as exciting as the Grand Canyon but far less populated (in fact, *un*populated) and private, with a more gentle beauty. The bare canyons jutting up from the streambed are impressive, and there is a definite visceral joy in perpetually climbing great distances straight up and down. Most of the muscles we have been "flexing" lately have been the ones hugging the auto seat contours, and our whole bodies ache for this labor (and definitely *after* this day's labor!).

We have fallen in love with this desert and Moab, even if plagued with too many motorcyclists and pink-faced tourists, and blanch at the thought of the return drive back to the cold slippery slide of Midwestern wintry spring,which seems to last until June. Everywhere we live we leave a part of ourselves, and we have lived many years in Texas. I feel a kinship with every part of the U.S., but especially for the dry stark startling beauty and the good-natured people of the Southwest, which sadly now we enjoy only in passing through.

Tuesday, March 23

Only one week to go on our tour! To wile away the endless hours of driving from Utah to Chicago, I write out a parody of the famous circles of Hell described in Dante's *"Inferno"*, which I label *"McDantLean's Touring Inferno Revisited"*:

First Circle (describing the tortured creatures who inhabit the different circles that ring the cavern to Hell): The Opportunists. Here you see glazed-eyed unshaven touring artists that look suspiciously like Barton McLean, who are driven to insensibility by scheduling tours to please everyone's schedule, so they race across Indiana four times, back and forth to Chicago twice, up to Michigan, down to Indianapolis, up to Ontario (this folly got dropped—it was too much: we call from Oberlin Conservatory of Music to apologize and explain we are having "car trouble", but it is only *map* trouble), etc. etc. I hope parties are listening…

Second Circle: The Crowds from Hell—snowy reveling New Years First Nighters clutching drinks, or lines of eager & impatient Earth Day Festival-goers, all eager and grasping, all elbowing each other to reach the synths and microphones, hour after raucous hour while we are too busy to find food…We waste away along with our equipment, worn down to nothing (substitute lines of school children from buses when appropriate…)

Third Circle: The Truth. Instead of Wasting Away, we have eaten in *so* many restaurants and at special lunches and dinners, we are now lumbering flaccid sloths, perpetually smiling (and burping) and bulging, on and on to the next greasy meal and late night munchies…

Fourth Circle: Here lie composers with ground-down teeth and worn-away ears, perpetually having to listen to their own music, forever and ever. John Cage once told us, "The only bad thing about being a composer is having to listen to your own music over and over!" When at the 1982 North American Music Festival in Buffalo, NY, the university had scheduled a five-hour concert of Cage's works, John looked horrified and said plaintively, "Why would *anyone* want to listen to my music for *five hours?*"

Of course, next to these composers sulk the ones with over-large underused ears, who wait eternally for someone to perform their music so they can finally enjoy the fruits of so much creative labor. Having been both people, I prefer the worn-out kind, that is, *if* the music heard over and over is not a piece you wished you had never written…

Fifth Circle: Those very enthusiastic people (and this part is a blessing) who come up to a composer after a heartfelt serious concert of works created in the heat of spiritual and intellectual ecstasy, and expound with great revelation, as if this were the first time anyone had ever thought of this idea, "Have you ever tried film scoring for horror or sci-fi movies? We heard some music the other night on TV that reminded us of your style…"

Sixth Circle: The, usually young and male, Technicians of the Future, who are always lingering nearby, cooing casually: "Oh, are you still using *slide projectors?* And only *two?* Why, we have used as many as a dozen in tandem, but that of course was years ago, since it's a terribly old technology…No one uses *them* anymore! Haven't you tried *Video* yet? Why, it's much (pick one: smaller, easier, more up-to-date, more elegant, interesting, etc.)

Later, when we include a new video on our concerts, "Oh—video—again? Everyone's doing that, aren't they? Well, here we have a special engineer who has been producing wonderful laser disk images on CDs, with multiple screens"…or "*tape* music? We *never* do that anymore. Have you tried the [insert latest invention here] for really fascinating live performance?"

Seventh Circle: Dante declares the beasts of nature to be the lowest circle in the Inferno, but, ah…here is where we disagree…Perhaps this level is the Circle of Mirrors, where we truly see ourselves, inside and out, stripped of all pretense, all illusions taken away, the Artist revealed, like dreams I have had of being out on stage with no music, no tech equipment, and no preparation, standing in front of a paying audience trying to remember a scrap of music to improvise on while the spotlight beats down…

March 23, cont.

After three long driving days, we are now in Chicago, amid torrents of rain, and are dragging our wet selves and covered equipment into the auditorium at Governor's State University. This is an auditorium like no other, distinguished not by its new design, as it is quite old, but by the fact that it is "raining" *inside*—an alarming prospect for our electronics! Wastebaskets and buckets are scattered around, catching most of the drips, thankfully none yet on stage. Who knows—today we may end our lives in an unanticipated "surge" of electronic "glory"…

Richard McCreary, the head of the electronic music studio here, a tall, slim black composer of our age greets us and helps unload, apologizing nervously for the situation. This university is just about to combine with Loyola University, and there is no reason to fix up an auditorium that will be abandoned soon. Richard gives us a tour of the electronic studio, and we realize after awhile that he has single-handedly bought and built this studio from his own paychecks, and has set it up for the students, who otherwise would not have one. For our concert he has run out and personally bought a four-channel reel-to-reel tape recorder (which we didn't ask for) in case we needed it. There are a few dedicated composer-professors around the country who give of themselves to the students, beyond all recompense, and surely McCreary is on the top of the list. Along with teaching here, Richard is also a fully ordained Baptist minister with a church nearby and an extremely active musical choir. I am awed and humbled by his energetic generosity.

We are treated to dinner at the student cafeteria and joined by the Dean and a professor of music education, all flamboyant handsome African-Americans in dark blue elegant suits. After our long drive, we feel incredibly scruffy and disheveled in contrast! My hopes of performing before our first largely black audience are not realized at the concert, however, because although African-Americans are the predominant student body here, only whites and a few Chicanos come, with a black person here and there.

This is one of our "mix and match" concerts, and we proceed on stage to a very enthusiastic audience of thirty, braving the deluge outside and inside, who look up at us worriedly. I launch into the banter of a late-night TV host and thank them profusely for allowing the "rainforest" to come into the auditorium and set the atmosphere for our first piece, *"Rainforest Images"*. The laughter puts everyone at ease, and the concert is a happy event, with large sales of our records and tapes afterwards.

After the concert we follow Richard McCreary to his palatial home an hour from Chicago in a wealthy suburb, so that we can store our Honda and equipment in his locked garage, instead of at the Holiday Inn where we are staying. This is a common practice for us, as we have no equipment insurance (nor is any possible at this stage). Richard drives us all the way back, and we celebrate the successful concert by waiting another hour for the staff at Denny's Restaurant to decide to serve us, at one o'clock in the morning (not all of us in the group are Anglo Saxon white)…Bart's comforting and restraining arm keeps me from going up to the nearest waitress and throttling her. But we spend the time in excited conversation, since Richard is such an interesting person, along with his physician-wife and college-graduated grown children.

Thursday, March 25

After a short drive yesterday to Angola, Indiana State Park for a soggy spring hike and rest, we are now at Oberlin College, Ohio for two days. Elizabeth Hinkle-Turner is hosting us. A composer and recent doctoral graduate from the University of Illinois, Elizabeth is a high-powered dynamo who has a year contract teaching in the electronic studio here. We are joined by friend and colleague Gary Nelson, and the four of us laugh and talk over a generous lunch at the Oberlin Inn, where the college is having us reside. By the time we are ready to set up our lecture performance for a roomful of students and teachers, we are both so content we are ready for a nice nap.

The performance goes well, but in the smallness of the classroom my singing of *"Wilderness"* has an effect of being in an elevator with a practicing opera singer, and I notice people flinching. Not the ideal concert space. The small budget that Oberlin has for these lecture-concerts is offset by the carte blanch restaurant food allotment and the elegant room, and we manage to explore some of their finest food and drink with great satisfaction—there has to be some reason for doing all this touring!

Friday, March 26

One of the pleasures of touring is visiting old friends, and we stay overnight with another touring duo, Burt and Celeste Beerman, in Bowling Green, Ohio. Burt is a professor at Bowling Green State, but more interestingly he was one of the original "Mix" back when we started in 1974, with David Cope and us. We all toured for a year until the distances between our four colleges spanning Indiana and Ohio became too grueling. Burt and Celeste have matured into a fascinating duo of electronic composer/clarinetist and dancer, and we have many long conversations about the touring biz and how our lives have evolved. We learn a lot from Burt, because he has always been more electronically inventive than we, and he inspires us. These days he is experimenting with virtual video images with Celeste, who is about to quit her Lilli Company position and work full-time as their touring manager. We wish them well.

Saturday, March 27

Now we are regressing, driving back through Indiana, through hair-raising thick fog on the crowded highway through Chicago and up to Wisconsin, to another friend, Don Malone, head of the electronic studios at Roosevelt University, who will be our host tomorrow. Sharon, Wisconsin is a tiny town where nighttime "refugees" from Chicago live, the last stop on the commuter train. Don and his wife Ginny are renovating an old house, and are being very creative about it. We step into a very spacious homey room with large woodstove in the center, between two gas stoves and behind a long trestle table, with ceiling rafters showing overhead. Walls that are in need of repair have become art easels for their two spirited small boys, and child art designs decorate the place. Off in a corner are a computer and many modules, Don's creative workspace.

Don has decided that the market for electronic tape music is so minuscule, and the corporate forces so indifferent, that it is better to create elegant custom works for individual friends who want to hear his music rather than produce thousands of copies of unwanted CDs and tapes for a non-existent mass audience, to be stored in one's attic or closet for eternity…This is too realistic for us, and we reject the thought. We definitely believe in the happy child shoveling the manure, looking for the pony. What is life but believing in special ponies that keep you smiling while you shovel?

Don is a large man in the style of Ernest Hemingway, with a long white beard, and both he and dark-haired Ginny welcome us in an atmosphere of utter calm and peacefulness, which we desperately need after our second drive through Chicago! We sleep tonight, after a rare and wonderful home-cooked meal, in the boys' upstairs bedroom, knowing how few homes we are invited to stay in overnight anymore, with everyone's busy schedules. The Malone's two boys, Willie and Joe, are being home-schooled, and the following day we all spend together exploring a local state park. Ginny prepares the food for all the meals, and from scratch. I am reminded of the early 70s when this was a much more common practice than these hysterical times. When we leave their home for Chicago we feel as if we have been on vacation, well rested and content.

Monday, March 29

At 5:30 a.m., Don Malone drives to the commuter train, the price of living in the far suburbs, and we follow slightly later in our Honda, gritting our teeth through the fog-bound bumper-to-bumper truck-filled highway close in to Chicago. Performing in cities is always an unpleasant ordeal, except for a few like San Francisco. Here at Roosevelt University we give a lecture and play some of our tapes, to a class of music students especially assembled for this purpose. One student is so excited, he runs out of the class to take money from his bank, in order to purchase our CDs before we leave.

We say a warm farewell to Don and colleagues and drive yet again through Chicago and up the interstate to northern Michigan. The highway becomes more and more rural and winding as we head toward Lake Huron. Alpena, Michigan is our destination, up near the Mackinaw Bridge. We have never been here before, and the country is densely tree-covered and wild, and I muse again on the dramatic extremes of the USA, and where we have to go to perform.

By 10 p.m. we are checking in to the Best Western motel in a state of exhaustion, after an eleven-hour drive. We marvel at the tiny size of Alpena and an arts council daring enough to hire us from our mass-mailing, because they want to be "more adventurous" in their programming, especially for the children in this very isolated lake town. So we are here for a three-day residency.

Tuesday, March 30

By 7 a.m. I am gagging down inedible oatmeal from the nearby restaurant (obviously not their commonly prepared breakfast), and walk to the Alpena High School, where all the events will take place, as it is the only auditorium in town. The town is so excited that we are coming they have scheduled a maximum number of busloads of eager children to participate in *"Rainforest"*. Although they have provided us with a good large screen and excellent sound system, there are 50-60 nine-ten year-olds in each group, each child allowed only about two minutes to perform—very frustrating and nerve-wracking for all.

The local high school students run the cafeteria and cook the lunches, which are surprisingly tasty, and some of the best school cafeteria food of the trip. We are finished at 2:30, and return to the motel, where I rehearse my voice and then take a long leisurely swim in the large motel pool, which is inside a separate metal building like a spa. I try to swim at every location I can, the last one being at Oberlin a few days ago. Bart naps, instead.

Quote from my travel log: "At 6:20 p.m. we were dressing for a pot luck dinner given in our honor, when they (the Thunder Bay Arts Council) called—'Hurry up—we're all waiting for you!' We hustled over to the Greenery room—and were greeted by a large roomful of applauding adults—I felt like Queen Elizabeth! These are jolly rural people, rotund and energetic schoolteachers, a minister, business people: the community Pillars. We gorged ourselves on homemade fatty food—fried chicken, ham rolls, salads, cakes, etc., while Bart expounded eruditely on anything anyone wanted to know." This is the reason we perform, to be with the *real* America.

Thursday, April 1

After another day of packed busloads of enthusiastic country children with *"Rainforest"*, and a fine meal at a lakeside tourist restaurant, we look forward to our *"Gods, Demons, and the Earth"* concert tonight. But it is April Fool's Day, and we wake to—oh God not again—another blizzard with high winds! I have heard that America has the worst weather in the world, and wonder for the thousandth time why we torture ourselves for a living.

We struggle to the high school and set up, not knowing if the concert will be canceled, as the snow comes down harder throughout the day. But the Arts Council assures us that people up here do not give up easily, and will come, no matter what the weather. Just before the concert begins, while the auditorium is filling up, we sit backstage wolfing down Arby's sandwiches, and the Arts Council treasurer hands us some press clippings, Girl Scout Cookies, and a check that is $350 too light. This gesture is so pre-meditated I am taken aback, almost accepting it without a word. After all, these are such lovely people! Before I sign for it I talk to Bart, who is with the lighting boy, and we approach the treasurer and ask her to rewrite the check for the proper amount. Without hesitation, she does so, thus endorsing my opinion that this wasn't a mistake…

The timing for all this is terrible, and with the knowledge that six inches of snow has now piled up outside, I with heavy heart go on stage to face—seventy hearty souls brimming with eager anticipation, twenty of whom are children, to hear the strangest and most avant-garde concert of their lives. We are so relieved that an audience has shown up that our performance is a very happy experience, with only one brief hitch with the slide projector during *"The Dance of Shiva"* that is inadvertently unplugged, as the cord has to trail underneath all of the seats to the back of the auditorium, where the projectors are.

To keep the children interested in this definitely adult concert, I ask them to tell me afterwards how many birds and animals they hear on the tape during *"Wilderness"*. Afterward, a tiny boy comes up and, overwhelmed by being on stage, stares at us speechlessly. His six-year old sister approaches and exclaims loudly, "There are nineteen!" I have purposefully never counted them, so I can be surprised every time a child tells me. Several other children come up and exclaim that they loved the concert, although they had expected not to. I am flabbergasted, because I did not think this was for children. The Arts Council people are surprised at the potpourri of small children, bearded lumberjacks, electronics buffs, and sharp-eyed women in the audience—quite different from their usual crowd, I guess.

After today we will drive down to Indiana for a two-day residency in Indianapolis, and on to our home, and my crystal ball tells me that on the "worst interstate highway in America", outside of Scranton, Pa., our Honda will give up a rear tire amid a flurry of wild flapping sounds, and we will just make it to the *only* garage open on a Sunday…

Tour Summary *(from travel log, chronologically):*

4 bad snowstorms—we drove through 3
1 spring blizzard of the century—we were inside, giving a concert
1 earthquake (mild) in Utah, near Moab
1 killer oil slick on Rte. 50 from California to Nevada, which we missed by 6 hours
1 parent's death—my beloved father
1 mild second attack of the facial shingles
1 headlong fall (me) onto cement pavement in Chico, California
2 giant poison oak scratches down my legs from the California hills, with my legs itching for a month afterwards
1 narrowly missed loss of $350 from our pay (Alpena, Michigan)
1 incident of leaving a tape box, the Sony Walkman, and aluminum foil *on top of the car* and driving through Indianapolis, arriving safely at the Inn garage, with all of it still on top of the car!
1 disintegrating tire and blown muffler
Excellent though smallish audiences (not unusual for this music)
14 performances, 3 radio shows & classes that all went very well
2 very exhausted composers who have gained nine pounds apiece!

◆ ◆ ◆

6.

To close this Section, I will relate a dream and elegy that sums up my early life and family, written after my mother died in January of 1990, and my father had collapsed and been placed in a nursing home.

On November 10, 1990 I returned to Petersburgh after emptying the family apartment at 26 Atlantic Avenue, Fitchburg, and seeing to Dad's comfort in the nursing home. I quote from my diary:

Dream: "I am high up in a large, airy, light house. Floating. My mother calls to me a message—a woman named Cindy wants me to substitute in her elementary school class, and she has left a phone number for me to return her call. She wants me to call immediately, for it is late and time is running out. I dally, reluctant to leave my airy high spaces and come down. I laboriously climb down, it seems, a labyrinthine rope to the ground floor, which is dark.

Now urgency is upon me. My money is low, and I must call immediately. There are several phones, all with different configurations of numbers. The written down number is so complicated I keep misdialing. Once a Japanese girl answers, but she can't speak English. I become more and more frustrated. Now I've lost the paper, and can't remember the number!

Suddenly I am standing by my parents, in a dark dining room, by the door. Mom says to Dad, "You've never seen Priscilla really cry before, have you?" I begin weeping uncontrollably, pressing myself against the threshold wall and sinking into a crouch. I cry for a long time, while Dad tells jokes.

The doorbell rings. I am in the back hall (an unfamiliar room—all the rooms here are unfamiliar), and a young man resembling my landlord from Hill Hollow (Petersburgh) is here holding his baby boy. He is talking to my parents' landlady, saying how he lost all of his money and he is desperate—can they loan him some? I am wary and fearful, as I know he is dangerous, and is about to pull a gun from his pocket and rob me.

I back into the family apartment. Just then in a flash I remember the phone number of Cindy, with total clarity: 343-7062. Then with horror I realize that that is the number of the 26 Atlantic Avenue home, and if I call it, no one will answer, ever evermore...(Song: "Get along home Cindy, Cindy")...

How does one leave a home of thirty-four years? Does one ever *really* leave it? Each piece of ancient furniture, each doorknob, each mirror holds thousands of stories, memories. Saturday morning hearing muffled voices in the kitchen while lying snugly in my double bed in my "apartment" room, with its large dark upright piano, its three-mirror vanity facing it, the ceiling with its checkerboard pattern, the private "inner sanctum" (my mother's name) off my bedroom of built-in bookcase, drawers, metal desk—the perfect study if only the TV didn't back up to its door…

Sunday mornings after church, when I would come home from choir singing and join them reading the newspaper, with fresh donuts from Dunkin Donuts and coffee, feet up on the coffee table and papers indulgently spread all about. Then I would steal away and try my hand at composing on the large dark piano in the days before composing consumed my life. Dad would keep the TV football game low, so it wouldn't disturb me.

The pizza Saturday nights in the kitchen, Dad all aglow from his all-day preparation from scratch of the masterpiece, Mom and I waiting hungrily for the cooking to finish, the rich cheesy-pepperoni smells filling the small kitchen. Just at the right moment Dad would bend down and sweep it dramatically out of the oven, all red, yellow, and bubbly, sizzling. The best pizzas I have ever had!

And Mom's pies! Sunday afternoon, after the roast: lemon meringue, tart blueberry, lattice-work apple, rummy mince (on holidays), pumpkin. I can still taste them all, see her working magic in that cramped Massachusetts high ceilinged kitchen with the large pantry.

And on the kitchen table, I slaved at my studies nightly, and late at night a few poems were born, and later, laborious music copying. That table was my desk, my muse, my meals, my games—strip poker one night until 3 a.m. with aspiring swain Dave Clancy, Dad coming charging out of his bedroom red-faced in blue pajamas, no glasses, demanding to know what we were doing, and why was I sitting there in my bra?!

My parents' bedroom, where all the linens were kept in the closet, and all the games. Mom kept every greeting card we gave her over the years, and all my letters. A vast pile. Stripping it felt like those rare times I would come into the room and catch one of them naked and embarrassed. It felt criminal to hard-heartedly pile up the cards and clothes for the dump…What value a life? What merit a pile of memories? How could I violate these? But I did, I did…

My sunny bedroom with the three tall windows lighting the dark mahogany-colored upright piano against the wall, always inviting me to play and compose. The mornings I would wake up filled with expectant joy as the windows revealed piles of new fallen snow in bright sunlight, ready for skiing. The mirror-vanity that saw me as a thin shapeless 13-year old, a buxom 18-year old, a bride of 25, a strong-legged woman of 40, 44, 48...

The parties, the babies of Conrad's running up and down the hall, the fragrant but emaciated balsam Christmas trees, the tap tap of Dad's drumsticks on the radiator to the Dixieland jazz on his record player in the room where he collected thousands of stamps, the call of Mom from the kitchen, "Come and get it!" every night, the sizzle and pop of the old radiators, the army of ceramic dogs on the knick-knack shelves, Dad's loud yawn and slamming of the crossword dictionary at night, the high piercing laugh of Mom's, the musical high ring of the hall telephone—343-7062, the early morning voice of Mom—"Just make a sound if you're alive," the pat-pat of Dad's cane on the floor, the quieter and quieter house with the years passing, the shadowy old people carefully moving along, trying not to fall, not to fall down...

Can it really be ended? Is it true that the house is finally empty, scraped bare? Or are only the physical house and people gone—aren't the real ones still alive in my heart, my very being—to be here as long as I am?

2

Becoming

1.

In Old Wachusett's Shadow
Our Alma Mater stands,
Her proud New England banner
She holds aloft to all the lands.

Hail to Alma Mater,
All praise her name!
Always may her sons and daughters
Justify her fame!

Official Fitchburg State College Alma Mater,
Words and Music by Priscilla Taylor, 1963

Although friends and classmates were dismayed to learn that I had enrolled at Fitchburg State College instead of applying for Boston University or New England Conservatory of Music, I made it clear that I had no intention of pursuing a career in music. Indeed, I could not conceive of such an idea, knowing how expensive the tuition and fees in good New England music schools were, and with no music major alternatives offered by Massachusetts state colleges in 1959. At first I felt very disappointed in the sea-change in music programs from my very advanced high school to this college which bred school teachers, but I discovered soon enough that the not-difficult courses and few extra-curricular activities gave me special extra time to develop other skills.

I began studying organ at the Christ Episcopal Church, which had a magnificent pipe organ and a wonderful teacher, Donald Wilcox, who also conducted the church's boys choir. I quickly switched churches (from Universalist/Unitarian to Episcopalian), and joined the choir, as altos were needed, regardless of gender. For the next four years I walked to the Main Street church from the college, and often after studies at midnight, as I had my own key. I would unlock the totally dark church, often with Bruce Goyette, a close friend I dated who enjoyed hearing me play, and ring the rafters with the music of J.S. Bach, Mendelssohn, Guillamont, Healey Willan, and many other great composers. I felt like a mix of the Phantom of the Opera and the ghost of Bach as the dark empty church reverberated in the wee hours of the morning! The organ introduced me to a variety of tone colors and the ability to change the timbre of a melody as it was played (the cornerstone to my working with synthesizers later), plus working the pedals. Many electronic music composers-to-be have had their appetites whetted by playing the organ. Perhaps it was the effect from the magical power of the great composers, as I have never written a piece for organ to this day.

After I had been in college for a few months, still living at home, I decided to write my first piano piece, *"Rhapsody in D Minor"*, which took me the next six months, laboriously slaving over the keys of the piano on Sundays. I had only the vaguest idea of how to craft a classical piece, and the work evolved into a kind of melange reminiscent of extremely bad Rachmaninoff and *"In a Small Hotel"* sung by Frank Sinatra. My listening repertoire was confined to two piano concerto phonograph recordings—*Piano Concertos #1* by Sergei Rachmaninoff, Peter Illych Tchaikovsky, and Edvard Grieg—given to me by Tim Krieger, a close friend I dated who lived in Lunenburg, the next town over. These recordings I listened to repeatedly the summer of 1960, while working on my own naive attempt.

What is important about this episode were the incredible feelings I experienced as I composed. I had never felt such a powerful force as the intensity of creating music, and this first attempt to create a work of complex artistic quality filled me with such passion, that I would lie awake nights and pray to God that the desire to compose would never leave me. Those months of writing when I was seventeen were to shape the whole rest of my life, even if I was not aware of it, and when I became aware, a few years later, I fought against this with all my strength.

The month of June was spent being fired as a waitress at a dying hotel in York Harbor, Maine, then being hired at The Sand Dollar—a Mom and Pop diner-style restaurant directly across from York Beach, which saw me endlessly roaming the cold beach and staring off into the ocean at the rocks of Nubble Lighthouse the hours I was not working. When it mostly rained or drizzled the whole time I was there, I quit and returned home in July to bury myself in music. After the piece was finished, I eagerly showed it to a friend who was an excellent pianist, who had been the choral accompanist my last two years in high school. Susan stared at the Rhapsody distastefully, and would say the most chilling words I had heard to date, ones that rang with such truth that they have never been refuted these past forty five years: "Why should I be interested in this? We pianists have enough great literature to last us all our lives. We don't need or want this music!" I raged bitterly at her at the time, but now I know she was oh, so right…

A compartmentalization began in my life. There was the college and its studies and social activities, and there was my secret life as a new composer and organist. After the Rhapsody, I had no idea what to do next, and I deeply felt the inadequacy of that work. So I went to the choral director, Dr. Richard Kent, a red-haired mustached man in his early forties, with his thick Iowa accent. Kindly, after looking at my music, he said, "It's not whether the work is good or not that counts. What is important is that this is how you commune with the Greats, because you are doing the same creative activity they did. Every time you write you become one of the selected visionaries who can feel the passions of the great composers flowing through you."

So began the opening up of my secret life, with special private music theory and composition lessons in Dr. Kent's small office, while he perused work I had created that week, puffing away at his powerful stogy cigar. After a few weeks he said, "Your next assignment is to write a college Alma Mater, to replace the old one we have now. Let's get started on this right away," and we racked our brains to plot out the special New England words that would make this a custom-made song just right for this school. This was my first compositional success. Easily sung and in the style of Alma Maters of the day, it was premiered by the college chorus in 1961, and to this day is being sung at FSC's graduation and other ceremonies, over four decades later.

A very comfortable life ensued through my junior year. I balanced my hours of study and classes every day with organ practice and writing poetry far into the night. On weekends, when I was not skiing or running off to dances or parties with boyfriends, I was working on my theory or composing, although my compositional efforts declined greatly after the first big piece. Summers I earned money waitressing or working in stores for the ridiculously low tuition, now up to $100 per year. I read literature voraciously. In fact, I did everything but think of the future. I was so content in my coiffured custom-made world that it never dawned on me that soon I would be thrust into a classroom and expected to teach all subjects to runny-nosed noisy little children who cared not a whit about my compositional efforts!

The first semester of my senior year at Fitchburg State was spent in student teaching, split up between two different elementary schools, which were part of the college's training program. Although I somewhat enjoyed the teaching—consuming all my time—the frustration with this life was building inexorably. I finished the term and received an A, but I knew now that my next step was to graduate, and "get thee to a music school!" When I sat down with my parents and with trepidation told them my decision, thinking that they would be aggravated, having seen me through almost four years of college (going in the wrong direction), they both looked relieved. "What took you so long?" was their question in chorus. They had known for years that I needed to pursue music training, but had patiently waited for me to decide for myself. Years later I would feel the pride of having propelled myself forward with no parental pushing, and found that my ambitions were fueled greatly by the wise restraint my parents had shown, letting me grow up and become my own person and make my own way, with their ultimate blessing.

Perhaps I have given the impression that I was a nose-in-book indefatigable student who basically studied, student-taught, practiced on the organ, and walked to and from the college those four years, but this is of course false. I was having the time of my life socially, and when I was nineteen, my junior year, I danced my way through five proms in three different colleges, with five different men. I had a happy balance between romantic boyfriends and good men friends who occasionally took me out, and at one point, after postponing yet another composition lesson with Dr. Kent, he barked in exasperation, "You know, *tranquility* is the mother of creativity, not endless running around!"

But I was preening in the joy of my late-blooming womanhood, and would hear none of it. A little warning bell in my head began tinkling when I began to feel more seriously about a special boyfriend, one of the industrial arts majors. I noticed that whenever I would talk about my budding composing career, he would change the subject. At one point he said that he really wasn't interested, that he knew he wasn't as musically inclined as I and didn't want to be reminded of it. I had begun writing religious music for the college chorus, and Dr. Kent wisely had the chorus "audition" each piece without committing to a performance, and I arranged the new Alma Mater for the fledgling college band. In fact, with organ practice and weekly performances with the Episcopal boys/mens' choir, I was now spending more time on music than on schoolwork, writing on weekends and late into the night.

About the time I had decided to continue my studies in music, Dr. Kent decided to introduce me to the Twentieth Century. It is amazing that the entire

Twentieth Century has passed, and a new composer still thinks about "classical music" in 18th and 19th Century terms, like a new writer penning in the style of Robert Louis Stevenson! And that the unsuspecting young creator must be forced to address her/his own century, and then be made even more painfully aware that the rest of the society not only looks backward for classical music pleasure, but is wallowing up to the neck in popular commercial music written right up-to-date! What happens is a kind of schizophrenia—the budding composer goes inward and fashions a daydream-fairytale-accepting atmosphere gleaned from films and novels of the last century's composers, and blinding him/herself to the real situation, feeling that all will change just as soon as enough "mature" good works are created by the new young creator. People will love the music—*how can they not?*

I who came from a working class background knew firsthand the indifference of the world, which becomes magnified exponentially by the newness of the classical music. I was not interested in creating something no one wanted, but an opportunity arose that was ideal for trying out some new sounds. The Drama Department was headed by brilliant teacher and optimist Eugene Casassa, who had built one of the first area theatre-in-the-rounds in a barn on his farm on the outskirts of town and staged several plays, including new ones, each summer. Preparing to stage William Shakespeare's *"Hamlet"* at the college with the Drama Club, Mr. Casassa decided it would be nice to punctuate in-between the acts with some original music written by a student from the college, and performed by a small student ensemble. Eugene approached Dick Kent, who approached me. I was honored and flattered, and immediately wondered how to write Shakespearean music without knowing anything about music of the 16th Century…Dr. Kent gave me that look. "No, Priscilla, this is the *Twentieth Century*, and you must write in your own time." So Dick handed me two books, *"20th Century Harmony"* and *"20th Century Orchestration"* by Vincent Persichetti, told me to read enough of each to get an idea about what and how to write, and hand him the music in a month.

I decided, after doggedly pawing through the books on the piano, to write the wildest thing I could imagine—I would pay all of them back for this outrage! Clashing dissonances and new effects, like flute flutter tonguing, mingled bitterly with hard high notes, for Bb trumpet, flute, and piano. When I finished and presented my "horror", Dick laughed and said, "Now you are finally acting like a composer. Welcome to the world!" The piece is still in my pile of early works, and today seems meek and naive, with more fanfare than form, but I was 100 feet tall the evenings when the trio of friends played the music before and between the acts, and my score lay in a lightened vestibule cabinet for playgoers to peruse during intermissions. I am sure the *"Hamlet"* production was also good, although I don't remember any of it!

◆   ◆   ◆

THURSDAY, APRIL 16, 1981

I walk the sunburned sands,
Bathed in the salt-fresh water,
Sunbathed, cooled,
Cooled by the pungent air;
Cooled, sunbathed, sparkling sea.

I touch the time-worn sands,
Damp from the ebbing water,
Wandering, swayed by the water
I turn my thoughts toward the sea.

What distant sands and water,
What wonders to lands across the sea?

"Summer Soliloquy" from
"Four Songs In Season", by Priscilla Taylor
(SATB, piano, Greenwood Press, 1967)

As I am sitting on stage waiting for the tape recorder to begin, I am wondering how I could possibly fool everyone into thinking I could play the piano well enough to give a premiere concert with Bart in front of the music students, doctoral included, at the University of Texas at Austin—? My left hand is just starting to recover from the ganglion cyst in the pad below the third finger, which has just been punctured and drained by the local hand specialist. This misery popped up a few weeks ago as I laboriously tortured my hands practicing my *The Inner Universe* set of pieces for piano and tape on the university's brand new and very stiff Steinway nine-foot grand piano on stage, the piano so new that we are almost the first ones to perform on it. And to top things off, this is a send-off concert for our first McLean Mix European tour, so I am very nervous and apprehensive, waiting for everyone to discover what a charlatan I am...

Bart has just performed his new piece *"Dimensions 8 for Piano and Tape"*, and I am astounded at his newfound virtuosity. As I begin rolling and bouncing the small rubber superballs on the open piano strings, which is the start of the first piece *"Landscape of a Coleus"*, accompanied by a giant electron-microscope slide of a coleus leaf on a screen in back of me, the old magic of performance returns, and I am totally consumed by the music—forgetting audience, nerves, hard piano, and even Bart's presence. To be a composing performer is to immerse yourself totally in your fantasy, breathe and wallow in your own created environment, willing your body to play the sounds the right way, the way you truly want them, the electrical force emanating (supposedly) directly from God to the composer, in one's good moments.

The mid-April date, late in the semester for busy college students, has cut the audience size down to 300, but they are very enthusiastic, and we are happy until the next day when we realize that the Austin American Statesman has not bothered to send a reviewer. This is not so terrible, since the last concert of ours that was reviewed showed no understanding of the music at all, which is worse…

Wednesday, April 22

I simultaneously launder and iron traveling clothes while memorizing French phrases and listening to a fascinating twenty-minute electronic dramatic musical poem, *"Genesis of Kazan"*, by good friend Pekka Siren from Finland. My nerves are strung to the breaking point, and I cannot believe that we are finally touring in Europe—Bart's first trip abroad!

Saturday-Sunday, April 25-26

We leave Austin (Texas) for Europe at 3 p.m.. After a long, sleepless night of flying and waiting, we land in Belgium the next afternoon. In Brussels we cannot find a cab driver who speaks English or who understands my phrasebook French, so we have to drag our wheeled suitcases in the rain about a mile to the Hotel-Pension Les Bluet on Rue de Suisse. The elderly red-haired lady is shocked that we are here: she did not receive my letter of confirmation, so has booked the room to others. Kindly she puts us up in two single rooms for the same price as the one double room, but we are so tired she could have laid us on the sidewalk and it would have been fine with us, we would have slept! After settling in, we eat at a nearby Indonesian restaurant, which I remember from my solo journey to Amsterdam two years ago has wonderfully tasty, spicy, and cheap food. When I go to sleep, I am still so excited to be here that I have forgotten to be tired, and have to take a sleeping pill finally to calm down.

Thursday, April 30

At dawn a blaring serenade of roosters and starlings wakes us, and we stumble to the window of our large handsomely wallpapered room at the Hotel-Pension Rubens in Antwerp, to see the black birds craning their necks in discordant song on the tops of the humped slate roofs stretching across the city. The rooster's cries come from underneath us, and we are told that the hotel mistress breeds hens and eggs in the basement. At breakfast we are served bread with cheese and bologna, and I ask please for one of those fresh eggs, cooked for two minutes, if you will. The proprietress glares at me, but soon appears in the dining room, set with little round tables and a long table for dinner hour, an egg in a tiny cup by my plate. I smear "Krumpy Nut" chocolate nut sauce on my bread (addictive) and prepare to daintily eat the egg with the little spoon by its side. Ah, but it is only barely warm, the white as transparent as a fibbing child…Bart laughs and says, "She dropped it in the cold water and heated it for two minutes, as you suggested." Ah, but I meant two minutes after *boiling*…! So I pour the raw egg over another piece of bread and—it really doesn't taste too bad. It is fresh, after all.

We are now very rested and relaxed, having just spent the past three days exploring Bruges, a gorgeous medieval city of canals, called the "Venice of the North", and are ready now to perform our first concert in Europe. The day is the usual dreary Belgian gray of cold rain, and we take the tram to the BRT Radio Station, where we are scheduled to play our first European concert, to be broadcast later in the month. Joris De Laet has organized our set-up, and we meet the director who hired us, to whom we have been writing for months—Karel Goeyvaerts. The concert room is tiny and circular, with our percussion set-up, and the strangest small grand piano I have ever seen. If a pianist played only on the keys there would seem to be no difference, but my pieces call for bouncing superballs[5] on the strings and plucking strings, along with many other effects. But *this* piano has a series of sympathetic strings raised above the primary ones, an octave higher! I realize that I have to invent several new sounds to make up for the ones that can't be produced with these sympathetic strings in the way, and I am at first terrified and panicked. After playing with the new strings for a while, I become fascinated with the possibilities of a whole new sound environment to complement the piece. Europe is a series of unexpected turns and twists, as we are rapidly learning.

After a long day of technical set-up and rehearsal, we are ready for the concert at 8:30 p.m.. A minuscule audience of ten indifferent souls dribbles in to fill the fifteen seats. Our first piece is an excerpt from a much larger piece for chorus, instrumentalists, and tape (which has never been performed) entitled *"Mysteries from the Ancient Nahuatl"*, composed by Bart and arranged for our duo. Bart has filled the harp of the piano with hard preparations, which takes an hour to set up: washers in-between the strings and other gadgets which make the piano sound like a drum ensemble, ala John Cage. He has also left some of the strings untouched, for straight keyboard playing. Acquiring a set of tubular bells has been a struggle: Bart made the error of asking for "a set of chimes", and when we arrived, we were handed a small set of wind chimes! So Joris de Laet has reluctantly but speedily rented the (large) tubular bells—not a happy last minute situation!

Bart performs on the prepared piano, tubular bells, and a soprano wooden recorder while I narrate and sing a series of existential-spiritual poems from the ancient Pre-Columbian Mexican texts, at times speaking in the Nahuatl language:

> We have come only to sleep,
> We have come only to dream.
> It is not true, no it is not true
> That we have come to live on this earth.
>
> As in every spring the grass grows green,
> So, too, do we acquire form.
> Our heart puts out shoots,
> Our body begets a few flowers
> And then lies
> Withered.

Ancient Nahuatl Poetry, trans. by
Daniel Brinton, 1887.

I love performing this piece, because it is very beautiful and meditative, with unusual sounds. Second on the program is my electronic tour de force, *"Invisible Chariots"*, three movements of mixed musique concrete[6] and analog synthesizer sounds, my most powerful electronic work to date.

Next, I perform five pieces from *"The Inner Universe"* for piano and tape, with the slides projected on a small nearby screen. The pieces go very well, and I am delighted with all the newly invented sounds I cajole from the unique piano strings. To end the program, Bart performs *"Dimensions 8 for Piano and Tape"*, which features deep bird calls lowered some octaves mingled in with other musique concrete and piano sounds. His music is played only on the keyboard, so he has not had to adjust to the extra strings.

This being our first concert abroad, we are very nervous and anxious to have some feedback from the audience. But this audience is not there. Perhaps they are so jaded with the endless variety of music available, but after hearing a local concert last night, and being part of the Gaudeamus Festival in Holland two years ago, I am guessing that our style is so different from European electronic music, that no one is "getting it". We do not create music to explore a new electronic technique or instrument, nor do we adhere to a pitch formula, as many earlier composers have done. To us, the electronic medium is just another way to create intuitive music while exploring new and unusual sounds—not an end but a means to produce the music.

Karel Goeyvaerts is happy with the concert and the music, so we are pleased. This is our fate in Europe, I'm afraid. The people who hire us love the music, and the audience is indifferent. The unfortunate part is that we cannot perform here enough to "educate" them so as to make the music more pleasurable…Who says that music is the universal language?

Happily, Anne Lebaron, a fellow American composer, is in the audience, having taken the train over from Germany where she is studying composition with the famous Hungarian composer Gyorgi Ligeti. We take her and her woman friend out to a pub close by, and laughingly drown our sorrows in two (unbelievably strong) Trappist ales apiece, to the incessant accompaniment of a roving cafe violinist. By the end of the second ale, my sentences are not connecting anymore, and I can hardly see the room…I stagger off in the direction of the "Ladies Room", which is out the building in the back, and past a long row of open urinals occupied by performing men. The European way, I have learned, is a kind of "blindness" in situations like this, and I obligingly keep eyes forward, trying not to land nose-down on the uneven tiles.

Saturday, May 2

We are refreshed from our day off yesterday, after watching a workers' May Day parade down the streets of Antwerp and enjoying the local zoo, awash in stunning tulips. But now we are on the train to Brussels, for our second concert performance, at the Palace de Beaux Arts, near the center of town. We are met by a tall, slender composer who seems to have leapt from the pages of an old Flemish book or painting, with his black goatee, wild dark hair, intense eyes and forbidding look—Godfried-Willem Raes, the director of the "24 Hours of Communication" concert series that is ongoing in the round theatre where we are about to perform.

This is a unique space for us, set in front of an indoor shopping center, with coliseum-like seating, and a piano in the center. There is an unnatural urgency to our setting up, and as we perform our piano-tape pieces, the mobile "audience" flows around us as they go in and out of the shopping center, a few stopping briefly to listen on the rim. I cannot imagine how any of them are making any sense out of what they are hearing, and come to the sad conclusion that none of them are listening anyway, only resting before resuming their shopping spree. As soon as the last note of my *"The Inner Universe"* is played, I leisurely begin taking the preparations out of the piano, when four extremely energetic young people come bursting out of the corners, practically throwing my bag and tools out of the way as they push me off center stage and leap into their act as the dancers/theatre people they are. The audience is immediately entranced, and begins to sit down and watch as the performers cavort in a centuries' old European street tradition that understands restless instantaneous audiences who gather and disappear like smoke swirls, and who have no patience for concert-hall productions like we were doing. I slink away, retrieving my scattered materials from the floor, reminded of "the hook" which pulled bad performers off the stage in Vaudeville days, resolving never to perform again as long as I live, and certainly not in Europe, and…Now how *are* those people attracting that audience when we couldn't? Ah, Europe is a vast learning experience!

Sunday, May 3

Weary and jaded, we take the train to Ghent today, which is the second beautiful sunny day in a row, although our gloom creates its own gray. The same host as yesterday, Godfried-Willem Raes, greets us at his house on Kongostraat, where our bad mood suddenly evaporates upon entering his astounding four-story ancient narrow Flemish house, filled with the strangest musical instruments we have ever seen. Upon entering the house, one passes by an altered piano with each key numbered, and as one presses down the different notes, a variety of bizarre sounds erupts. In the next room we are treated to a self-performing variety of cacophonous bell alarms, mounted on a box.

Later, Godfried demonstrates his trumpet-trombone combination, the trumpet with its valves going in one direction, and the slide trombone in another, all played through one mouthpiece. There is also a bicycle wheel mounted on a platform with plectrums that pluck the spokes as the wheel is manually spun around and amplified. On the same platform is a very large bicycle horn. Godfried is the only other "wheelist" besides Bart that I have ever met, and I am completely charmed. Many of the instruments are self-performing, exploring all kinds of electronic, bell, horn, and completely original sounds, and the only corollary I can think of is the popular performer decades ago in the U.S. to whom we loved to watch and listen—Spike Jones and his Orchestra!

We meet Moniek Darge, Godfried's tall, willowy wife. The two of them also perform internationally, Moniek playing the violin and contributing poetry while Godfried composes and plays his wonderful instruments. After sharing tea together, it is time to prepare for our performance in the basement of his home, where he has set up about thirty seats around a cleared area where a grand piano sits. He holds over 300 concerts a year in this space, featuring artists from all over the world—a completely unbelievable schedule of almost a performance every night! I wonder who comes to this perpetual flood of concerts, and all new art music—Hmm. That warning bell is ringing again…

We dress, warm up, and enter the stage to see…six people, including Godfried and Moniek, all of whom are smoking in this small, airless basement room. I sing the first piece, *"Mysteries from the Ancient Nahuatl"*, and find myself gagging on the dense smoke, the audience only five feet away and puffing merrily. At the end of the last piece, Bart's *"Dimensions 8 for Piano and Tape"*, it begins to pour outside, and the sound of the pounding rain on the metal roof tiles blends in with the taped bird calls, creating a rainforest-like atmosphere and an enchanting end to Bart's impressionistic nature piece. We are all thrilled, and try to forget that there are only four people in the audience who came voluntarily…Soon we are returning to Antwerp on the train, having been to one of the most famous cities in Europe, which houses the famous Ghent Altarpiece in the Gothic Cathedral, and not having seen it or the church…Ah, the life of the roving musician!

◆   ◆   ◆

2.

End of *"observations on a winter's day"*
Priscilla Taylor (1965)

doors open   i hear a clarinet wail
violin screech   rising soprano laughs
home for the musicians

pathetic in study
but gay gay
as the abandonment of a creative dance
or the soulsuffering search of a single harmony
to make a song "perfect"—
crazy life and as fleeting as

the winter's

snow

My search for an appropriate music school for continuing study was very short. I could not yet conceive of majoring only in music, without the goal of teaching, and found that if I did post-undergraduate work in one of the other state colleges in music education, I could perhaps finish in two or three years. I did not feel I could ask my family for any money, as they had finally pulled themselves out of debt, but had none left over. I had financed my own way through the first college, which at the end of the fourth year was an incredibly low $200 tuition, having quadrupled from the $50 per year when I started. As the University of Massachusetts did not yet have a major in music, the only choice was Lowell State College, forty miles from home and reasonably priced. I would have to save every penny from summer work to afford the $500 a year for tuition expenses and living there, but at least it was possible.

I was accepted at the third year level at Lowell, exempting out of all academic and most of the music courses, due to my studies with Dr. Kent. However, I would have to take the full semester's load of student teaching and all of the music education courses. I went from being the resident composer and favored musician to being an over-aged, financially strapped student with some glaring deficiencies in my knowledge of the music world, which would haunt me in future.

After a hard summer of waiting tables at a Howard Johnsons Restaurant five days a week, I moved into a small room on the second floor of a three-story yellow clapboard house at 360 Wilder St., about a half-mile from Lowell State College. Two young women were in the other rooms—Nancy Robinson, a special post-bachelors student like myself, and Merryl Butler, in her junior year. All of us were enrolled in the music education program, but only Merryl actually ended up teaching music for longer than just a few years. Mrs. Pourier, our landlady, installed a refrigerator on the second floor landing, and we heated chicken pot pies and TV dinners on our hot plates, and washed our dishes in the communal bathtub. When the fire inspector came to visit, Mrs. Pourier would bellow up the stairs, and we would all hide our hot plates in our closets, as the house was not licensed to have cooking facilities in the rooms. This way we were able to spend only $10 a week for room & board for the two years we lived there!

On the twenty-second of November, I was cashing a check in the local bank branch when the tellers all started weeping. To my shock and horror, I learned that President John F. Kennedy had just been shot, and I stood at the counter in mute embarrassment, unbelieving. Sadly, it was the first of many national shocks to come, even penetrating my student cocoon, which became more opaque the more music took over my life. I settled into a life of classes and study, composing furiously on the weekends in the deserted practice rooms housed in an old building, one of the first ones built when the college was Lowell Normal School. This was basically a commuter campus, and weekends were very quiet. I drove home about one weekend every two weeks, as this was my first time living away from home, and I missed the family.

I began taking voice lessons. The only voice teacher in the college was an old woman who immediately recognized that I should not be singing alto and was really a high soprano, but had adapted to the lower range through teachers who had exploited my music-reading ability over the years. I could not sing any high notes and was dragging my chest voice up into the soprano range, because I felt my voice should be sounding like a heavy contralto's. This made for agony on any notes over an octave above middle C. She knew I had this problem but did not know how to help me relearn how to sing. So I ended up being assigned mezzo-soprano art songs and coughing my way miserably through them, my throat full of phlegm. On my own, I continued to sing alto in the college's concert choir and when I returned home to sing in the otherwise all male Episcopal Church choir.

One of my courses was orchestration, taught by Robert Shawnessy, a nearly blind jazz musician who wore dark glasses and taught a very freewheeling course. He called me into his office one day, said he heard I was a composer, and for the next assignment he wanted me to write for my voice and the instruments in our class, in the style of Arnold Schoenberg's *sprechstimme*, which I learned was a kind of speech-song. This was my first introduction to Schoenberg's music, but rather than listen to any of his, I began just to explore the idea of "speech-singing" and made up my own style, which I sang in class a few days later, accompanied by class musicians. It was a cross between a badly injured wolf and 19th Century German composer Hugo Wolf, and the class went wild. I terrified myself by my own daring, and fearing complete ostracism by these students, all younger than I and a bit suspicious already of me, I backed off of this new (fasci-nating) style and reverted to the traditional, not trying anything like this again until I had graduated from Indiana University and was a safely married woman!

Shawnessy directed me to study privately with Dr. Hugo Norden, as he wanted me to have some music theory training apart from Lowell State. Weekly I drove on Rte. 128 around Boston to Roslindale where Dr. Norden lived, and we sat together on a sofa by his grand piano while he taught me 16th Century species counterpoint. Dr. Norden was a sweet old elf who taught at Boston University, with a shock of white hair, a round pudgy face and glasses, and a lovable lisp, plus unbounded enthusiasm for music. He especially loved J.S. Bach and all the ways Bach used the German chorales. He taught me the Fibonacci method of calculat-ing structural points in one's music, and all the (to him) delightful ways one could use counterpoint, his favorite being double counterpoint at the octave.

After a couple of years I produced a very contrapuntal string quartet according to the strict rules (and deadly dull), and Hugo became transfixed with joy, sug-gesting that we form a duo, as he was also an accomplished violinist. I could write violin and voice music, which we could perform together, forming a duo that would tour the various coffeehouses in Boston! I tried to imagine the '60s coffee-house crowd, after listening to Joan Baez and smoking hashish, being enchanted by a round old white-haired professorial elf and his nervous female student (wear-ing the owl-eyed heavy eyeglasses of the day) playing double counterpoint at the octave in the style of Bach…hmm…Hugo was a dear man, and I enjoyed my years of study with him, but that arrangement (fortunately) never came to pass.

During my two years in Lowell, I learned more than the study of music, important as it was. Perhaps the greatest lesson of all was how not to ruin my life by marrying the wrong man…

When I began at Lowell State, I was placed with students younger than myself, who knew that I already had a degree. Therefore, I was obviously a very strange person to be studying for another Bachelors degree immediately after-wards, and they tended to shy away from me. Subsequently, I was very lonely and isolated, despite living with two other women. In my class was a very charming, slender and tall young man who seemed, unlike the others, intently serious about his music study. We both played baritone horn in the college wind ensemble, and along with being a fine horn player, Bill financed his way through school by forming a folk trio and playing guitar in the Boston coffeehouses on weekends.

Soon we began dating, and I wrote a hootenanny[7] song for his group, which I heard performed at the coffeehouse, to my great pleasure. One day in November, while walking along the banks of Walden Pond in Lincoln, Mass., Bill proposed to me. Instinctively, I knew something about this was wrong, but was not sure why I felt so uneasy. I accepted, with the provision that we wait to marry until I graduated in two years. Soon after, at our engagement party in Fitchburg with some of my new friends from Lowell, we announced our plans to wed. There was dead silence. Gradually people began to converse with each other, but not one person congratulated us, or even acknowledged our announcement!

It became quite clear why, very soon afterwards. Bill lost his charm almost immediately, and became more and more verbally abusive. He ordered me around; he wanted every waking moment of my time to focus on him and his actions. He was unbearably rude to his and my parents, and very emotionally unstable. Never had I had such a difficult relationship with any man, and on top of this, he did his utmost to impregnate me (so I could not back out of the engagement). Marriage to him would have destroyed any chance of future composing or graduate school, or peace of mind! I did a great amount of praying that semester, and finally summoned the courage (he was mesmerizingly dominating—hard to combat) to break off our relationship.

I mention this experience because so many women have fallen into this trap, becoming single mothers and struggling to survive and write down a few notes, or artworks, etc.. At the end of that first year away from home I knew definitely whom I would never marry, and why—probably the best "course" I ever took! After our breakup, Bill almost immediately became engaged to the singer in his group. She became pregnant[8] and dropped out of school. They were married, but later he turned out to be far worse than I ever had imagined…As soon as I was free, my friends jubilantly told me of their great joy and relief. How very fortunate I was to wake up in time!

That summer I celebrated by taking a basement apartment in the Beacon Hill section of Boston with two women friends–Nancy Robinson and Nathaly Heselton–and waitressing, within a note's throw of the Boston Public Gardens and all the summer events taking place there. We rented a piano, and for a few weeks I lived the life of a city dweller, for one of the only times in my life. I began writing a piece for the college symphonic wind ensemble. The apartment was largely underground, dark, and dank, surrounded by other flats where the women were in a "slightly" different profession…Soon, Nathaly quit her job and went back to safe suburban Somerset. Nancy and I could not swing the extra rent, so we had to abandon our lovely city life. But I had gotten a very good job as waitress at Anthony's Pier Four Restaurant on the docks, one of the best restaurants in the city, and paying large tips.

I tried to stay in the area by moving into Nathaly's house in Somerset. This, too, was to end in failure. Each day before going to work I would enthusiastically compose my wind ensemble piece on the upright piano in Nathaly's family dining room, to the agony of her mother in the next room, who loathed me. After two weeks, Mrs. Heselton asked me to leave, as she was "near to a nervous breakdown" with all the cacophony! So I finally retreated to Fitchburg, and for another few weeks drove the hundred mile round trip five days a week, arriving home as late as 3 a.m. on weekends, and once becoming stranded at 2 a.m. as my ancient Chevy's ball bearings froze to the front axle and my whining lurching car ground to a smoky halt in the middle of the highway…Ah the perils of youth!

When college classes began again, I proudly showed my symphonic wind ensemble composition which I titled *"Holiday for Youth"* to Dr. Willis Traphagen, the director of the ensemble for which it was written. He helped me revise and reshape it into a much better piece, and I set about copying the parts, as he had promised to perform it the coming year. It was my first large ensemble work, patterned after Paul Creston's music, which we had performed, with his driving rhythms. This was a huge step forward for me compositionally. My mother, who had never written music before but could read music from her piano lessons of long ago, gamely agreed to help with the copying, and years later, after it became published by Bourne Co. Inc., she would look through the printed parts and shriek joyously, "I know that note! I copied that part!"

Unfortunately, I had not practiced the baritone horn since school had ended, as I had no instrument, and a very excellent freshman auditioned and was chosen to be a partner with Bill Ryder instead of me. I was in shock. I couldn't be in the ensemble I had just spent months writing a piece for? Willis Traphagen took pity on me and made me an extra percussionist, which meant I played all the odd percussion and instruments that only occasionally made an appearance. This was actually a wonderful development for a budding composer, as it led to a fascination for these instruments, and eventually to my creating new sounds.

To perform these instruments, one had to be extremely alert in reading and counting rests in the music, then instantly coming in and playing perfectly, a skill that took a long time to learn but which sharpened my musical abilities considerably. I remember playing the tambourine in George Bizet's *"L'Arlesienne Suite"*, which involved repeated rapid attacks, and my tired hand would gradually slow down, thus dragging down the rhythm of the whole ensemble, as I was "timekeeper". Then I would hear a hoarse yell, "Taylor! You're slowing down the group again!" and I would strike with renewed vigor, like one of those wind-up monkeys with the cymbals.

Speaking of cymbals, I took mine home and shined it up like a mirror for my debut in my own piece, *"Holiday for Youth"*, the premiere of which was scheduled during an exchange concert at Fitchburg State, my old Alma Mater. This was a big moment for me, and I wanted to do my best. At the concert I came very close to breaking my nose when I grazed its tip during the big climax with a thundering cymbal crash, and I found my eyes watering from the impact. The picture of the alumna-composer smashing her nose in the middle of her celebratory composition in front of several hundred people was not the way I wanted to be remembered in the college annals!

About children. That summer when I was twenty-two and working on the symphonic wind ensemble piece at my piano in Fitchburg, my mother came into my room and said, "You know, Priscilla, you are going to have to give this all up when you have a child. Otherwise your child will grow up with baby sitters instead of a mother's care, and that isn't right. A child needs the total attention of its mother, which is far more important than writing down notes on paper." I agreed with her. I would just give up the children, then, which is what I did not say aloud. My mother's edict was a bit hypocritical, as she had worked at an outside job since I was six years old. She evidently did not want me repeating her mistakes. Everyone was afraid of where my composing was leading, including myself...

More statements. Dr. Kent once said, "If you want to continue composing after you are married, you will probably have to hide your work, doing it after your family goes to bed, or in the kitchen in the early morning. It's not something that a man can accept easily." Dr. Hugo Norden said, "I think the most successful women composers are rich. Then they have enough money to hire servants and nannies, and can have the leisure needed to compose. It's a tough world for a woman composer." His statement was the truest, but at the time I couldn't imagine even *knowing* a rich man, let alone wanting to marry one.

MONDAY, MAY 4

So far our concert tour has been disappointing, to say the least. No audience, no reviews—only money! We leave Antwerp today on a train crowded with holiday revelers going home, and reach Paris in mid-afternoon for a mini-vacation. Bart's wallet is bulging with ten bills of $100 each from our concerts, and as we are walking through the train station, we hear a loud barrage of excited French directly behind us. Turning around we are horrified to see Bart's wallet on the ground, with the hundred-dollar bills gently wafting across the station, and the middle-aged couple who called to us striving mightily to collect all the bills, which they return to us with a stiff lecture (in French) on our mishandling of the money. All of the negative, foreboding stories about the coldness of the city and its people evaporate in a second, and I am almost in tears of gratitude. We have to do better than this in future, however!

Thursday, May 7

We have been enjoying ourselves, touring areas of Paris I have yearned to see for decades—Notre Dame Cathedral, only a few blocks from our hotel Henri IV (25 Place Dauphin), also visiting the Sacre Coeur Cathedral where we purchased a still-wet painting from a street artist, the Tuilleries—a public garden of massive rhododendron and azalea bushes that was made famous in Modest Mussorgsky's great orchestrated piano piece *"Pictures at an Exhibition"*, and all the Left Bank that our sore feet could manage after three days of constant walking. A difficulty arose with the concert money that we can't seem to send back to the U.S., and we spent half a (precious) day arguing with the people in the post office about how to mail a bank check in dollars. Our lack of speaking French paralyzed us and we finally gave up, and Bart now places all of the present and future money earned in a sock pinned to the inside of his underpants for the duration of our tour, which eventually makes him look as if he is gaining weight! We have learned too late the importance of procuring money belts, which we had not been able to find easily back home.

Today we arise early and take the Metro to IRCAM. Bart has made an appointment with David Wessel, the director of Pedagogy, for a short tour. This is France's premiere headquarters for computer music, and is stationed in one of the strangest buildings I have ever seen, in the center of the commercial section of town. A phantasmagoric array of brightly colored pipes of different hues wrap around the building, the plumbing designed to not be concealed as in every other building, but displayed as art here. It resembles a giant next-century robot, completely standing apart from its traditional neighbors. David meets us upstairs, and leads us through the different rooms lined with reel-to-reel tape recorders and computers, where composers from all over the world come to study and create new music. The rooms seem cold and mechanical to me until we are led to the huge auditorium space, which has giant modular wood panels to create any acoustic shape the ensemble desires. Then I am struck with the image of a benevolent arts-oriented country that finances such a monumental gift to its creators, something unheard of in the U.S..

I am impressed by the musical excerpts of the visiting IRCAM composers that David plays for us, and a little envious. But I do not think I could work in such an austere environment, however government-friendly. At a sidewalk cafe on St. Michel we eat Greek sandwiches in grape leaves and drink beer, spend the afternoon at a park with the only grass I have seen (with many signs warning to keep off of this rare entity), and after dinner sit watching the left bank people stroll by at Pont Neuf. An interesting event has been occurring across the street from our hotel. A small film company has staged a scene on the street in front of a flower shop, with a beautiful actress who holds an umbrella while stagehands pour water over it as she poses. They repeat this scene endlessly, gesticulating in rapid French, and we never know if it is a television commercial, a "foreign" film, or an act for models. They are there for at least three days, pouring gallons of water over that same scene!

We muse along the banks of the Seine in the sunset, then return briefly to our hotel to pick up our packed bags, sadly say good-bye to Paris and hike the few blocks to the train station. By 10:40 p.m. we are in a sleeper on the Arlberg Express, bound for new adventures at the Zagreb Muzicki Biennale (international new music festival), Yugoslavia.

Friday, May 8

At 6 a.m. the train porter wakes us, asking if we want coffee or tea, but I would rather have more sleep. After only four jolting hours of sleep, I am quite groggy, and after our coffee stumble to the tiny washstand in the sleeper cabin. We are roused out about 6:30, and the sleeper cars are removed from the train. At 9 a.m. we change to a more luxurious train, with a dining car that has leather seats. Here we eat breakfast and watch the magnificent peaks of Switzerland fly by, wishing we were up there wandering in the Alps. Amid the many new-looking Swiss houses the meadows are covered with dandelions, blazing yellow in the sun. When lunchtime comes, we switch to dark Austrian beer and our own sandwiches, reluctant to give up the wonderful dining car with the big picture windows.

Tonight becomes afternoon as we head east, disembarking in Salzburg, and exchanging enough money into Austrian currency to buy dinner in town. Since we have several hours, we roam around the incredibly beautiful and ornate streets of Salzburg amid loud motorcycles. The Americanized Austrian restaurant is mediocre and the people are loud and pushy. Perhaps we are just over-tired. We head back to the railroad station by 9 p.m. Austrian time, and exchange all of our francs and Austrian marks and some American dollars into Yugoslavian dinars, trying to anticipate just the right amount we will spend, since we have been told that the dinar is useless outside of Yugoslavia. Then we sit on the platform and watch the modern, sleek trains go by filled with travelers.

At 10:40 p.m. a dirty, ancient, lurching and screeching train comes in. Surely this can't be–but it is–bound for Zagreb. There are no first class sleepers available, so we have to settle for a second class "couchette". We enter the train and are overwhelmed by the smell of urine coming from the public toilets. Our couchette is very filthy and blazingly hot, with two narrow seats we are supposed to lie down on, surrounded by enthusiastic hot radiators. It is almost impossible to sleep, but I manage about three hours.

Around 5 a.m. I am so excited and curious about this new country that I dress and run to the railing outside the rooms. There I watch the sun rising over a post-card view of Ozark-like mountains, deep green forests and mountain streams. A young Croatian man watches along with me, and I find I can converse with him in German, his command of the language being about like mine, and we speak to each other slowly and carefully, thrilled to be able to communicate.

The farms have long narrow buildings, and many of the houses are also this style. This country appears to be older and more run down than the rest of Europe we have seen, and I realize that Yugoslavia was not bombed in World War II, which has resulted in a crisp new and clean look to so much of Europe—a benefit I had not thought about before. At 8 a.m. the train comes to a fingernails-on-blackboard halt inside an ancient station, and we disembark. This is truly another world. Beggar women in head shawls holding babies confront us, which is a surprise, as we are now in a Communist country that I thought took care of all its inhabitants. Perhaps this is a custom—held over from previous days? After enduring a long outside line to show our passports to a clerk at a win-dow, we grab our bags and walk to the Hotel Esplanade, across the street and a very large square. As we bump along in an exhausted haze, suitcase wheels bang-ing on the cobblestones, I stumble and drop my carry-on bag. Something like blood oozes out of the bottom, and to my horror I realize that I have just broken our expensive bottle of French wine dragged all the way from Paris, and it is now soaking through all of our dirty laundry, coats, and umbrellas that are wrapped around it for cushioning!

I am mortified to be entering probably the most elegant hotel we have ever been in, dragging a duffelbag that is painting the pavement maroon in a wide swath. The Hotel Esplanade is huge and luxurious, in Victorian style, with sump-tuous ballroom, dining rooms, bars, and columned foyers with ornate seats. Waiting for us is our guide for the week—a young woman from the university who will escort us around here and help with the language problem, since Yugo-slavs generally do not speak English. It is a great relief to see her. All the musical groups have been assigned guides.

The porter pretends not to notice our hemorrhaging bag, and we somehow make it to our large spacious room with private bath. The price, which includes breakfast, is normally $60 per day for two, but as part of the Zagreb Muzicki Biennale Festival we pay only $28. As soon as the porter leaves, we fall onto the beds in a coma, and are asleep in one minute, and stay that way for the next three hours.

The afternoon is spent, after a small lunch of delicious curdled cheesy milk over bread at a luncheonette in the hotel, washing all of our red-stained clothes and umbrellas, which takes hours. Fortunately, all of the wine comes out, but what a loss as we see it run down the drain never tasted! We dress and walk to our first real meal here—at a Hungarian restaurant on the way to the main concert hall where the first event of the Festival will begin at 7 p.m.. The food is wonder-ful, very spicy—hot pepper salad, goulash with much paprika (paprikash), choco-late pancakes for dessert and Turkish coffee, which is my first experience with this syrupy sweet, thick drink with an intense espresso flavor.

I am doubling as journalist for this festival, as I am on assignment writing a major article for *Musical America Magazine* about the Zagreb 11th annual Muz-icki Biennale. I feel obligated to go to as many events as possible, which will be daunting in the next eight days, as each day has events from 7 p.m. until 1 a.m.. The first concert features two ballet companies, and the most memorable one is the Ballet of the National Theatre of Sarajevo, performing *"Kreature"* by Japanese composer Shin Ichiro Ikebe—a fascinating dance of conception and life, where the whole ensemble creates a mass movement like one animal, using texturally rich orchestral music and a setting which includes a paper-mache moon and huge mobile balls.

Sunday, May 10

At the opulent breakfast in the hotel dining room we sit and talk with a good friend from the U.S., Yvar Mikhashoff, who is the pianist for the Sylvano Bus-sotti opera *"Le Racine"*, scheduled for tonight at midnight (!). Yvar has extensively performed Bart's *"Dimensions II for Piano and Tape"*, and we have spent many hilarious hours over dinner at our house with him, listening to his escapades as he tours constantly all over the world playing new music, and teaches full-time at the University of Buffalo, with seemingly indefatigable energy. It is good to see some-one here whom we know.

After breakfast we walk to the Biennale Cultural Center and introduce ourselves. My journalistic status enables me to have free Turkish coffee and pastries with the other "honored guests", and the people at the Center give us a thick book profiling contemporary Yugoslav composers along with many recordings. It is far nicer to be a press agent than a composer! A young composer, Branco Starc, introduces himself and invites us to visit his home as soon as we have some free time. We return to the Hungaria Restaurant, a block away, and meet Yvar for another great dinner, which has us so engrossed that we find ourselves starting late for the next concert, and having to take a taxi. This is a concert of Slovak and Polish orchestral music, all good pieces, but the ones that stand out are Branimar Sakac"s *"Matrix Symphony"* and Milko Kelemen's *"Mageia"*, the latter inspired by Mexican culture. The concert is a long five hours, and during intermission in the lobby a piece by (American) Jacob Druckman is being performed by English composer Barry Guy, a double bassist, who gamely plays to an audience involved in drinking hard liquor and talking (I am to learn that putting the English and American composers in the lobby to perform their music in-between the *real* events is unfortunately typical). I feel sorry for Mr. Guy, but this sorrow will become bewildering anger in the days ahead…

Not allowed to collapse, we must take a taxi to the opposite side of town to attend the Bussotti opera at midnight. Bart writes later in his journal, "The Bussotti *'Le Racine'* is a bunch of pompous fluff which is supposed to herald the *triumphant* return of serial music. Bah!" We leave after fifteen minutes and return to the hotel.

Monday, May 11

We have a decidedly "chilly" breakfast with Yvar, who is unhappy over our opinion of the opera. Just as gloom is setting in, another friend joins us at table as Yvar departs back to the States—Melvyn Poore, the English virtuosic tubist who performed my tuba & taped whale ensemble piece *"Beneath the Horizon III"* at the Gaudeamus Festival two years ago. Melvyn is here to perform Trevor Wishart's music tonight. The three of us, plus Pekka Siren–composer from Finland, and a Rumanian composer, Horia Ratiu, chummed around at the Gaudeamus Festival for the nine days, laughing, drinking, and cavorting through the streets in the various Dutch cities like over-aged teenagers out on a holiday, and not the married-with-children-serious people we really (?) were…

Tonight the Stockholm Cramer Ballet performs four dances of uneven quality, and during one of the less inspiring pieces I hear a sound that becomes very common throughout the festival: someone loudly honk-blowing his nose. This, I am told, is the way the audience shows disapproval, instead of catcalls or boos! At 10 p.m. in a small theatre hidden away in the recesses of Zagreb we are treated to one of the best events of the festival: Trevor Wishart's fantastic theatre music.

Later, for Musical America Magazine I will write: "Another 'Spectacle' was the production by Trevor Wishart, a young composer from York, England, who with his band of three performers (Melvyn Poore, tuba, Kathryn Lukas, flute, and Martin Mayes as improviser on the french horn in-between pieces) put on three theater works of black humor. There was hilarious appreciation from the few English-speaking members of the audience, and bewilderment from the others. Wishart's ideas are basically grim: humanity crushed by technology and bureaucratic thought control. These concepts are realized through fantastic and stifling tuba mutes in '*Tuba Mirum*' where the tubist is a political prisoner in a cell, boxes filled with 'technologically' taped flutes confusing the improvising soloist in '*Fidelio*', and an Adam and Eve, the tubist and flutist in body suits, trapped in a 'utopian' giant music-box clock with stuffed birds, animals and 'rain' in '*Walden II*'. The integration of message, wit, and music made for a memorable late evening." I smile with irony that this message of technology taking over and rules of behavior being tightly controlled should come from an electronic music composer...

Tuesday, May 12

At breakfast I interview Trevor Wishart about his theatre pieces we experienced last night, for background on my *Musical America Magazine* article. Then we walk down the main street to the Center for Cultural Information to buy some more recordings and talk to the people gathered there. The streets are lined with heavy long buildings, very official-looking. At one point we walk past a city park with the loudest frog pond I have ever heard. Today Bart is wearing a silk shirt with Disneyland castles on it, and Yugoslavs passing by whistle "Yankee Doodle", which upsets him to the point that he won't wear the shirt again...For me there are moans and clucks from the women who do not approve of my pants. They are all wearing dresses, obviously the accepted style here. It's amazing what can be understood without language! We stop at a tiny grocery store and point to a loaf of bread cheese, tomatoes, and chocolate, which the storekeeper adds up on paper. We hand him our money, like pre-school children who cannot add, and he takes what is needed.

We have now to go to the civic auditorium where we heard the orchestral concert, which lies outside the ancient Roman wall surrounding the city, on the other side of town, to rehearse for our own concert tomorrow night. Bart studies the map as we make the long walk, in back of the railroad station and down many winding streets and under the wall via the highway bypass. We practice in separate rooms in the very modern building, and Bart finishes before I do and returns to the hotel. It is raining outside when I finish, and I leave and immediately become lost. I cannot follow the map (written in Serbo-Croatian) and although I can see the wall, I have no idea where the bypass under it is located. Before I lose sight of the auditorium, I return to the main desk, and they patiently in thick broken English try to explain the map. Our student "guide for the week" mysteriously disappeared after our first meeting at the hotel and has never returned. We had inquired after her at the front desk, and the student had left a message saying that she had final exams and would not be able to escort us anywhere. So much for hospitality! (We were to learn later that every other party had a guide, and this was an unforgivable sin to leave us in the lurch.) So I set out on my own again to try to reach and conquer the Wall.

I reach the wall but there is no opening. I can see the railroad station from here (it is now pouring rain) and know that the hotel is on the other side of it. I decide, with time running short for returning to go to dinner, to try a bus. A bus halts, and I hop on. The driver mumbles in Serbo-Croatian, and I turn and ask the passengers, "Does anyone speak English?" No, no one does, or German either. The driver orders me off of the bus. I stand there in the pouring rain holding my dinars with the bus gone, and burst into tears, like a four-year-old child. A kindly old lady approaches and tries to be of help, but of course she doesn't speak English either. So I have no other recourse but to return to the civic auditorium again.

I ask the very concerned front desk clerk if she would call the hotel and have Bart paged. She does, and soon I am begging him to pick me up in a taxi. He is disgusted, but agrees. After all, how could anyone not read a little map and figure out how to get back? Soon we are back in the hotel, and I am changing into dry clothes, but I remain upset about this long after the incident is over. Actually, I am *still* upset about it, and would like to try that Wall again sometime. There *must* be an opening…!

Tonight we endure a very dramatic, heavy one-act opera, *"Jakob Lenz"* by German composer Wolfgang Rihm, in post-Alban Berg style. The performers are wonderful, but the room is so small and the music so loud that it makes my head ache. Late at night we have a lively discussion with Keith Potter, who writes for the British *"Contact"* magazine. By now I am enjoying myself again.

Wednesday, May 13

We arise early and after a quick breakfast walk the now-familiar route to the civic auditorium. Our rehearsal and level-settings go very well, and we have time to walk back together and rest during the afternoon. That is good, because the *worst concert of our lives* is about to happen. Back in the lobby of the auditorium, where our concert is scheduled (this sounds familiar…), we watch as Daniel Lentz and his assistants set up for his part of the concert, which comes just before ours. Daniel Lentz is a young composer from California whose style of music is a mixture of minimalism, cocktail piano, and soft rock. The concert begins with Yugoslav orchestral music in the main hall, and as last time continues for several hours. I grow more and more nervous waiting, and wonder how much more music the audience can endure in one evening. They seem to have a giant amount of patience, and the concerts so far have all been crowded to the last seat.

After four hours, it is time for the audience to file into the lobby, where the bar has been setting up, and everyone immediately joins a line for refreshments. It is Daniel Lentz's turn to perform on the piano. Daniel's piece is forty-five minutes long, and the audience, who seems totally unfamiliar with this style, begins to pelt him with green cocktail napkins wadded up and concert programs. This is too much for me. I retreat upstairs to "warm up" before I break into tears once again!

By the time I return for our part of the concert, it is 11:30 p.m., and the (by now much smaller) audience is quite drunk and talking and laughing loudly. Lentz's strategy was to turn up the amplified volume and drown them out. But I do not like to be covered with green paper balls, and when it is time for me to perform *"The Inner Universe"* on the piano, after the first piece where we perform together *"Mysteries…Nahuatl"* (which is incomprehensible to the audience), I decide to play softer and softer, barely breathing on the keys. For awhile this idea works, and there is a hush which lasts until they get tired of being polite, or until they have actually heard the music and decide it isn't worth it, and their volume rises again. Bart manages to get through his *"Dimensions 8",* but before his last note, Paul Possner, a German video artist who works in the Belgrade studio, blasts on his video and music, totally erasing Bart's delicate ending.

In my diary, over a bottle of rum and coke, I write early in the morning in the hotel room: "I feel devastated. At this point I cannot see much sense in writing any more music. No one seems to care—what we do doesn't seem to matter in the slightest. Performing in Europe has been one crowning bad experience…I don't know why they (the Zagreb Biennale committee) bothered to have us come if they think so little of us. We are like two wounded animals, crawling in a corner away from each other. I don't even want to go to any more concerts, or review the festival. I just want to go home."

◆   ◆   ◆

3.

In June 1965 I graduated from Lowell State, and immediately rented an inexpensive three-room apartment in a run-down neighborhood in Cambridge, Mass. with Carol Schiavone. Carol was a brilliant, talented girl who had performed in my voice/composition recital as well as for most of the groups on campus and who graduated summa cum laude. Before the recital, I hardly knew her, but she was the best student pianist in the school, and she enthusiastically agreed to play my pieces. At the recital I sang several original songs, Robert Perry and Carol played my trumpet sonata, and Cecilia Miles, on the piano faculty, played my piano sonata and accompanied my singing. I organized this recital mainly for my benefit, as it was not required, but it proved an invaluable learning experience, and gave my friends and family a chance to see me as a composer/performer for the first time.

The added bonus was getting to know and become friends with Carol. We both wanted to live and teach near Boston after graduation. I applied for six positions teaching music in the public schools, and after several interviews was accepted by all six! I chose the one closest to Boston, in the prestigious school district of Lexington at the Adams and Munroe Schools, near where I had done my student teaching, and which had the highest starting pay–$5500 per year. Carol found a job teaching strings in the Medford public schools (she also was a budding violinist). That June I took a cocktail waitress job with Carol at the U.S. Air Force Base, which allowed us during the daylight hours to completely paint and remodel our dingy (but promising) apartment.

We painted the living room and bedroom beige and hung green burlap curtains, which went with the cheap bright turquoise sofa and easy chair we bought for $100 total. We had heard that our next-door neighbor was a furniture mover, and he helped us move our furniture in, then invited us to his house next door for a celebratory glass of wine. The whole family of French Canadians—grandmother, children, dog, mom, and dad gathered in the large kitchen, and Carol was invited to sit at the well-tuned upright piano there and play some songs. She played some Chopin, and inquired about us renting a piano from them. "No!" thundered the owner. "You are much too good for that! Please—take piano home with you and use it until you move from your apartment. It will be an honor to have someone like you playing on it. And, please, also take this (three foot high) carafe of Chianti as a welcome present to the neighborhood!" He even moved the piano for us, and I had another lesson in the true Christian spirit, which wrapped around that big family like a warm cocoon. So we were blessed with our very own piano for as long as we wanted it (and enough wine for a year).

We moved into our renovated apartment at the end of August, paying $90 a month. Besides the nice French Canadian family next door, we faced a complex of low-income "projects" on the street opposite. The house we lived in had two apartments, ours being on the ground floor with a wooden porch and area for a garden. Upstairs lived the landlady and her husband and mentally challenged son, who was fully grown and six feet tall, but gentle as a kitten.

Carol set an artistic tone by placing a large photograph of the Los Angeles Symphony conductor, Zubin Mehta, on the kitchen wall by our table. We divided up the housework by each cleaning one of the rooms, and Carol agreed to do all the cooking, since she was from a Northern Italian family and hated my New England food. I can thank her for making me aware of spices and exotic flavors, which revolutionized my life!

This is a picture of a typical day teaching. I would awaken, rising three feet straight up in the air to the *"Star Spangled Banner"* at 6 a.m., blasted out of the clock radio, set by (sadistic) Carol. I would roll over and go back to sleep until 6:30 when she vigorously practiced the violin. By 7:30 I was driving my brand new red Volkswagon Beetle with the sunroof, maneuvering through heavy traffic to Lexington and one of the two schools assigned to me. At 8 a.m. I conducted either before-school elementary school chorus or band, then had a packed schedule of classes from grades one through six, plus two classes of mentally challenged and one class of emotionally disturbed children (they were my favorite classes, because they loved music so much). There was a half-hour for lunch. The school continued until 3 p.m., and then I taught free private instrumental lessons in trumpet, trombone, and flute, as part of the job. This continued until 4 p.m., at which time I would plan my lessons for the next day and drive home, arriving by 5:30 or 6 p.m..

Being young and just out of school, exposed to the wonders of the Boston area, I was not going to allow a little thing like the murderous schedule of teaching full-time discourage me. So I scheduled something to do every night. Monday nights I went to a three-hour rehearsal with Alfred Nash Patterson's Chorus

Pro Musica at the Old South Church in Boston, where I sang soprano. Tuesday nights Carol and I reserved for Harvard Drama Club productions, attending each event in their theatre-in-the-round. Wednesday nights I composed, preparing for my lesson with Dr. Norden on Thursday nights in Roslindale, where I was writing simultaneously *"Symphony #1 for Orchestra"*, a piece for symphonic wind ensemble for Willis Traphagen, and *"Rainer Maria Rilke Poems: Three Songs for Voice and Violin"*, the only piece of the three still extant today.

Saturday morning I took a French horn lesson, which I had started that autumn. Friday and Saturday nights were reserved for (the rare occurence of) dates, and Sunday, when I wasn't composing or working on an oil painting that I was creating, I collapsed and tried to find strength to do it all over again the next week. Mostly I would run in from teaching, gobble down Carol's wonderful cooking, dash out the door to return at 11:30 p.m. or 12 midnight and, with a tiny, reluctant hot water heater, try to make the water warm enough to wash the dishes by 1 a.m. or so. Often the dishes sat in the sink for days untouched until Carol would bitterly complain and refuse to cook anymore!

As the year wore on, I became busier. I was expected to produce a large musical production for the Christmas season for both schools. This was before the government law barring prayer and religious songs in the schools, and I wrote a pageant about the first Christmas, and involved all the classes in it. In the Adams school there was a fifth grade student, Thomas, who had advanced muscular dystrophy. This was the last year he would be able to attend school, and by the end of spring was in a wheelchair. He was a large boy and loved music, so to involve him and give him something special to remember, I made him one of the Three Kings and had him lead the long line of fifth and sixth graders who were going to see the holy birth in the manger. He had two lines to memorize, which was very hard for him, but he did it, and marched slowly but proudly down the center aisle, the two grades trailing along behind him. Everyone knew why I had chosen him, and all were rooting for him, which made him the center of attention for a few weeks, anyway. Whether it had any lasting effect on him is questionable, the disease taking its toll soon after, but it had a wonderful effect on the children and me.

I dressed up the mentally challenged children to be Christmas elves, so that they could come on stage and sing, and the audience accepted their strange looks and manner (in those unenlightened days) with good spirit. I arranged all the carols into two and three parts, and wrote several special songs to go with the story. Right in the middle of the preparations, there was a district-wide brownout, following on the heels of the biggest blackout in Boston's history about a month earlier, where Carol and I ate by candlelight and took turns playing the piano in the dark for fun. With this inspiration I wrote *"Candlelight"*, the first of a set of *"Three Children's Night Songs"*, later published by Silver Burdett Co., Inc.,[10] and performed the spring of 1966 by a special Childrens' Chorus, conducted by my former training teacher—Deanna Kidd. Along with these activities, the Chorus Pro Musica gave several concerts in the Boston area. This was an elite group, all of whom could read music at lightning speed. We had three rehearsals for every new concert, and then would perform the concert at different churches and people's homes, while rehearsing for the next new concert. The chorus was made up of top musicians, music students from the New England Conservatory of Music, doctors, lawyers, and graduates such as myself. A large part of our repertoire was contemporary music. I remember with great fondness plodding through the deep snow along Beacon Street to reach a lovely old church where we would perform a Christmas program on Sunday morning, eat lunch there, then drive en masse to another church for an afternoon concert, and then to a party at Patterson's elegant home.

During the spring of 1966 we were the chorus for the Boston Symphony, performing a concert version of Wagner's *"Parsifal"* at Easter time in Symphony Hall (we were on the third balcony as angels), and in May, Carl Orff's *"Carmina Burana"* with the BSO and a trio of dancers on stage of Symphony Hall for three nights. In June we sang Verdi''s *"Requiem"* with the Boston Pops Orchestra in the same hall. I was very proud to be part of this ensemble, and since then have never sung in a chorus as good or as interesting as this one. This group really saved my spirit, which was flagging from the exhausting teaching load.

> "Strange violin, Why haunt me?
> In how many cities calls your
> Fearful, lonely night to mine?"

> from Rainer Maria Rilke's poem *"Der Nachbar"*
> (The Neighbor), translated by P. McLean,
> "Three Songs for Voice and Violin"

By May I had made up my mind to find a graduate school and to major in composition. I had taken my fledgling symphony to a conductor friend of Carol's, in whose community orchestra she played violin. He looked at it and said, "This is a very promising piece, but you know nothing about the orchestra.

When are you planning to go to graduate school? If you don't go immediately, your talents will be lost, perhaps permanently." This pushed me over the edge of decision. I had been carefully saving my money, and had just enough to attend one year, if I sold my new car and everything I owned of any value, but my choices were limited to the Midwestern large universities that had low tuition.

I knew that I needed to make a move before I met a future husband, and although this year had been a barren one socially, the time would undoubtedly come, as I was nearing my mid-twenties. Willis Traphagen, the symphonic winds director at Lowell who had become my friend after I graduated, advised me to apply to Indiana University, where he had received his doctorate. I knew nothing about this or any other Midwestern school, but had faith in his judgment, as I admired him very much. That night after showing my symphony, I sat in my car for an hour, then came in, sat at the kitchen table, and at 1 a.m. wrote for an application to both Indiana University and the University of Illinois, another top music school that had been recommended to me. I sat stunned, for I had made a very large decision, that would lead me away from everything I had grown up to emulate—teaching young children, living in New England, motherhood, perhaps even marriage—and direct me to God-knows-what around the corner into the questionable future.

At the end of May I awoke to a horrible pain in my intestines, and diarrhea. I took a sick day from teaching and lay in bed. The next day I was no better, and took another sick day. By the third day the diarrhea had stopped, but the racking pains continued. After several days of this, I fearfully dragged myself out of bed to go to a doctor in Boston. After examining me, he said that I was suffering from colitis, and he recommended a bland diet given at that time to people with ulcers, which was to have a great deal of milk, soups, bread, mild food, and no roughage or "rough food" such as legumes. Today the medical establishment knows that this is totally the wrong diet for "spastic colon", as one needs a large amount of fiber, fruits, and grains to combat the compulsive intestinal grinding, but not in 1966. I immediately shopped for all the recommended items and began the diet, thinking to be well again in a day or so and able to go back to teaching.

The pain did not go away. In fact, it got worse, and I was now constipated. I lay in bed with the heating pad on my writhing intestines, wanting to die, day after day. I gave up the diet and went back to what little regular eating I could manage, although I was still hungry and the pain would abate for a few minutes during and after meals, then return with increased vengeance. My family did not know anything about this, as I had no energy to tell them. Carol became very worried. Finally, three weeks from the beginning of this disease, I began to feel better.

I returned to school the third week of June, which was the last week of the school year. I must have looked like a ghost, because everyone was extremely nice to me and solicitous, including the worst acting children in my classes. The year before, the young man teaching music in these two schools had had to resign because of unending splitting headaches. I also resigned, but I do not think the murderous teaching schedule changed any for the next teacher/victim. It wasn't entirely the fault of the school district, however.

I had worn myself down with too many grueling after-school activities and late nights, and my colon rebelled, weakened by the absence of healthy bacteria from all the antibiotics of the summer before, when I had had a run-away wisdom tooth abscess (and subsequent operation) and ended up in the hospital for a week. I managed to survive the rest of the school year, and with Carol—who had also decided to go on to graduate school at C.W. Post College, Long Island University—disbanded the apartment, sold our furniture and returned the piano. I returned home to begin the momentous job of gathering as much money as I could and studying several hours a day in order to pass the entrance examinations in music history and theory and basic piano skills that both universities required.

Before I left Cambridge I made out an application form and paid a small fee for "Data Mate", which was the first computer program to match couples of like intelligence and interests together. The men I had dated this year had not interested me, and I began to realize that not only were they scarce in my field of elementary education, but hardly available in the larger world, either. The Vietnam War in 1966 was escalating, and the draft had been reinstated, the National Guard called up. Single men my age were taking refuge in graduate study at colleges and universities in record numbers. My "Data Mate" lined me up with a very intriguing group of males. I had put "superior intelligence" and "high musical interest" on the form, and I was sent a list of five men who were nuclear physicists and engineers with a hobby of music listening. So at the end of my first teaching year, having been involved with children's minds all year, I was now being courted by men whom I could hardly understand and talk to at all!

I now was taken to dinner, driven to Tanglewood to sit on the lawn and listen to the Boston Symphony, treated to watching one of the dates build a pair of loudspeakers, and taken dancing, in a social whirl rivaling my early college years. They were all gentlemanly and charming, if too cerebral, and one even continued seeing me after I returned to Fitchburg. His name was Jim, and we had begun to get genuinely fond of each other, but by that time I had been accepted in the graduate program at Indiana University School of Music, and I left, nipping our relationship in the bud. If Data Mate still exists, I highly recommend it, but just make sure to live near a large gene pool, like Boston...

The whole summer I stayed home in Fitchburg, did not waitress, and studied. In the morning I would compose and prepare my music to show the professors at Indiana University. I then practiced harmonizing melodies at the piano in twelve different keys, and worked on a hands-only organ piece by Bach for the entrance exam. The afternoon was spent relearning page by page my book of music history and working out theory analyses of a variety of pieces written in different time periods. Late afternoon I would wander over to the tennis courts north of town and play with anyone who was willing, which resulted in a nice summer romance spent swimming at night and tennis playing. Coupled with my Data Mates, it was one of the most pleasant summers I had ever had, and a great relief from the teaching year.

By July I had been accepted also at the University of Illinois, but chose Indiana because Illinois wanted me to take two remedial courses, since I had no strictly musical undergraduate degree, and Indiana allowed the entrance exams to determine any remedial work. Gradually I sold my red Volkswagen with the sun roof and stereo FM radio for $1500—only $300 less than I had paid for it new, sold my two-burner hot plate I had had at Lowell, and sold my clothes, keeping only my old black second-hand English bike. Tuition and dorm expenses came to $1800, and I figured that I could afford one year, leaving to the gods my future after that. At least I would finally be going in the direction that had been pulling at me for so long.

At the end of August 1966, my father drove me to the bus station with four suitcases. The bus went to Boston, where I transferred to another, which went to Philadelphia, where I transferred at 3 a.m. to one bound for the Midwest. I hadn't been west of New York State since I was six, and had to look Indiana up on the map to see where it was. I remember looking blearily out of the bus window at the dirt roads in Dayton, Ohio, which at that time was very rural, and with distaste at all the flat farmland stretching in every direction, and utterly straight unpopulated highway. I barely slept an hour during the whole trip, which took a day-and-a-half, and around 6 p.m. on a Sunday the bus dropped me off at the 10th Street station in Bloomington, Indiana, just north of the university.

The bus station was closed for the night, and I inquired at the local cafe about cabs. There were none running after 5 p.m. on Sundays (!), and receiving pointing fingers for directions to the graduate dorms, I picked up my four suitcases, and dragged them along, two by two, shuffling back and forth, inching towards the dorms in the sunset. I felt utterly alone and abandoned, my raw nerves jangling on one hour of sleep, and at one point kicked the bags along.

I arrived at a several-story undergraduate dorm, and struggled inside to the information desk. There I learned that the graduate housing office was closed for the weekend, and that I would have to find a motel to sleep for the night. The motels were on the other side of town, I had exactly $6 in my pocket (before the days of credit cards), and there were no taxis running, anyway. So, bitter but not defeated, I shoved and dragged my bags to an elevator, taking it to the basement, where I intended to crawl behind the laundry machines and go to sleep. I was just settling in, having spread my coat on the floor and preparing to nap when the dorm housemother came rushing down in great exasperation, and offered me her living room couch for the night, plus dinner! Who says that ingenuity doesn't win the day?

The next day I learned that my housing application had never arrived, and the only housing available was in a conclave of old World War II barracks, in the middle of the campus, which had been temporary housing for the army personnel, and now was used for college misfits, late applications, and lost souls such as I. These were unpainted one-story rooms with bunk beds, but I had a room, which was a great relief. My roommate was a lovely woman of thirty, Feeya Androvina, from Thailand, who was studying inorganic chemistry. Across the narrow barracks hall were Margaret Luedtke from Florida, studying comparative literature, and Neda Tomasevich from San Francisco, studying world history. Next door was Angelique from Argentina, related to the Argentine president. I mention this because our situation was so traumatic that we all became good friends, and I am still good friends with the American women, almost forty years later. The barracks had no air-conditioning, and the weather was very hot, but I was so happy to be there, amongst such interesting women, that I didn't care.

After a week my bicycle arrived, plus a trunk with the rest of my clothes, and one more week saw us finally integrated into the graduate dorm, with private rooms and air-conditioning. My first weeks in the music school became a time of ecstatic rapture for me. Never had I been near student virtuosi who practiced all over the school, seven excellent student orchestras, several choruses, and eminent teacher/performers such as Janos Starker, cellist, Josef Gingold, violinist, Menachem Pressler, pianist, and many others. There was (and is) a wonderful all-wood recital hall, where one afternoon I sat and listened to one of the student orchestras rehearsing. Tears coursed down my cheeks out of sheer joy for being here to hear this music. For the rest of the year, I followed the orchestras around, attending all the rehearsals I could fit into my schedule, and all of the concerts.

My composition teacher was Dr. Thomas Beversdorf. There were three in our class. Richard Heiniger was a Masters student, as was I, and a rustic but mild fellow from northern New York State who wore homemade check camping shirts and wide khaki pants named Barton McLean, who was working on his Doctorate. Each of us received about a half-hour of undivided attention from Dr. Beversdorf, while the other two sat and listened. For the first lesson I had hoped to show my new symphony, but I had sent it through the mail in a large packet of manuscripts, and it had gotten lost. It took the post office three long months to find and return it to me. Having had to endure several jokes from Dr. Beversdorf and the others about my "lost symphony", I was so eager to be showing it that I tried to reproduce it from memory, but that proved too difficult. When finally it came, I stood by the elevator with the manuscript, heading to my composition lesson, with Bart McLean by my side. I accidentally dropped it just as the elevator door swung open, and the whole manuscript disappeared down the slot between the floors! That lesson consisted mainly of Dr. Beversdorf, Richard, and Bart doubled up in laughter, while I waited until after class to retrieve it from the basement, with the janitor's help (Afterwards it was decided that God was trying, in a kind way, to tell me about the piece)…

My naiveté became apparent in remedial music history class when Dr. Malcolm Brown, a virtual Simon Legree whipping us very reluctant weak students into shape, announced that for the midterm we were expected to know all of the composers' names we had been studying. I asked if that also meant "all of the obscure composers". His mouth curved in an evil half-grin, and he asked, "Okay, Taylor, which composers are you talking about?" I swallowed, then answered, "They are so obscure that I don't remember their names!" There was that sound again—of unrestrained laughter.

But I was shaping up as a scholar, through long nights of study, and mornings of composing—presently a woodwind trio and a string quartet. My library listening had stretched my musical interest as far as Bela Bartok's string quartets, which I now loved, my own quartet trying hard to be a clone. The *String Quartet #1* was performed by an excellent pick-up student ensemble at the student composition concert in early spring, and recorded on the fledgling university electronic studio's stereo Ampex tape recorder, a big thrill for me.

During Christmas vacation I joined a car pool of students going back to New England, and arrived home at midnight after a day-and-a-half sleepless ride. I entered my home to have my parents greet me at the door with champagne! They were prouder of me than I was of myself, and we talked until about 2 a.m. When I finally went to bed, I slept until 4 the next afternoon.

During that vacation I visited Carol Schiavone, staying with her in Great Head, New York for about a week. We attended a very interesting party at her theory teacher Joseph Marx's house in Manhattan. There was Charles Wuorinen[11], a young man of twenty-nine, drunkenly holding up the corner of the foyer, peering at me suspiciously. Then I was introduced to Benjamin Boretz, about whom Carol had told me, and I said confidently, "So you are the editor of *'The Spectator'* Magazine." "No, young lady," he replied, "*that* magazine went out of business about four hundred years ago. Mine is called *'Perspectives of New Music'.*"

Joseph Marx was a virtuoso oboist, and performed in Wuorinen's premiere New York ensemble, the Group for Contemporary Music. Marx, a refugee from Germany during World War II, had a huge collection of artworks and ancient musical instruments, some of them sent to him from other European Jewish refugees, and he showed Carol and me his vast collection of paintings and sketches by the famous German artist Lyonel Feininger, about whom I stated, "I love these paintings by Heinigen!" (No, dear young lady, that is a popular Dutch beer...) And to top this off, while every other woman was wearing black, I wore a skin-tight bright blue sequined short dress above the knees, and Joseph's young children kept running their hands over my dress, murmuring, "Fishy, fishy..." I never wrote any of this memory down, but I never forgot it, my ultimate evening of unabashed embarrassment.

THURSDAY, MAY 14, 1981

This morning I am feeling very low. Bart reminds me that the Zagreb Festival is the best paying "gig" we have ever gotten abroad, $1500 plus a discount hotel price and free tickets to all events, and of course the rare opportunity to be here at all. After each day of concerts, the next morning is taken up with a press conference, with the festival heads and the ensemble directors sitting together on a platform in front of microphones. We have attended one of these, as they are open to the public, and were unimpressed with the interviews, which are answered in the language of the participant and laboriously translated into Serbo-Croatian for the audience of local and national news media. The atmosphere was very stultified, with deadpan expressions on everyone's face, and we had the distinct impression that what the participants on stage said was not translated exactly, but was changed to reflect the festival in the best light.

This morning is our turn to be interviewed, along with Paul Possner, moderated by Igor Kuljeric, the composer-director who had hired us. At one point I complain that the American and English ensembles have been relegated to the lobby of the concert hall in a role that seems to be an afterthought of the festival, that our student guide has never appeared, and that no one seems to care how we fare. I know from the way this is being translated that this message is not being sent out, and come away realizing that in a Communist regime, freedom of the press and the right to free speech are not constitutional virtues. Later that day, Mr. Kuljeric calls us into his office, and lavishly praises our performance, stating that he would like to set up a future concert tour of The McLean Mix around the different states of Yugoslavia, after this festival is finished and things settle down again. We are pleased and flattered, but that wretched little bell in my head is warning that this sudden enthusiasm for us may be only a way to ameliorate us (which turns out to be the truth). Not good to stir up the Americans, fired up with puritanical justice as they are...

When we return to the hotel, the mezzanine is filled with the Dresden Opera Company, here for their performance tonight. They can speak no English, so we exchange crude German pleasantries. They seem ecstatic to be able to converse with an American, and delighted to meet us. Many of the groups here are from Communist countries and are experiencing euphoria from being allowed to travel outside their homeland.

Tonight is an extra-special treat: Udo Zimmermann's three-act fairytale opera *"Der Schuhu und die fliegende Prinzessin"* (Shuhu and the Flying Princess). Everything is wonderful: the writing, the singers and the orchestra! It is all in German, with no English notes in the program, only German and Serbo-Crotian, so we never quite figure out the story-line, but the opera is so filled with flying singers, exotic props, rapidly changing scenery and great music, including tape echo, which creates a dense musical texture with the arias weaving in and out of it, that we don't care. The opera receives a standing ovation, one of the few given the entire festival. There is a cabaret after the concert, but we want to savor the memories of this music and return to the hotel, happy for the first time in two days.

Friday May 15

Today is the last day of the Zagreb Muzicki Biennale. We walk to the Cultural Center and meet the young composer Branco Starc, who volunteers to help us mail our recordings (and also a package of unused clothes) back to Texas. Also, to our intense joy, Udo Zimmerman is here, and Branco introduces him to us. Mr. Zimmermann, along with being the resident composer with the Dresden Opera is also in charge of the state electronic studio, and invites us to perform there. He is a tall, slender man with grayish-black hair, my age, and quite attractive. His wife is Polish and he laments in German to Branco (thinking that we do not understand German) that she can leave the country freely, but not he, and that she carries out recordings and publicity about him when she takes her trips. He says, "No one knows how terrible it is to live like this (trapped in a Communist regime)", and Branco agrees with him. I am silently sympathizing, but am also trying to remember when there has been a resident opera composer in the U.S., or an international U.S. new music festival which, well-supplied with money, paid the performers, housed everyone, and made the event the focal point of the country's attention…

Branco, Bart, and I walk to the main avenue of downtown, which has a tram-line running down the center, and in the distance can be seen Zagreb's castle, with a funicular running to it from the town. Many of the composers are planning to make a holiday outing to the castle tomorrow, which is everyone's day off. After mailing the packages and having some free time, Branco again invites us to his home, and we go with him in his car to a more modern part of the city, beyond the medieval walls. Branco lives in a small flat with his wife and baby. We are treated to plum brandy and cookies and Branco's scores, of–of all things– American Negro spirituals he has arranged for chorus! We are bewildered—surely Yugoslavia has a wealth of folk music we Americans have never heard. Why doesn't he use this as material? The air becomes decidedly chilly. Everyone knows that *America* is where the action is, not Yugoslavia! He will become wealthy, writing spirituals for the mass market…My head is beginning to hurt.

Later, back in the Esplanade Hotel lobby I make a phone call to Shirley Fleming, Chief Editor at *Musical America Magazine* in New York, asking when I should mail the information about the festival, and she says immediately—they are planning to use it in the next issue. Thinking to write up the article after we return home, I realize that I shall have to take all of tomorrow, with the Zagreb Cultural Center's help, to write it up, thus using up our only free day in Yugoslavia—the life of a journalist is not an easy one!

Tonight is the last marathon five-hour concert, and after hours of mediocre Yugoslav choral and instrumental music, the audience is moved to a smaller ensemble room and treated to a wonderful percussion group from Paris–Le Cercle. They perform Mauricio Kagel's *"Dressure"* for *"Three Hooligans and Wooden Instruments"*, a music street theatre piece involving dance-like movements, threatening and cajoling each other, clomping rhythmically on the floor all around the audience along with a battery of wooden percussion—a very humorous piece. Then Camerata Strumentale, an Italian ensemble, performs Gyorgi Ligeti's *"Aventures"* and *"Neues Aventures"* in a highly dramatic manner, which involves myriad instruments, three singers, and tearing up paper. The singers speak gibberish as if it made sense, and at one particularly frantic moment, the soprano runs off stage, comes over to Bart, who is sitting in the front row, tears off his glasses and throws them into his lap, all while singing at the top of her range. It nearly frightens him to death!

Afterwards, Bart talks with the fellow next to him, who is Per Jordal from the Holland NCRV Radio. Mr. Jordal invites Bart to present his whole "Dimensions" piano and tape series on the radio. So from the ashes of our concert rise up three possibilities of future engagements—the way it goes in show biz!

Saturday, May 16

Today is a grueling day. A beautiful sunny warm day, perfect for sight-seeing the city and taking the funicular up to the castle towering above the city. Instead, we are elbow-deep in the press office of the cultural center for nine hours putting together the festival article for *Musical America Magazine*. I type while Bart, who has sweetly agreed to stay here all day and help me, edits. When I tire, I write the article longhand, and Bart types. The typewriter is strange, with all kinds of characters we don't use—umlauts for German, accent marks for French, and other characters for Serbo-Croatian, and the keyboard is a different configuration. I have to type with two fingers instead of the typist's way, which slows me to a crawl. The people in the press office are wonderfully friendly, buoying us up with Turkish coffee, giving us five excellent 8x10 inch photos of the different concerts, including our own, and during breaks kibitzing with us over endless cigarettes.

They ask, "Do the people of America like their president (Ronald Reagan)?" "Isn't it dangerous living there with so much crime and guns everywhere?" (a common question that comes up again and again in Europe). When we ask about their contentment with their own country, their answers are guarded, except for overwhelming, almost religious love for their president Tito, whose giant photograph hangs in every building. The Yugoslavs are envious of our material wealth, but leery of our freedom that allows for the more dangerous side of life. Later, when we pass a house on the street, we glimpse the TV show "Dallas" spoken in Serbo-Croatian, and wonder no longer about their preoccupation with our guns (On a later tour in Holland, during a cafeteria lunch we have a brief encounter with the custodian. His English is limited, but when he finds out we are Americans, he says, "America? Oh—Bang, bang!" In Bergen, Norway we are asked by a shoe salesman if anyone is alive in New York).

By 9 p.m. we finish, completely exhausted. There is a concert of English music down by the river, but we can barely crawl back to our hotel room and flop down on the beds comatose. A very busy week!

Sunday, May 17

The dining room is deserted, as just about everyone has left. We have most of the day to explore, as our train to Austria doesn't leave until 6:30 p.m.. I am eager to see the shops, the castle, the restaurants, but today is Sunday, and we relearn the sad truth that on Sunday Europe is closed. So we decide to walk as far out of the city as we can, since we cannot ride the buses without knowing the language. Before we do, however, there is the business of lunch. Most of the restaurants are closed, even the Hungarian pizza parlor we are so curious about. Down a back street, the alley opens into a courtyard of a restaurant doing a brisk business, and we sit down gratefully. We are surrounded by Yugoslavs, and no one comes to wait on us. Others are waited on, and it becomes obvious that this slight is not an accident. There is real danger that we will not ever be waited on, and we are both ravenously hungry. I whisper to Bart, "Let's move to the other side of the court-yard, and say nothing. I will talk to you in German, because I think the problem is that we are Americans." Bart, puzzled, agrees, and we quietly move to a table far away from the other.

The waitress comes immediately, and I order in German, the menus fortu-nately being in Serbo-Croatain and German. Our dinners are tasty, and we talk (in English) happily, feeling that we have outwitted these strangely hostile people. However, when dessert and tea are brought, I taste my tea to discover—that it is dishwater! I spit it out, and know that we should leave immediately. Something is wrong here, and we do not want the rest of our tour put in jeopardy. Why this blatant hostility, I have never been able to figure out, but we do know that Zagre-bians are very capable of covertly showing displeasure, and perhaps our country's anti-Communist stance has caused this anger (or is it also antipathy towards Ger-mans?). We pay up and leave quickly.

We have a few hours left for exploring. Past Zagreb are beautiful southern New York-style trees, but taller, and on muddy ground. The parkland is littered as we follow paths along a mountainous stream, and the rivers have a foul odor. Once I slip and fall in the mud. We dare not hike too far away, so return to clean up and pack, and buy a cold meat sandwich, popcorn, and orange soda for our next meal, aware that the train will probably have nothing to eat on board (which is correct). We board the Beograd-Basel Express to Innsbruck, and find in our sleeping couchette three other passengers, all middle-aged men with lunch boxes. One of them speaks some English, and he takes a fatherly interest in my welfare.

Tonight there is a full moon shining on the steep hills over a rushing river, glinting silver, and we stare out the window entranced while one of the other passengers spreads a whole toilet paper roll on the floor. The public W.C. (toilet) is overflowing into our couchette! This is all taken in stride, and about this time all the men pull flasks from their boxes and begin to drink heavily. As I make my way to the one working toilet, I notice that about 98% of the people on board are men, all drinking themselves into a stupor quietly. Next to us is a cabin of young German men, and I carry on an animated conversation with one of them at our door. When he asks me to have "Lust" with him, I know enough German to point to Bart resting on the top bunk in our compartment and say, "Mein Mann ist da!" (My husband is there). His eyes bulge and he instantly disappears, to my sorrow, as we were having such a nice conversation. The fatherly Yugoslav clucks his tongue and instructs me to be more careful…

It seems that everyone falls to sleep instantly, sated with the tranquilizer of drink, but I cannot. The train is extremely bumpy and old, shaking from side to side, and I sleep only two hours. At about 3 a.m. we are abruptly awakened by a deafening intercom screaming in Serbo-Croatian, and three men with guns burst into our room. I am instantly awake and terrified. Surely this is a World War II movie and this is the Gestapo? They want to check passports. We sleepily grovel for them, but they look at us in disgust and say, "NO! You Americans. Only Slavs, please!" Boy, I would not want to have the wrong passport here (the natives can travel for a very limited time to Austria and longer through the other Communist countries, and security is very tight)! Thus ends, on this strident note, our experiences in the Eastern bloc.

Monday, May 18

From my journal: "It is so nice to be back in civilized country! The Austrians are infinitely cleaner than the Yugoslavs, and one can read the signs. The Tirolean district here is *heavenly*, with deep forest, wells to drink from, rugged snow-capped mountains. Up here on the Hungerburg Plateau, are all Austrians (in houses and hotels), and down below in Innsbruck are Americans rushing through…"

For the next six days we have a wonderful time exploring Austria, romping in the mountains outside of Innsbruch, riding a tiny train to its furthest point, just to experience a small village, visiting Salzburg with its huge overhanging castle and birthplace of Mozart, whose house is only a few steps away from our hotel. Of Mozart's home, I write, "The rooms are small and simply decorated, with the petite delicate piano of that time, and it is hard to imagine all that great music with its beginnings here. The place feels like a shrine, with lines of worshipful onlookers." Later we have a simple soup and salad dinner, then walk to the other side of the Salzach River, where white swans are feeding in the growing twilight. On this side of the river is a path between houses that climbs up to a monastery and eventually to the Frankizosch Castle. We have time before dark only to reach the monastery, which is high enough to overlook the sparkling city with its silver river in the sunset. Then we must return to pack, our visit much too short for all that Salzburg offers. Until next time…

Sunday, May 24

We arise at 5 a.m. to myriad birds singing and dozens of Austrian church bells ringing, breakfast on the buttered bread and coffee left for us last night by the hotel, and take a taxi to the Hauptbahnhof. We board the train at 6:08 to Munich, and with one more change ride to Holland through the whole of mid-Germany. Germany's "breadbasket" is pretty—hilly farmland and woods, and that thought is the only "bread" we see all day. Being Sunday, there is no food available. After fifteen hours of fasting, alone in our compartment (the Europeans are too wise to travel on Sunday), we finally arrive in Utrecht, and feast at the train restaurant, which is surprisingly excellent—potato salad, boiled eggs, herring, anchovies, sardines, and tuna fish placed on greens with dressing.

Then we take a small suburban train to Bilthoven, and are picked up by a young man from the Gaudeamus Foundation, which has their headquarters at an incredibly quaint and charming ivy-covered, thatch-roofed house and offices in Bilthoven. We stay for the night in a front room, with luxurious bath and, for the first time, a television set. This is a very nostalgic time for me. Two years ago I stayed in this town at the family Springer's home while having meals, conferences and rehearsals in this Gaudeamus house, as part of the Gaudeamus Musiekweek—my first trip ever to Europe.

Gaudeamus Musiekweek is an international music festival, during which several young composers are chosen from around the world to have their music performed by ensembles and soloists who have been the winners of a performers' competition. It is a wonderful residency of several days attending rehearsals, concerts, lectures, and becoming acquainted with young composers and much music one would probably never hear at any other time.

My journal states, "I have mixed feelings—like coming back to a deserted house and no festival—everyone gone!" All except old Walter Maas, who founded the Gaudeamus Foundation after World War II and had the house, offices, practice rooms and composing cabins built, donating it all to the Foundation, in gratitude for the Dutch people hiding him and saving his Jewish life during the war. He vaguely remembers me, and I look upon him as a crusty but darling old German "saint", and smile hello to him the next morning at breakfast in the large dining room with a jungle of hanging plants and ornate furnishings.

Monday, May 25

We are off to Hilversum for a radio interview. The VPRO Radio is taping a program about ourselves and our music for 1 1/2 hours, directed by Han Reiziger. Han is on the same "wavelength" as us, and the interview is slow and relaxed, from 2 to 6 p.m.. Afterwards, Han treats us to very special "Reistaffel" dinner at the Bouda Indonesian/Chinese restaurant. This is a dinner with many small courses of very elegant and tasty Indonesian food, over a hundred different combinations of minute portions, plus the bottle of the best white wine the restaurant offers. It is such a treat to talk to someone who understands our music and ideas, that we want the day never to end! A rare meeting of the minds in Europe.

Tuesday, May 26

I take Bart on a tour around Bilthoven, one of the most beautiful suburban towns in Europe, with its many elegant, expensive houses of brick or stone with thatch roofs that look like Dutch caps, or orange-tiled roofs. Flower gardens abound, and bicycle paths. It reminds me of the better neighborhoods of Seattle, Washington. We say good-bye to Bilthoven and leave with our bags. This afternoon we visit the Utrecht Studio, one of the oldest electronic music studios in Europe, with large reel-to-reel tape recorders, and giant analog synthesizers, mixers, and effects processors invented by the studio engineers. We meet composer Jaap Vink, who plays one of his compositions for us, using beautiful-sounding mass structures with very slow evolution.

After a bite to eat at the train restaurant, we board for England, going to the Hook of Holland to catch the overnight ferry to Harwich. This is a massive ferry, and we hurriedly reserve two places in a group cabin, Bart in men's and I in women's. We are late, and only the lowest floor level is still available. There is a vast crowd of people aboard, mostly young. It is already midnight, and we descend to the bottom floor, near the engines, to ride the waves all night, but somehow this is comforting, and I sleep exceptionally well, about five hours. Our tour of Europe becomes all pleasure at this point. We will spend several days in London and York, take a train and a small postal bus to Scotland, return to London and fly to Finland, visiting composer friends all along the way. This will turn out to be the most life-changing tour we will ever have. Not only have we been introduced to another continent, the fascinating people and countryside, and all the different ways of thinking, but ultimately, Bart will lose his university position (partially) because of this tour, throwing us out into the world permanently. More about this in Section Three.

♦   ♦   ♦

4.

Indiana University offered not only a pool of brilliant young men studying in myriad professions, but young males from all over the world. I immediately became enamored with more "exotic" men than I had ever even seen in my previous life. Considered as one of the best music schools in the world, the university draws foreign students from Europe, Asia, and the Middle East in large numbers. For over a semester I wandered through this field of sterling male talent, dating avidly, hanging around and conversing tirelessly, enriching my repertoire of experience while secretly compiling a list of marriage possibilities.

There was one man with whom I had grown so close that I never considered him as husband material. Almost from day one, Barton McLean was by my side. We started as rib-pulling classmates, jangling each other while waiting for our composition lessons. This progressed into friendship, with the marker being his invitation to myself and one of my close friends, Margaret Luedtke, to see his slides of the New York countryside around his home in Potsdam and his backpacking trips to the New York Adirondack Mountains. With him was Elmer (now Takeo) Kudo from Hawaii, and he treated all of us to a jug of wine hidden under his bed in his dorm room that Saturday afternoon in November. A tiny light went on in my brain, then. An unmarried composer who loves hiking, camping, and nature, and who owns his own home. Hmmm…

Later we improvised together in a practice room, but I was terrible with jazz, a medium about which I knew little. At the Christmas dorm party Bart played the double bass in the dance band, and I became more interested. Being in different programs, I in masters and he in doctoral, we only saw each other during the few hours of composition class a week, but he repeatedly helped me with music copying techniques, cheered me on and genuinely liked my music. I had more reservations about his, as it was strongly influenced by Paul Hindemith[12] at the time, and only gradually over the year worked itself out of that into more originality. He had no problems with insecurity or jealousy about his or my composing—a very refreshing difference from every other man I had known well! By late February, and after a particularly depressing period of chasing after and being rebuffed by a wonderfully virtuosic German cellist, I prayed for divine guidance, for a sign to guide me in the proper matrimonial direction...

The next day Bart joined me for the dorm's lunch and dinner, for the first time ever, as he always ate much earlier than I, and with his own friends. Margaret, sitting next to me, noted that he would make a good "catch" and that I should be looking closer to home for my "entertainments". I decided to ask him to a party. Our first date was a classic case of faux pas, mostly on his part. Meeting him outside his dorm room, he brought me in for a glass of wine and to show me a blurred photo of his white-haired old mother, saying, "This is Mom. Isn't she beautiful? I really love her, and she lives with me back in Potsdam. She's had a hard life, and she lives with me now, and will always have a home with me." Uh-oh.

At the very juvenile party of ex-remedial music history students, we were sitting in a circle playing a game of remembering the last person's animal call, and the one before that, etc., when it came to Bart's turn. He hated this game, so made up a "turtle" sound that no one could reproduce, thus stopping the game dead in its tracks and gaining the enmity of the whole party! Okay, he overly-loves his mother and can't socialize. Oh...Boy...

The next week Bart took me to a Ben Johnson play at the Drama Department's theatre, and for some reason I dressed up in a tight black knit dress rising far above the knees, as was the style. Our relationship abruptly changed. We spent a late Saturday night dancing and talking at the Ramada Inn lounge, and the old adage, "If you want to know how a man will treat you, watch how he treats his mother" came to mind. This was a man who was a gem of a son, sharing with his mother a home they both paid for, so she could enjoy her own home for the first time in her life. His father, who had been a hopeless alcoholic, was deceased. Even now in graduate school Bart sent money home—sabbatical income he had earned teaching in the State University of New York (SUNY) at Potsdam teacher-training schools for six years, while he had worked for his masters at Eastman School of Music during summers. This enabled his mother to retire from the endless heavy work of waiting on tables she had done for decades.

At the beginning of April was a week's spring break, and I caught another car-pool home for a few days, and then took a bus to Potsdam, New York. When Bart met my bus at the station, I was impressed about how handsome he was—mediumly tall, broad-shouldered and slim, with deep brown hair and strong chin. His mother was better than I expected, at age 58 rather slender and independent, letting Bart alone, and friendly to me. His home was a new ranch house on a quiet dead-end street, and they put me up in the guest room/sewing room. That evening, after dinner, we took a walk in the woods. This was no ordi-nary walk, for Bart was carrying a sleeping bag, with no intention of slumbering at all...

The rest of April and May were spent solely with Bart, the other boyfriends evaporating like early morning mist. Along with concert-going, studying, and hiking in the state parks all around hilly Bloomington, we explored a beautiful spot by a lake to rendezvous in Bart's Ford station wagon, and took to spending several evenings on the (dark) local golf course. One night there, lying by the put-ting green, we declared our love for each other, and as in response, along with an earlier bright orange full moon, a glorious (very auspicious) aurora borealis formed in the sky, lasting most of the night. I have only seen three others in my entire life, but nothing like this one.

Neda Tomasevich and I, deciding to escape from the dormitory, found an apartment to share in the town of Bloomington for the next year, with two large bedrooms, and signed a lease before school ended. By the last weeks of school, I had run out of money, and had nothing left to buy dinner with on Sundays when the dining hall closed. I took a waitress job that lasted one day, until Bart talked me out of it, saying that the concerts and events at the university were far more important than eating dinner! So I fasted until my parents sent some money, and they promised to donate $500 for the second year. Squirreled away in the savings bank was another $500, the product of a loan I had procured for Bill Ryder, my ex-fiancée, and had never given to him. This was still not enough to pay for the year, but I planned to waitress all summer, also.

My diary states, "This has been the year of my awakening. Never have I lived so much—felt so much—improved so much!" At the end of May, Bart, I, and two other students, with Bart's double bass in the far back, returned to New York State. We took a short backpacking vacation in the Adirondacks, sleeping in the three-walled camping shelter by the Johns Brook waterfall, the first night of which was spent bashing ten mice over the head with our small camping frying pan, because they were crawling in our sleeping bags with us! It rained all three days, but we hiked the mountains anyway, and being in the haze of love cared not at all.

The second part of our time together was spent in Fitchburg, where my parents immediately fell in love with Bart, and their eyes sparkled with secret hope. After a few days at York Beach, Maine and down to Boston, on June 15, Bart, who was sleeping in our den on the couch, was joking about this being, in his future biography, his "Taylor" period. I lay awake worrying that all of this was just a temporary fling for him, and at 3 a.m. could stand the suspense no more. I crept into his room, woke him up and asked what he meant by this being his "Taylor" period. He started to apologize, then blurted out, "What I mean is, will you marry me?"

We announced our engagement the next evening at dinner. Dad broke down and cried, saying over and over, "Oh, you dolls!" (What a tremendous relief he must have felt). By the end of the meal both men were crying while Mom and I, dry-eyed, planned the wedding. This has been our only marriage, soon to go into its fifth decade, so I can remember all this with extreme joy and satisfaction. After all the years of misfiring, I finally had accomplished something successful and found a lover and soul-mate for life, no matter what happened to any of my music.

Bart had dreams of an outdoor wedding in Bloomington, with friends of his playing horn calls, and perhaps the god Pan leaping through the bushes as we wove garlands through each other's hair…This was not to include parents or any friends except the ones in Indiana. I could see the terrible disappointment that this would create, and stalled. We had to wait a year, anyway, because I had signed a contract to live with Neda Tomasevich in a student apartment in Bloomington, and we must honor our commitments…

Right after our engagement, I was scheduled to drive to Lenox, Mass. and work as a waitress with my friend and ex-housemate Carol Schiavone. Carol's future husband Giora Bernstein, who played violin in the Boston Symphony, had given us complimentary passes to all of the events at Tanglewood, including a couple's pass for Bart and myself. The next week I drove to Lenox, and Carol and I rented the only apartment we could afford on our waitressing salary—a shabby flat with small grimy kitchen, tube-shaped bathroom, and a warehouse area divided into living room and bedroom by a shower curtain, on the second floor over a greasy diner, in the center of town. My job folded after about two weeks, but I stayed on in the apartment, since we had already paid the rent. Carol took to living with Giora at Tanglewood, and except for a brief visit from Josef Marx, Carol's elderly professor, I spent the time alone, composing a large orchestral piece, and waiting for the weekends, when Bart would drive the 500 round-trip miles from Norwood (his home in northern New York) to stay with me while we partook of the many excellent Tanglewood concerts and lectures.

The many dreary, lonely nights alone in this slum in the center of wealthy Lenox made my head much clearer for the future. I could see Bart still living in the men's dorm, over two miles from the apartment I had rented in the town of Bloomington, and both of us being too busy with difficult school work to see each other very much. Gradually, the difficulties would erode our relation-ship…We would see each other less and less, and he, the one big love of my life, would fade away—just as my life was fading in this horrible smelly slum-in-the-midst-of-plenty here in Lenox!

So with these emotions running high, I drove hurriedly the next evening, in early July, to the center of Lenox, where there was a telephone booth in the little park, and phoned Bart in Norwood. When he answered, I blurted out that we should get married *before* we returned to Bloomington in a month. Bart was sur-prised but eagerly willing, and in this hyper-state of terrified bliss, when Bart was again in Lenox, we went shopping for wedding rings. Bart bought us two match-ing white gold wedding rings, for $25 apiece, with inscriptions. I wanted no engagement ring—I was a flaming feminist and aspiring composer at this point, and wanted total equality, and cared nothing about spending money on a wed-ding (I was also living on student loans, with no summer job). Then Bart returned to finish his summer school teaching at SUNY Potsdam and prepare his mother for the monumental change in her life that was about to happen (She was less-than-happy about this marriage). I informed Carol that I would be moving back home to be married, and she agreed to be my bridesmaid. I managed to con-vince my two Indiana University friends, Margaret and Neda, to be housemates, thus absolving me from the binding contract, while I called Mrs. Bates, the land-lady in Bloomington, and contracted for a tiny three room apartment I had admired when looking with Neda earlier. By the first of August I returned home to finalize preparations, and our wedding was set for August 26.

After returning home I drove downtown with my mother, and picked out a short white wedding dress that cost all of $10 on sale, plus a $5 lace tiara, and white high heels. My parents, always cautious about expense, agreed to host a wedding in our front entryway of the home apartment, and hire a caterer for cof-fee, tea, a huge wedding cake, and champagne, to be set up in the alternate living room used for Dad's stamp collecting. Only the closest of local friends and rela-tives would be invited. We also arranged printed wedding invitations, which would arrive only about the week before the wedding. To prevent problems, I called everyone up in advance and invited them.

Weddings are a frightening experience. I had nightmares for two months; Bart had insomnia and irritable bowel syndrome. The day before the wedding, Bart and Grace McLean, his mother, arrived in Fitchburg. All day the florist assistants arrived with armloads of flowers, turning the wide colonial hallway into a marriage bower, with garlands framing the French double doors on both sides of the hallway which separated the two living rooms.

The caterer came the following morning with silver coffee/tea sets and crystal for the reception. By evening, the tension had built up to the breaking point, and when all parents were out of the living room, we started arguing over whether we were going to have children, or would I go for my doctorate, and if we had children, would we be too poor to ever travel out west, which was a dream for both of us? Neither one of us knew the answers to any of this, but ended up yelling at each other, anyway. Bart kept running to the bathroom with diarrhea, and finally, our wise parents entered the living room with armloads of wedding presents and instructed us to open them *now*. Thus, with hands and arms doing something constructive, we mercifully dropped the arguing and settled down to good old American consumerism!

Do not ask me what the weather was like on my wedding day. I was in a state of complete apoplexy, and sat like a statue while Carol styled my hair. By noon all was ready. Reverend Richard Huff from our First Parish Universalist/Unitarian Church had arrived, a Mozart string quartet was playing on the record player, my relatives were standing in the living room by the French doors—the two mothers, Aunt Ethel, my ninety-year-old grandmother Marie, my uncle Dick and his daughter Helen and second husband Charlie Roddy—who also was our photographer (with his Polaroid camera), my brother's wife Peggy and six-year-old daughter Darlene. Bart's best man was my brother Conrad. Our small wedding party marched down the hallway and stood under the floral wreath over the other French doors to the stamp room. Except for a very long five minutes when I broke down and wept in the middle of the ceremony (the closeness of everyone in that small hallway was overwhelming), we were wed in the short Protestant ceremony.

People laugh when we talk about our homemade thrifty wedding, but as I look at the faded almost-40-year-old Polaroid prints in my album and the two fading color wedding portraits, I see that we are still married and still happy, a small miracle that no money or photos can capture. Perhaps an artist's life can be seen as a continuous adventure, strange and dangerous, penurious yet exotic, exasperating, terrifying, and ultimately very, very satisfying.

> My eyes already touch the sunny hill,
> going far ahead of the road I have begun.
> So we are grasped by what we cannot grasp;
> it has its inner light, even from a distance—
>
> and changes us, even if we do not reach it,
> into something else, which, hardly sensing it, we already are;
> a gesture waves us on, answering our own wave…
> but what we feel is the wind in our faces.

(from *"A Walk"* by Rainer Maria Rilke)

Grandparents Cora and Frank Lesure and their three Daughters, Ethel (back), Alice, and my mother Grace.

Grandfather Conrad Taylor and two sons, Dick and Conrad Jones Taylor, my father (c.1914).

My parents Grace and Conrad Taylor at the beach, c.1935.

Grandmother Marie Taylor with brother Conrad, Jr.
and me, ages 12 and 8.

At the Farm—my mother, brother, and I, 1951, Binghamton, NY.

Me playing toy piano with my niece Darlene in
My Fitchburg home, 1962.

"In Old Wachusett's Shadow"—
me conducting the graduating class of 1963,
Fitchburg, Massachusetts State College

Demonstrating (1981) how I used to compose
in my bedroom in Fitchburg.

The McLean Mix in their first performance, St. Mary's College,
Notre Dame, Indiana, 1974.

"Ah-Syn!" for electronically-modified autoharp and
Arp 2600 Synthesizer (1974)

Synthi-100 Synthesizer and Scully Tape Recorders,
Indiana University at South Bend—a cutting edge studio in 1974.

Our home (analog) electronic studio, Austin, Texas, 1980.

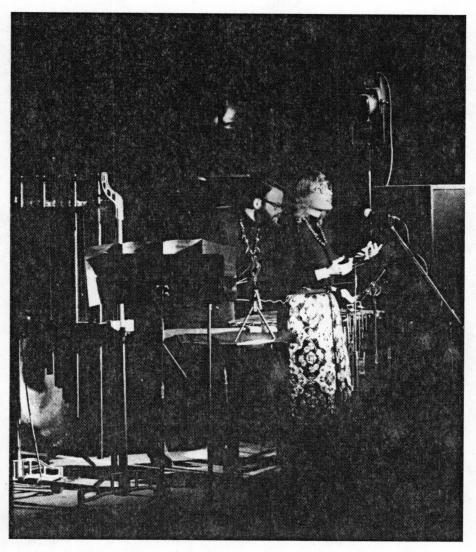

Us performing Bart's "Mysteries from the Ancient Nahuatl" at the Zagreb (Croatia) Muzicki Biennale, 1981. Photo by Davor Siftar

Me composing "The Inner Universe" in Kirby Cabin, The MacDowell
Colony (Peterborough, New Hampshire), summer, 1981

Our 1790 rental farmhouse in Petersburgh, New York.

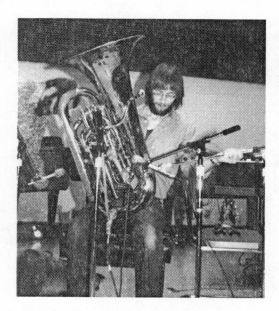

Melvyn Poore preparing to perform and record "Beneath the Horizon
III" at the University of Texas at Austin, 1982

Barton McLean performing on bicycle wheel,
Alternative Museum, New York City.

The McLean Mix plus two local friends, "Rainforest"
Installation, Kirkland Arts Council, Clinton, NY.

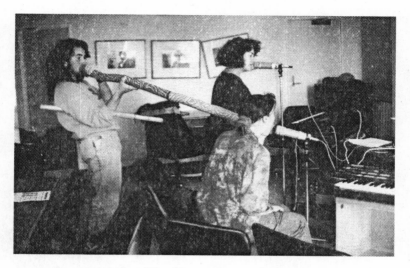

Brendan Dickie—didgeridoo, Ivana Troselj, and Kerrie Ryan, singers, ("Rainforest Images" CD) at Canberra School of Art and Drama, Australia.

Hasnul Jamal Saidon, Video Artist at Rensselaer Polytechnic Institute, RPI iEAR Studios, Troy, NY.

This buffalo skull we transformed into a digital sampler,
for our "Desert Spring" installation.

Borneo—inspired ceramic gongs, painted by artist Ann K. Lindsay for "Jambori Rimba" premiere—Siena College, Albany, NY 1997.

Illecillewaet Glacier, British Columbia

Conrad Taylor and his son Jeffrey Conrad (left), future wife Marissa, (step)daughter Eleisha Panteleo and friend, 2001, Petersburgh Pass.

Our 1830 home on Coon Brook Road, Petersburgh, New York.

3

The Composing Life

CREDO

(from April 16, 1977 Journal):

I believe in passion. I believe in the passion and joy of creating and comprehending beauty. I believe beauty must be a combination of color, interweaving structure, and live energy to produce that combination of passion, euphoria, and high intellectualism we call great art or great natural beauty.

I believe in the permanence of energy and life in the universe, and the common energy that courses through all living things.

I believe in the sympathetic energies between living beings, binding them together.

I believe that the intricate and delicate beauty of an electron microscopic view of a flower petal is as beautiful and purposeful as a Miro painting.

I believe the devotion of an eagle to his mate is as much a part of love as the human bond.

I believe humankind is only a part of the universe, that the spirit of love and life flows through all creatures, and all are important. And all are unimportant.

I believe only the life-force is basically the Importance. We comprehend this as Love.

I believe in my own ability to create, and to evoke sympathetic bonds of passion and joy in others through my music.

I have two styles, as befits my dual-identity as a Gemini. The first is that of delicate, flowing color and clarity of line, simplicity of melodic and often harmonic idea—a late 20th Century "Mozart". These ideas are undulated energies with their own special line, often connoting light and sometimes humorous moods.

The second style is a union of colors, producing blends that are music "compounds". Sometimes the result is a "cloud" effect of mass combination. Sometimes a quality is produced that is partially abstract and partly imageric, referred to as "imago-abstract" in some of my writings. This second style can also be delicate, but generally is thicker in texture and less melodic (re *"Invisible Chariots"*, movement 1, or the beginning of movement 2). This style is darker, more passionate, and often evolves in and out of the first style. This is a keystone of my work.

I do not believe in stylizing my style, of freezing it. To cauterize my pitch-rhythmic manipulations is to mannerize them, and I will not do this. I cannot compose serial music, now or ever.

I shall use my music to project my beliefs about passion and life, as I have done, and I shall keep my music free to develop its own specific character with each piece, providing only the seeds of a style and my philosophical understanding of life, joy, passion, and beauty.

How to Obtain a CD of Musical Excerpts for Section THREE— The Composing Life

It is strongly recommended that the reader, upon reaching Section THREE, listen to an excerpt of each piece heading the chapters for greater enjoyment and understanding of the text. All thirteen musical works have excerpts the reader can access free of charge, following these simple directions: On the Web, go to the American Music Center's "New Music Jukebox" as follows— http://www.newmusicjukebox.org/composers/ After registering according to AMC's guidelines, click on McLean, Priscilla. List of works with icons will appear. Click on Soundfile icon for the piece you intend to hear. Excerpts are from two to seven minutes long.

To obtain a high quality CD of the excerpted musical pieces of Section THREE, the reader is asked to send a check or institutional purchase order for $15.00 to: Priscilla McLean, MLC Publications, 55 Coon Brook Rd., Petersburgh, NY 12138. Make check out to "Priscilla McLean", and include a paper with your name and address and request for "CD for Section THREE".

1.

"VARIATIONS & MOZAICS ON A THEME OF STRAVINSKY"

The formation of this piece was like a journey through a wormhole in space, emerging into a different world and time from where I began, the components of me having shifted and re-formed unwittingly. It was a dissolving and tearing apart, searching for myself. I began as a young, unmarried, giddy graduate student and ended eight years later, transformed into a wiser, more cynical yet far better composer, married and struggling in the world. The misspelling of *"Mosaics"* is mine, as I felt that the Byzantine quality of the word and its meaning called for a more exotic look. Fortunately, I rarely arbitrarily change spellings, but I did this time.

Back in Dr. Thomas Beversdorf's advanced orchestration class in 1966, containing the same three students who were in his composition class, he set us to studying the incredible orchestration in Gustav Mahler's *"Das Lied Von der Erde"*, along with other works, prior to our own attempts. That piece burned the retinas of my eyes, ears, and heart, transforming me to the outer atmospheres of sonic adventures, which I never forgot.

At the same time I browsed the Indiana University Music Library to find a small score to orchestrate, and came across an obscure collection of three Russian folk songs adapted by Igor Stravinsky for baritone voice and women's three-part choir. The last of the three, *"Master Portley's Complaint"*, has three very short but memorable and distinct melodic/harmonic sections repeated in each verse—first, the baritone solo, like a cantor's, then the answer by the choir, who extend it with the three different phrases. The piece fairly explodes with compositional and orchestrational possibilities, and has the very important trait of being virtually unknown, but with Stravinsky's clarity of style and of course the appeal of his name...At the time he was my favorite composer, so I was ecstatic to find this set.

The assignment was only to arrange for full orchestra a short chamber work of a famous composer or a short piece of one's own. Barton McLean and Richard Heiniger, the other students, did the assignment as asked, but I became entranced, and by the end of the semester had written three variations to go after the theme *"Master Portley's Complaint"*, and then had orchestrated all of them, making a 15-minute piece with many intricate orchestral filigrees, strange doublings, and solos, inspired by my study of Mahler. About seven minutes of the piece were completely finished, and I was given the notice to have all twenty-six orchestral parts ready, with multiple copies for the strings, in about two weeks, for the end-of-semester readings of student works by an assigned student orchestra.

Anyone who has never copied an orchestral score or parts by hand cannot have any conception of how long a time it takes, and how difficult it is. I certainly had no idea, and left until the last few days the writing, thinking it would take only a few hours. Bart, by now my almost-fiancée, grew more and more agitated, and finally agreed to help copy the parts, giving me much instruction on how to put fountain pen to score paper, which was waxy ozalid ("onionskin") in those days, and how to take a razor blade and scratch out any mistakes, one of the most arduous tasks invented and enough to make any composer question her life's choice…The day before the reading, I still had about fifteen parts to go, and my blood red eyes managed to see the sun go down and come up again before I finished, while Bart proof-read the parts. After that, he needn't have proposed, because I would have married him on the spot anyway!

The reading went well, and I obtained a tape of the piece. To anyone walking into the orchestra room, it would have sounded like a rough reading of a student work, complete with copying mistakes and flaws, but to me it was the opening to a vast unexpected universe. I was enchanted, thrilled, the long night forgotten. The concertmaster was David Mallory who introduced himself to me after the reading and became my lifelong friend. He now lives in San Miguel, Mexico and has become a prominent painter, with his studio right on the town square, giving violin lessons after hours. So life turns and twists, around unsuspected corners.

"Variations on a Russian Folk Theme", as it was called then, quietly was thrust into a drawer while I prepared the next year, my second year at Indiana University, to work on my Master's thesis. On this ill-begotten piece I slaved daily, grimly trying to be profound and intellectual, even writing a fugue as one of the movements, emulating the great symphonies that hung like scabbards over my pathetic cowering brain. The best thing I can say about this piece is that, mid-year, I went in tears to Dr. Beversdorf and begged him to allow me to bury it and resurrect the *"Variations"* I had written the previous year. He grimaced, then said grudgingly, "All right, but I'm giving you a B!" (I didn't know enough to laugh, since theses do not receive grades, anyway.)

My last year at I.U. basically was spent finishing the thesis and copying it with all its parts in ink. Basically, the form of the music directly relates to Stravinsky through melodic motives and repetitions, unlike themes and variations of the past, which use the same harmonic structure as the original theme for each variation. In my work, each variation uses its own formal design, developing fragments of the original theme, interplayed with my own melodic and harmonic themes and motives. A section in the middle, between *Variations III* and *IV*, was written eight years later and called *"Mozaics"*. *"Mozaics"*, a much more jazzy and light-hearted variation, displays the techniques of alternation of brief sections and interruption, using melodic and harmonic motives often directly taken from the original *"Theme"*. This movement, inspired by Stravinsky's *"Agon"*, is a tribute/parody to the later styles of Stravinsky. The last variation begins with an introductory section and gradually evolves into a recapitulation of the original *"Theme"*. The theme expands with repetition until the broad climactic section that juxtaposes the original folk music and a slower variation of it, found in the horns, ending the work in a grandiose gesture of affirmation.

At the end of that third year I managed to persuade a doctoral conducting major, Eduard Forner, to find a pick-up group to read and record the whole piece, now eighteen minutes long. Since it had already had a reading, albeit only partially, two years before, the faculty would not support this, but we found that no student readings were scheduled that spring, and the orchestra room was available. A few minutes before the reading, we discovered that we had no cellists, and I frantically barged in on Janos Starker's [13] lesson, pleading for his help. He dropped everything, and ran around the practice rooms, dragging out all his doctoral students and ordering them to the reading. Subsequently, I had the most amazing cello section, eight virtuosi, for the best reading of anyone's music ever! Bless you, Janos Starker.

The reading/performance of *"Variations"* was slow but inspired, and during a moment of brief rehearsal, I crept into the string locker room and broke down, weeping with joy. This is one of those moments a composer lives for.

I graduated with a Masters of Music in Composition in 1969, and back went the thesis into the drawer. What does one do with a Masters thesis after that? The cold world was beckoning me, and we had many student loans to pay. The scene rolls ahead five years, past the hours/days/months I sat at the dining room table in our house in South Bend, Indiana copying Bart's doctoral thesis, a wonderful work for orchestra entitled *"Metamorphosis"* (ah yes—pay back time), and to the choosing of his piece to be played at the Indiana State University National Orchestral Symposium, by the Indianapolis Symphony, Oleg Kovalenko conducting. Bart was one of the honored composers for a week of rehearsals, panels, press sessions and concerts in April of 1974. A suggestion box was placed in the hall asking for questions for the panel. I asked anonymously, "Have you ever chosen a work by a woman composer?" The next day the question was read to embarrassed faces, and my net was cast.

The next year I submitted my work, but with the bright new addition, *"Mozaics"*, featuring a virtuosic clarinet part, for a performer preferably who understands jazz, and who can smoothly glissade up a scale even higher than *"Harlem Nocturne"*. I patterned the solo for the Symphony's daring clarinettist Howard Johnson, having heard him at the 1974 Symposium. I re-titled the revised orchestral work *"Variations & Mozaics on a Theme of Stravinsky"* and again worked almost all night finishing the parts for the submission deadline. It was chosen, though with some reluctance because of its length, now grown to over twenty minutes.

So the spring of 1975 saw a new phenomenon—back-to-back years of composers from the same family having orchestral works premiered by the Indianapolis Symphony and honored guests of the National Orchestral Symposium. This was the first and last time anything like that ever happened, to us or anyone else, as far as I know. The orchestra loved my piece, and because of its length, it received too much rehearsal time to the detriment of the other six works. My happiness was tempered with regret for the others, who had become my friends over the week together. During the concert, at intermission after *"Variations"* had had its rousingly successful premiere, people were flooding me with congratulations. I found myself choking up again, and raced to the ladies' room to keep from bursting into tears in front of my well-wishers. As I entered the ladies' room, a group of violinists from the orchestra clamored up to me, full of compliments, and for the only time in my life I felt like a rock star, although I don't think that rock stars cry so easily...

The summer of 1975 I sat down, revised, and polished the whole orchestral piece and recopied the parts, then mailed a copy of the score to Jorge Mester, conductor of the Louisville Orchestra. In those rare days, now extinct, a composer could dare to send an unsolicited score to an orchestra known for performing and recording contemporary music, and have it actually seriously looked at. After waiting about a month, I called the manager of the orchestra and asked what the status of my piece was. Jack Firestone said, "Well, it has progressed from the pile of scores reaching from floor to ceiling to the pile of scores that only reach to Mr. Mester's desktop!" He suggested that if I wanted more real progress towards a performance, that I "donate" some funds to the orchestra to help the piece along. Oh. *Welcome to the Real World.* I was furious and shocked, and hung up numbly. I had no funds to give anyone, and felt if I have to pay to have a piece of mine played by an orchestra whose members are salaried, they who are in existence only because of composers, that my whole reason for writing would be a falsehood and I should stop composing right now. One must remember that I was only a few years out of graduate school and hadn't yet learned the basic capitalistic issues of supply and demand, even for "exalted" art. I still feel this way, although I understand and sympathize with the many composers who so desperately want to hear their hard-earned music that money becomes an unimportant factor, equal to buying that computer or extra car. Unfortunately, orchestras are extremely expensive.

During the summer of 1976 Bart and I moved to Austin, Texas, where Bart had been appointed Director of the University of Texas Electronic Music Center. On November 30 I was talking with Karl Korte, head of the composition department and now our decades-long good friend, who offhandedly mentioned the new Martha Baird Rockefeller grants for young composers of orchestral music, as an aid towards recording fees. The deadline was December 1, the next day! I raced home, called the grants office in Washington, D.C., receiving all the information, made out the application, which stated that you had to have a willing orchestra just waiting to record your piece. So I then called Jack Firestone again, stating that I had found a funding source, and that there would be no problem receiving the grant, and the orchestra could count on it. The Louisville Orchestra was involved just at that moment in a meeting to choose the next year's pieces for their annual phonograph records, as it turned out. A half-hour later Jack returned my call, stating that my piece had been chosen for a March 1 recording and a performance at Kennedy Center, that it was "a beautiful piece", and I could go ahead with the application!

I mail-grammed the grant application, then sent the parts to the orchestra, and waited. In mid-February I received an answer from MBR Foundation—my application was refused.

Such is the black heart of a struggling composer who has choices: inform the orchestral of the grant's failure and accept defeat, pay $10,000—the price at that time for one side of a phonograph recording with that orchestra—or keep quiet and pray that life will steamroll on and a recording will result, anyway. My 1977 Journal states: "I have not told the orchestra yet, but I figure they probably know by now" (pure fantasy, of course). "Two days ago they asked for final program notes, and the first rehearsal was March 6th. So I doubt if they'll cancel now." Then, to improve further upon my arrogance, I wrote a letter to President Jimmy Carter, inviting him to the Kennedy Center concert!

So I arrived in Louisville for the final rehearsals, and upon entering the orchestra's office, was heartily approached by Jack Firestone. "And when will they be sending the grant money?" he smiled. "Oh, yes, I forgot to tell you…the grant didn't come through. That won't make any difference, will it?" I syruped in reply. Pale, through clenched teeth, he asked, "Why didn't you let us know *in time?*" Hmmm. In time for what—*to cancel the recording?* I made a feeble excuse and decided it was time to vanish until the rehearsal later in the day. I sit here now, twenty-eight years later chuckling over the once-in-a-lifetime opportunity to foil an orchestra bent upon making composers pay. Now I am not an ungrateful wretch: the Louisville Orchestra has been the premiere orchestra in the United States for championing and recording new music by living composers, which up to 1977 had been at the orchestra's expense. And this is not a major metropolitan orchestra (who probably would not have even opened my envelope) with huge coffers of money. This irony of composer versus orchestra, with scores of unwanted new pieces being written daily and orchestral boards trying to keep their ensemble alive by programming familiar classical and/or pop-related works the audience will come to and pay high prices to hear, is a pathetic phenomenon of these non-classical times. My bravado and trickery on this occasion ultimately had its dark side, as from that day on, no unsolicited scores were ever again accepted by Louisville.

My next act of infamy came with the Louisville radio interview. During the live broadcast, the announcer asked me how I had received permission from the Stravinsky estate to use his song as the theme? Suddenly there was silence. He shut off the microphone, tuned into some music for the audience while I whispered tightly, "I never thought to ask for permission." Ohhh. This was glossed over on the air, and the next hurdle came the day of the recording, when, on my way into the recording room, the engineer Leonard Kasdin (who also engineered at Columbia Records) asked about the copyright. "You do have permission, don't you?" "Oh, yes, certainly!" I lied, almost fainting with terror. Nothing else was said, and the recording session went beautifully. Jorge Mester is a thorough, exacting, sensitive conductor who made the piece glisten with clarity. He obviously loved the piece, telling me this many times, and I loved him, every performer, the radio announcer, even Jack Firestone! The recording came out six months later, with Hector Villa-Lobos on the "other side", with his *"Bachianas Brasileiras No. 4"*.

The last installment of this deception came a few months later when I submitted the *"Variations"* to the Alexander Broude Publishing Company through its new music editor, William Sisson. Finally I had to admit that I had never dared to obtain copyright permission, the songs not being in public domain because Stravinsky was too wise to let this happen and would slightly revise or re-score a piece in order to extend the copyright another 26 years. So began the frantic search for the publisher of the original songs. From a March 24, 1977 entry in my journal written just before the recording session, I commented upon this same copyright mess: "I feel like I'm sitting on top of an atomic bomb with a rose petal, and drinking cherry juice. Such a beautiful dream is happening, that could turn into something so ugly! The only question is when..." But the God of Wayward Musicians was smiling upon me, for I received an ecstatic call a few days later from Sisson: the copyright holder of the Stravinsky Russian folk songs was—(drum roll here)—*Alexander Broude Co.*! Broude also owned Brietkopf & Hertel Publishers in Europe, and the *only* Stravinsky piece they had in their entire catalog was this set of songs!

Bill Sisson was so enamored with the piece that he nominated it for the Pulitzer Prize in February 1979. I would like to report that the piece continued to grow in performances and fame, and that it was now ensconced in the main repertoire of major orchestras. But anyone who has been reading this would know that the life of this piece was circuitous, with a continuous hefty push from its inventor. My music cannot be pigeon-holed into a category such as serialism, or minimalism, or third-stream, or neo-classical, or any other style that people can hang onto to figure out what it is I am doing. I was not ivy-league educated, had no contacts with influential people, and pushed my music as far as I could uphill on my own. In 1992 I gave up writing for orchestra, because all the doors had slammed shut and I had grown very, very tired of the battle.

"Variations & Mozaics on a Theme of Stravinsky" was performed at Kennedy Center, unattended by Jimmy Carter but had a full house, anyway, of mainly Brazilians who had come to hear the Villa-Lobos pieces. Since then, it has had a dozen performances by different orchestras. One of its main deterrents, it appears, is the fiendish clarinet solo in the *"Mozaics"* movement, plus its length of twenty minutes. American composers should write easy short pieces that require a minimum of rehearsal time, so the brunt of the schedule can be set aside for the *real* music of Brahms, Mozart, Tchaikovsky, et al.

2.
"INTERPLANES FOR TWO PIANOS"

"A restless, dramatic atmosphere pervades the first movement, as two strong, divergent personalities with their own planes of music compete for dominance. Within the individual parts restlessness is also encountered, as brief motivic ideas are reiterated, gaining and losing pitches, sometimes expanding into ostinato[14]-like melodies. The calm section about one-third of the way into the movement gives only brief respite as the two individuals soon begin again their forceful restiveness.

"The second movement suggests a different scenario. Instead of two individual competing personalities, the two merge into one broad, complex atmosphere out of which melodies, motives, and arpeggios emerge and fade, moving in space as from one large integrated instrument. Inspired by the stratification and alternation of musical ideas and moods (the unutterably calm chords versus the blatant, violent rhythmic attacks) in Charles Ives' *"The Unanswered Question"*[15], this movement is a collage of superimposed contrasts."

I wrote these program notes shortly after the piece was finished, in 1970. Now as I listen to it from a distance of over thirty five years, I see a woman, one foot nailed to the ground, the other flailing forward, as she lurches with her whole body toward a freedom she cannot have, and is forced to lurch in circles around the captured foot, with melodies and harmonies that keep repeating and alternating between great gusts of screaming and quiet plaintive cries for help...

Bart and I left Indiana University after I finished my Masters degree in May of 1969. Bart had finished his course work towards his doctorate, and had accepted a teaching position at Indiana University, South Bend. We returned to Norwood, New York, where Bart's mother was living in the house that she had given to us as a wedding present two years earlier (she and Bart had jointly owned it). That summer I painted an expressionistic work with bloodied face and hands becoming claws, surrounded by a bombed-out world of disembodied faces screaming, inspired by the recent horrifying assassination of Robert Kennedy. The work was called *"Assassination #3"*, in remembrance of President John F. Kennedy and Rev. Martin Luther King. Working arduously on this proved to be too much on top of composing, and I never created another oil painting after that. We spent a great deal of time that summer hiking and backpacking in the Adirondack Mountains, quietly saying good-bye to Bart's mountains and our lives in the Northeast.

By autumn 1969 I had found a teaching position at John Adams High School in South Bend, Indiana, dealing with eight ninth-grade required choral classes and a before-school volunteer ninth grade chorus which met at 7:30 a.m. in the choral room. Renting a house in town from Mrs. Daube, mother-in-law of the head of the I.U.S.B.[16] Piano Department, Robert Hamilton, we drove daily to our respective jobs, and became normal citizens. But I began to die inside. While Bart became an esteemed member of the small but talented faculty at I.U.S.B., I was greeted with rowdy classes and spitballs from bored 14-year-olds who planted chewing gum between the pages of music I handed out and giggled, talked out loud or whispered, sang in barely audible voices while shouting at each other across the room, and all those other tortures a class of young teenagers do when their teacher is fresh out of graduate school and has just finished a large erudite orchestral composition. There was a racial factor here, as well, as this was 1969, and South Bend had seen race riots in the summer. John Adams High School contained newly bussed black students from the inner city who felt very uncomfortable with the suburban whites in class, and acted out with loud bravado. I was as suited to this job as being an astronaut, and suffered from spastic colon so severely that I was doubled up between classes when I wasn't running to the bathroom with diarrhea, and spent my evenings lying on our couch with a heating pad.

I consoled myself by immersing my mind and heart in Stravinsky's *"Rite of Spring"*, Morton Subotnick's *"Silver Apples of the Moon"* (his first major electronic music recording), Iannis Xenakis' *"Orient-Occident"*, and many other pieces, studying score and record as I lay on the couch. I was determined not to let my mind atrophy. By winter, the high school principal made my life infinitely easier by allowing me to remove the rowdiest students from my classes and to place them in study hall, thus reducing my class size by half and freeing up the students who were at least somewhat interested in singing. The alternative was to fire me, since I would not quit, as I desperately needed to pay back our loans, and the volatile high school had gone through too many teacher changes already. That winter was frigidly cold. I would awake at 5:45 a.m. from our tiny icy bedroom under the eaves on the second floor, and prepare for school with the temperature outside being 20 degrees below zero. After a cold breakfast in the large drafty kitchen I would drag out to the old Ford, which often wouldn't start...Once I spent my early chorus period in the middle of Main Street with a dead battery. The children dutifully arrived at 7:15 for their choir rehearsal—they were a wonderful group of spirited singers, and the next half hour would be the high point of my day. By 9 a.m. the sun would finally decide to come up and it would warm to almost zero.

On weekends I tried composing a concerto for violoncello and orchestra, writing on an old upright piano in a downstairs bedroom. I even went so far as to drive back to Bloomington to show it to Dr. Beversdorf, who praised its progress in style from the *"Variations"*—more atonal and "modern". But away from Indiana University, with no performers for inspiration, the piece was retired to a shelf, aborted. By February 1970, I began a two-piano piece, first conceiving it as a piano & percussion work, hence its very percussive beginning. It became my solace and joy, composing on weekends and some nights, now that I was less plagued with IBS (irritable bowel syndrome).

Another piece I was fascinated with at the time was Luciano Berio's famous avant-garde orchestral piece *"Sinfonia"*, although when Bart first played it for me at the breakfast table, I hated every note. But he played it over and over, and the sounds began to make sense and creep inside my mind. I hear Berio's first movement in *"Interplanes"*, along with Stravinsky, but more McLean was beginning to emerge, the woman with the nailed-down foot in the classroom, hands aspiring to what was just out of reach for now, back in that wonderful university filled with music and learning and life.

During Christmas vacation, after visiting family back in the Northeast, we returned to South Bend with Mother McLean, who had sold the Norwood home and was coming to live with us permanently. This was a difficult situation for all of us in this small rental house, and during April vacation, with the house sale money we bought a 60-year-old comfortable farmhouse on almost an acre of woods surrounded by a pretty white fence, on the edge of town. This property included a tiny cabin-style house where Mom McLean could live and cultivate her extensive flower gardens. The three of us worked together as a team during the next seven years in South Bend. Bart and I renovated the old property, painting and roofing, while his mother did the gardening and laundry for all of us, and fixed up her own cottage. That spring vacation was consumed with painting most of the rooms and moving in, Bart's and my first jointly-owned home.

The summer of 1970 we returned to I.U., Bart needing to finish up his course work and I to take a couple of doctoral courses of my choosing. We both enrolled in a brand new electronic music course taught by Iannis Xenakis' assistant, Michael Babcock, a doctoral student and his assistant, Jay Williams. The electronic studio had been locked and moribund until Mr. Xenakis arrived in 1969, and the music faculty so disliked the idea of him coming that he was allowed to teach only mathematics courses, which of course ruled out just about all of the music students except the most intrepid and scientific. So it was left to his student assistant to teach this one electronic music course. Mike was a great teacher. He came into class one day and threw a large metal spring on the floor, then asked what that would sound like if recorded and the tape recorder slowed down to half its speed. Thus whetting our curiosity, he introduced us to the beginnings of European electronic music, back in radio days with sound effects, evolving into a style of "found sounds", like the spring, that could be altered with the tape recorder and disguised, made into fascinating musical events that defied standard logic but evoked a fire in the brain. This kind of composing was called *"musique concrete"*, and I fell in love with it the instant I heard it.

Along with being introduced to the whole history of the medium, Bart and I also worked on the Moog Synthesizer in private session with Jay Williams, who was a doctoral trombone student and blind, who would come into our sessions and wave his hands gaily over the synthesizer and say, "If you press this button and this button, I don't know what they are called, but you will get the most amazing sound!" His boundless enthusiasm infected and inspired us, way beyond any technical agility we were to gain.

I composed a little piece there called *"Experimental Landscape #1"*, which used smooth sine waves undulating and cascading up and down, a boiling coffeepot, the vibrations of a ruler plucked while held on one end over the edge of a desk, and in tribute—an excerpt from Iannis Xenakis' orchestral piece *"Pithoprakta"*, slowed down to half speed on the tape recorder, creating a musical pedal under the mass of bubbling sound over it. I also moaned plaintively into a mayonnaise jar, to blend it all together. The piece took one day, and I recorded it on the studio's old two-channel Ampex that night. It was definitely not a good piece, but immense fun, and I was hooked. Composing had never been so much pure joy!

Along with electronic music, I studied composition with Prof. Bernard Heiden, as Dr. Beversdorf was not teaching that summer. With his guidance and a whole summer to compose, I finished *"Interplanes"*, and gave him a copy of the final ink score. We lived in married student housing, and alternated listening to our latest discovery, Oliver Messiaen's *"Turangalila Symphony"* while squashing cockroaches and enduring the neighboring couple's new baby's constant wails.

Bart presented an evening of his music as required for his doctorate, and one of the main events was Bart's *(Carl)"Sandburg Songs"* for soprano and piano. Bart performed while I sang on that glorious recital hall stage, our first public performance together ever. Afterwards, Dr. Horace Reisburg of the theory faculty came up to me and said, "Well, you'll never do much as a singer, but you have a lot of spirit!"

1970 was a pivotal year in my fledgling career. The music studied and the skills learned were to shape all my future creative activities, much more than I would have ever dreamt.

When we returned to South Bend in the autumn, I took a job teaching alternate weeks of art and music to fourth, fifth, and sixth grade classes in the next town over, Mishawaka. I found myself thoroughly enjoying the art classes, where we invented projects in all kinds of media—toothpick sculpture, wet colored chalk, plastic straw sculpture, charcoal drawing over watercolor pastiches—the art projects were so popular they were hung all over the school, to the students' delight. The neighborhood was made up of working class people, and many of the families had migrated up from the southern mountain regions. Traditional music teaching was impossible, so I took a poll for the twenty pop songs the children liked the best, bought the sheet music at the music store, and adapted the songs for the classes. I discovered that the harmonies and intricate melodies of Simon & Garfunkel, the Beatles, and others were far more sophisticated and charming than the pedagogic tunes in the textbooks, which I used only for the folk tunes scattered throughout. I arranged songs in parts for the children, also. We painted pictures to music of Stravinsky, Bartok, and other classical composers. I worked relentlessly hard, and by mid-year had turned into a mature teacher with devoted classes and friends among the faculty, who also worked extremely hard. Elementary school teaching is the most arduous and exhausting of all the grades. I know. I have done it all.

So I had turned into a successful teacher. But alas—my composing died.

In the spring of 1971 *"Interplanes"* was premiered at I.U.S.B. by Robert Hamilton and his best student, Christine Larson Douberteen. This is a fairly atonal piece, quite dense and complex, and the audience was mystified. During intermission, after the performance, groups of people stood shouting at each other. "Well, I liked it!" "It was horrible!" Etc. etc. Audiences in 1971 tended to be large and really involved. Fellow teachers from my elementary school sat there with saucer eyes, mumbling sadly to me later, "You're not going to be teaching little kids very long, are you?" No. They were right. This year was the last time I ever taught children. For me it was time to move on.

In 1976 *"Interplanes"* was recorded for Advance Recordings, a small record company operated by Barney Childs in Arizona. Bob Hamilton and Christine Douberteen were the pianists. They recorded on a bitter cold January day in the college auditorium with the central heat off, since the heating system's fan made noise. Christine could not eat before a performance or recording, so she sat all day without food or heat, playing her best, while I feared she would keel over and justify what many people thought about contemporary music! Bart was the recording engineer. The pianos were unequal: one was a nine-foot Steinway and the other was a seven-foot Baldwin. Bob took the smaller piano, as he had the bigger sound. In spite of all these woes, their recording was a thing of joy—clear, spacious, musical. Robert Hamilton is one of the greatest pianists I have ever heard, and had he recorded extensively in his career, would be world-famous today. All of the recordings he has made are voices of beauty.

3.
"DANCE OF DAWN"

thunderous sun roaring away the abyss
riotous life-noises scream the air
            senseful
rougeyellow leers white light   eyeprying
footfall din is lost in

            the jeers of the catmoon

(Priscilla McLean, for *"Dance of Dawn"*)

A June morning in 1974. I awake at dawn in our South Bend country house, all the windows open, and am enveloped in waves of cardinals singing, then hoards of robins, then finally all the other birds so plentiful here amid the forests and swamps of northern Indiana countryside. The sliver of crescent moon still shines in the sky as the earth fills up with sun, and a poem is born. So began my fascination with natural sounds amid composed music, the poem written after the music.

I.U.S.B. had just begun an experiment with creating an electronic music studio. Because of Bruce Hemingway, who was an ambitious young recording engineer in the Division of Music, the school ordered from the EMS Studios in London one of only two Synthi-100 Synthesizers in the U.S. at this time, the other one sitting disconnected in the Columbia-Princeton Electronic Music Studio in upper Manhattan. No manual had been written for it, and the engineers at Columbia-Princeton were flummoxed on how to operate the real-time digital Synthi-256 Sequencer, the first of its kind, which would only run round and round in a tight constipated loop. Bruce figured it out, however, and had the synthesizer and sequencer up and running shortly after their arrival. The slight cloud on the horizon of this new studio was that it was not paid for: a down payment of $6,000 had been sent, which bought the sequencer, but the remaining $16,000 was held in promise as soon as the university could afford to pay. The EMS Company in London, eager to set up shop with the Synthi in America, accepted the wait, for at least a time.

By the autumn of 1971, we were sufficiently caught up in our loan-paying that I could afford to leave full-time public school teaching, and I accepted a two-day a week position at Indiana University at Kokomo, driving the 90 miles south to teach undergraduate theory and sight-singing to about twelve students in the new-born music department. This left five days a week at home, so when the new studio at I.U.S.B. arrived, I was ready to try my hand at electronic music. By 1971 we had begun our own home studio, purchasing from Boston a new Arp 2600 Synthesizer and three reel-to-reel tape recorders: two two-channel half-track Revoxes and a four-channel quarter-track Sony, and borrowing from the college a small Synthi AKS Synthesizer—an update of the EMS Putney, with a ribbon keyboard and 256-note real-time sequencer.

Just before the I.U.S.B. studio arrived, I went into our little home studio and in a frenzy of complete joy and froth, created a chamber electronic piece, and recorded it, all in one day! I neglected to write down how I had gotten the sounds, however, and the analog synthesizers of the day had no exact settings. This made for an impossible situation, without any diagrams, of reproducing the same sound later or the movement between sounds. So when I went back to the studio, the piece naturally needed fleshing out and revising, and I had no idea how to re-create the sounds. It took two more months to discover how to do this, and a little six-minute piece was born, *"Night Images"*. I also wrote a poem for this one:

> What are in the images of the night's eye?
> some drift by clearly, focused, lucid.
> Others are mere phantoms, vaporous ghosts
> that wander in the half-sensed twilight.
> The night belies and jests with reality—
> a cosmos apart.

Bart went first to learn the new Synthi-100 at the university, with help from Bruce, and convinced me to try my hand at it. I was very leery of my ability with no manual, but he was adamant that this was an important step into the future of new music. Although I had written for various ensembles in the small music department, our performance opportunities were limited, and one had the feeling that another new piece in an old medium was just more unwanted baggage for the performers, involved so deeply with the Past Masters…

When Bart introduced me to the new studio, I stared unbelievingly—here was a huge synthesizer, along a whole wall, with hundreds of "push-pins" (a matrix setup for connecting sounds, rather than the old patch cords), and twenty-two oscillators! Next to it on the right side stood a four-channel Scully reel-to-reel tape recorder with half-inch-wide tape, and next to that was a gigantic eight-channel Scully tape recorder with one-inch-wide tape. It could almost have been an upright piano! When I compare this monster machine with the tiny DAT (digital audio tape recorder) of today, I am floored—how quickly our tech civilization has evolved! Vastly better and tinier. Astounding.

The Synthi-256 Sequencer was a full-sized keyboard, standing alone diagonally to the analog synthesizer, but connected internally. Bart handed me a long sheet he had written, an abbreviated "manual" to get me started, and I was supposed to begin with the first instructions and methodically proceed down the list, learning the techniques of sound-alteration through analog synthesis. So I began with #1. After ten minutes, I grew so fascinated with the sounds I was creating that I abandoned the sheet, and immediately launched into a new piece, using all twenty-two oscillators in a mass-sound event, ala Iannis Xenakis, my mentor. I ran around the matrix board, gleefully pushing and pulling the pins, altering the sounds and connections in wonderfully mysterious ways until it built to a huge climax.

My approach to electronic music has always been this total frenzy of joy. I don't know why. The computer age has been harder to handle for me, because I am not a calculating-kind of person, but now with the sampling instruments paralleling the old analog days of musique concrete, I am again happily playing. I love creating new sounds and exploring new sound-worlds, and now in my predotage am doing the same with video images and loving that, also.

Bart was appalled at my unscientific approach, discarding his "manual"! He warned me that I would always lag behind every composer in the field if I didn't learn the basics of electronic sound production. So whenever we went anywhere he would drill me, "OK. How is ring modulation produced? What happens if you modulate a square wave with a low-frequency sine wave, modifying its amplitude?" Etc. etc. We would be driving to the Chicago Symphony concerts, an hour-and-a-half away, and tears would be blurring my vision of the road as I drove and struggled to visualize these techniques. He was relentless. I was not going to be an ignoramus! I fought him internally. Couldn't I be excused from all this? After all, I was playing with *dolls* when I was seven—not taking apart radios!

So we three—Bruce, Bart, and I—worked all our spare time, alternating with each other, in the I.U.S.B. Studio. Bruce would work all night, and drag home at 5 a.m. to grab a couple of hours sleep before his workday. Bart would arrive at 7, on the days he didn't work. Two or three days a week I had the studio to myself—there were no classes yet, as there were no interested students yet, and the studio could be whisked away to England any day for lack of payment, thus no courses were scheduled. So I spent whole days there, sometimes 22 hours long, working and working to get just the right sound-combinations and record them.

In that studio with the giant machines, one raced from one end of the room to another to play and record the sounds, never sitting down, and in removing unwanted noise or editing out a recorded section, the composer had to take a metal splicing block and sharp razor blade, and pressing down very hard, cut through the 1-inch wide acetate tape in two places, remove the unwanted time segment, and rejoin the two remaining ends with special splicing tape. Vladimir Ussachevsky[17] and many earlier composers created whole pieces using hundreds of splices in abrupt collages, using the medium of splicing as its own art-form. I was content to use it as sparingly as possible. A few years later saw electronic splicing supplanting this arduous process, and it is used only as a teaching tool in some colleges these days.

In January of 1974, during a bitter cold below-zero spell, the power supply for the Synthi-100 failed. I desperately wanted to continue working, and brainstormed with Bart and Bruce on how to get the synthesizer up and running again, since the power supply had to be removed and taken to a repair dealer in town, not to return for a few weeks. They came up with an ingenious method: twelve automobile batteries wired in parallel, enough to run the synthesizer at least for a few hours a day. So for the next two weeks, a surrealistic scenario evolved—a late twentieth-century state-of-the-art music synthesizer enveloped in an industrial hum of its twelve car-battery power supply, lying in a great line in back of the instrument, an artistic installation all its own! I would enter the room at midmorning, turn on the batteries and power, busy myself for a half-hour until the power rose to correct pitch-level in the synthesizer, then begin my day's work. Around noon, I would notice that my oscillator pitches were wavering, and descending in pitch, and shut down the equipment, so the batteries could regenerate and run again for a few more hours in the afternoon. Many mornings I would be so eager to start that I would stand over the huffing batteries, cursing them and making impotent fists in the air.

The first concert of electronic music ever presented at I.U.S.B. came during the autumn of 1973 and featured Bart's first major electronic piece, *"Genesis"*, my short *"Night Images"*, and *"Mandala"* by Bruce Hemingway. *"Mandala"* used two sound waves vibrating close together, which produced beautiful lissajous animations on film. The audience and I were thunderstruck by Bart's piece, played in the dark, with huge dramatic sweeps of sound, with discernible melodies and harmonies. Later played in the municipal auditorium in Akron, Ohio, *"Genesis"* was praised by John Von Rhein of the Akron Beacon Journal as a "minor master-piece" (strange contradiction of terms).

"*Dance of Dawn*" took a year and a half to create. During the summer of 1973, after working continuously on the piece for months, I took a short vacation with Bart—a ten-day canoe-backpacking trip along the lakes of Algonquin Provincial Park in Ontario, Canada. To our happy surprise, we were treated to a volley of loons singing from lake to lake. At sunset I would sit on a rock and sing with them, often getting them started on their nightly jamboree. One dawn, after a tremendous drenching thunderstorm that lasted all night and left us exhausted and sleepless, the noise stopped and in the brief silence started the most sanguine chorus of voices I had ever heard. I knew this had to be the ending of my piece. The "loon" chorus, made up of sine and triangle waves (no musique concrete in this piece) became a focal point of the piece, triggering the beginnings of new sections, and ending the piece after a drum-like rolling section, on four channels of loudspeakers ("thunderstorm"), with a slowly building chorus of "loons" which gradually die away into silence.

"*Dance of Dawn*" is not a programmatic piece. I did not intend to imitate loons or thunder. The thunder-like sounds happened unconsciously, and I was after the ululative quality of the loon singing, using cascading sine waves on the sequencer, controlled by finger pressure on the keyboard.

To explain my way of creating, I wrote an article entitled "*Fire & Ice: A Query*", which describes combining an abstract sound with an imageric one to become "imago-abstract", a multi-layered musical idea possible today with the new technology. Also featured are diagrams of "*Dance of Dawn*". The article appeared in *Perspectives of New Music*, Fall/Winter Issue, 1977, and later became a chapter in Robin Heifitz's book "*On the Wires of Our Nerves*".[18]

On the CRI Recording of "*Dance of Dawn*" that came out a year after the piece was finished[19], I wrote these liner notes for those who wanted to understand the piece better (the lead words stem from the poem):

"*Lifenoises:* An alteration and subtle change of motivic ideas propels the work, beginning with string-like minor seconds, gradually coalescing into a repeated rhythm which then separates itself by silences and slowly widening intervals (the interval of a second is a major cohesive factor throughout the work).

Thunderous: Rhythmic propulsion, distilled from the early percussive sounds, gains strength by the second half of the work. Highly filtered 'jew's harp' sonorities (beginning 13 minutes into the piece) and marimba-like qualities combine and invade the returned string-like fabric until shattering cross-rhythms and brittle timbres explode into a panning effect of violent drum-like (timpani) rolls.

Sun Rolling: An evocative melody of undulating character keeps recurring in different guises, usually at or immediately after structural climaxes. This melody, altered, becomes a polyphonic 'choir' of sounds approximately one third of the way into the piece, eventually fusing with clanging repeated tones and rhythms in a section of dense polyphony.

Leers White Light: Emerging from the beginning texture is a static chord-cluster, structured from previous sonorities, which recedes and reappears at key temporal locations. At times this becomes a ring-modulated chord gradually fluctuating and subtly changing, occurring as the antithesis to previous 'chaotic' and complex sections. These areas of stasis are the peace, the philosophical reflection, the calm that accepts and sorts the 'senseful' experience into a coherent intention; the transparent white light."

In June of 1974 I was approaching the end of the piece. Word was sent by Bruce Hemingway that the EMS Company in London was tired of waiting for that next payment of $16,000 from the university for the Synthi-100, and had decided to send over a crew to take out the studio and ship it back to England. They would be here in three weeks. I dropped everything else and virtually lived in the studio day and night to finish the piece, because otherwise I had no way of producing the same sounds, and two years of work would have been aborted!

The last day, I was recording the final sounds when in walked the men, ready to roll it all away. I begged and pleaded for one more day, to polish up the ending, and they kindly agreed. By midnight I had finished everything, my spirit and body numb to the core. This was the last large synthesizer I ever had the opportunity to work with. Perhaps my style might have been different if I had not been forced to return to found-sounds for the brunt of my material over the years. On the other hand, perhaps it would not have been so original and unusual, or even nature-oriented. One will never know.

Birth of *The McLean Mix*

The McLean Mix was born on September 19, 1974, in our World Premiere concert at St. Mary's College, Notre Dame, Indiana. My job at I.U.S.B. Kokomo came to an end that summer, due to budget cuts that wiped out its fledgling music department. I had grown tired of the long distance driving, alternating with taking the bus back and forth to central Indiana, anyway, and applied to teach elective piano and theory at St. Mary's College two days a week.

The college was just north of South Bend, on a very peaceful parochial campus, just across the highway from Notre Dame. My students included young Notre Dame men also, and the teaching was enjoyable, forcing me to work hard on my piano technique for my teaching. St. Mary's College was liberal in its thinking about contemporary music, and several of the music faculty performed old and new music together on their recitals. The Chicago Symphony Chamber Players and other prominent groups, such as the Boston Musica Viva Ensemble, regularly gave concerts of new music in the auditorium. Prominent guest composers had residencies, with master classes and conducting student concerts of their works.

So the faculty was delighted when I offered to perform with Bart our new electronic music. Our concert consisted of four pieces. The first was *"Gone Bananas"* by Bart, as he soloed on the Arp 2600. This was a light piece, and ended with Bart, having set the synthesizer to play the music by itself on its "sample and hold" controller, sitting on the edge of the stage eating a banana! Second was my *"Night Images"* six-minute stereo tape work. Next came a short demonstration on this new music medium of tape composition, and then my *"Dance of Dawn"*, 22 minutes long. We finished the evening with a jazzy piece by Bart called *"Groove"*, which had us jamming on two synthesizers—the Arp 2600 for me, and Bart on the Synthi AKS. These early live-performance compositions suffered the demise of all such pieces of the period, but fascinated the audience at the time—they who had never heard any live electronic music. The works for stereo tape lived on, however.

"Dance of Dawn" has had a long history of performances, as it became a staple of our McLean Mix tours through 1978. It appeared on a Composers Recordings Inc. vinyl record, with flip side being Bart's new *"Spirals"*, also 22 minutes long. Later it was re-mastered onto a CD under the CRI label.[20] During the halcyon days of the 70's, when all electronic music was enthusiastically received and the audiences large and eager, before personal computers, video recordings of films, 500+ television channels, e-mail, Internet, Web, etc., when the electronic medium was fascinating and new and people not so strung-out and exhausted, this album garnered a dozen reviews from all over America, and the composer was looked upon as a courageous explorer into a vast musical continent unknown and beckoning.

3a.
In Transition—Indiana to Austin, Texas

In August of 1976 we moved to Austin, Texas. After the Synthi-100 was removed from the Indiana University, South Bend Electronic Music Studio in 1974, we were left with its sequencer (paid for), a small ElectroComp 101 Synthesizer, the mini-synthesizer Synthi AKS, and the tape recorders and mixer. This wasn't enough to continue any quality work, so we added our own home studio equipment, and turned back to manipulating found sounds—steak knives bouncing on violin strings, tennis balls on the piano harp, banging pots and pans, etc. All of these sounds in addition to ones from the synthesizers and sequencer I used in my next major electronic piece, *"Invisible Chariots"*[21]. Because of the unwieldiness of the musique concrete medium, composing the piece was glacially slow.

For instance, the first sound is a scrape up a bass piano string with a metal bar. I wanted the echo from the piano to last over thirty seconds, so I had to record it onto a master tape, then re-record the echo from this tape to each of four channels of another tape recorder, recording each successive one a few seconds ahead of the last one, over and over, until thirty seconds evolved. Then I combined the beginning piano flourish, recorded at home, with a similar keyboard flourish created on the Arp 2600 Synthesizer and performed, playing (forwards and backwards) on the Synthi 256 Sequencer…Much more was involved to complete this complex beginning sound, and two months of time—for thirty seconds of music!

I was given a small stipend by I.U.S.B. as their "Composer-in-Residence" for 1976, and along with my teaching at St. Mary's College, I secretly gave private synthesizer lessons to Kay, a middle-aged woman student, since there were still no classes in this limping half-studio. I was not allowed to teach at I.U.S.B. even as a desperately needed adjunct lecturer, because of the nepotism rules of the day—no person (read: woman) could be hired, even for part-time work, if the spouse was already teaching in that department. This meant that many very talented graduate school-educated women had to drive 50-100 miles to other colleges, while the local university hired whomever else they could find locally or pay a high price to a special performer/teacher to drive in from Chicago…

Bart was growing more and more irritated by the limitations of his position, the studio, my situation, and South Bend in general, when we were attending an American Society of University Composers convention at the University of Iowa the spring of 1975, and over dinner with our new friend Karl Korte from Austin, Texas, learned about a possible opening for the director of the University of Texas at Austin Electronic Music Center.

Imagine—directing a real electronic studio at a major university in a large and culturally exciting southwestern city! We had never been to Texas, and the prospect was thrilling, breath-taking. It was a major music department, with seventy full-time faculty.

My only real regret would be in abandoning our new group *The McLean Mix*, which had evolved from our original quartet of David Cope, Burton Beerman, Bart, and myself for the 1974-75 performance season to just us two in 1976.

David Cope taught at Miami University, Oxford, Ohio, Burton Beerman at Bowling Green State University, Ohio, with the two of us teaching in Indiana. The four of us performed together in round-robin concerts at the three universities, calling ourselves *The Mix*. These were free events, mainly to present our new electronic and electro-acoustic music to a living, breathing audience, for some feedback on our work. Burt Beerman even composed "Reflections", a piece for all four of us: Bart and I on synthesizers, Burt on amplified clarinet and David on amplified cello, and we processed their sounds through our equipment. It was tremendous fun, and the audience loved it, but the logistics of driving between states for each rehearsal/concert became much too impractical.

1975 and 1976 were exciting *McLean Mix* beginning years, with many performances in Indiana, Ohio and Michigan, and we had even begun charging a fee. For me it was a special treat to perform this way, as my whole life was behind a small door teaching one student at a time or facing a bank of glittering electronic eyes. My orchestral piece had just had its premiere, also. I felt very ambivalent about the move to Texas.

The day we arrived in Austin, August 11, 1976, it was 110 degrees. Bart drove the U-Haul, I our new Toyota, and Bart's mother her aging Chevrolet, all without air-conditioning, in tandem, stopping sometimes just for ice cream sodas for dinner, being too hot and thirsty for regular food. The move took four days. We had bought a beautiful brick and stone house on the outskirts of town, in Westlake Hills, and were adding on an efficiency apartment for Mother McLean. The view was of the (Texas) Colorado River flanked by steep hills, with the lights of Austin twinkling in the distance. Our back yard was basically a cliff, and we lived in what was then called the "rattlesnake hills". This should have been Paradise, but on June 7, 1977 I wrote in my diary:

"In thinking over our year here, I see more losses than gains. It pains me to write this, but I believe we made a mistake moving here. Austin is a pleasant place if one likes sun, relaxed living, and recreation. *Losses:* 1. Bart's lovely sabbatical, to come up the year after next. We had planned to travel to New York City" (my perpetual dream) "and Europe for the semester, plus a ski trip to Colorado. Now that is gone forever—no sabbaticals in Texas, and not enough money to go even if he had the time off. 2. Money—about $1-2,000 less a year. Enough for record subsidizing, travel, etc. 3. Chicago, and nearby places—there is no center around here even *approaching* Chicago. No Univ. of Illinois, Univ. of Iowa, etc. Texas is the *pits* as far as culture goes…The South is regrettably, sickeningly conservative. We are feared and unappreciated. I feel myself dying daily…Texas has no Avant-garde, only Derriere!"

Of course, this report was very exaggerated. I had lost my job, and the nepotism rules were even stricter here. I was not allowed to work in the university studio unless I enrolled as a student. This didn't appear too awful at the time, because Bart was merrily throwing the studio down the third-floor old wooden stairs of the ancient junior-high school building that housed the strangest electronic studio ever created…The previous "director", Tom Wells, had faced a studio containing an old Moog Synthesizer, mixer, and a few tape recorders, even worse than I.U.S.B.! With *no* support from the university, he went to the nearby air force base and collected any electronic gadget he could get his hands on, using some and piling the rest in the corner of the cavernous old choral room. By the time Bart came, the room was practically filled with derelict machinery, and no one would authorize help for removing any of it (Tom had escaped to the University of Ohio by that time, and had found a really fine position as director of their large, modern Electronic Music Center).

So Bart solved the dumping problem by suspending all classes in the studio for the semester, then appointing the students to come daily and throw down the stairs as much junk as they could handle. When enough piled up at the foot of the stairs, and the chemistry department on the second floor began hollering to the maintenance crew about the fire hazard, the mess was removed from the floor. But not from the studio, so Bart had to keep this up all semester. He had built up a considerable amount of muscles by December! I was surprised that Bart was not fired on the spot for his insubordination, but there was a war going on in the department—did they really want an electronic music studio or not? He was finally promised a modest budget for some equipment, and by the second semester the Electronic Music Center was opened again in a gala week-long installation event called The Electric Sinfonia, where students and faculty could come and play with the sounds Bart had set up using the Moog and tape loops he had created, and each of five days his students and I set up installations of our own sounds with which the audience could interact.

We also performed a McLean Mix concert that autumn in the half-cleaned out studio with no air-conditioner, the three evenings we performed being 96 degrees in the room. Free tickets for the concert had to be obtained, due to the limit of 75 people per event, and each night a long line of students waiting for tickets snaked down the narrow stairs and into the hall. Bart was proudly considered, by the students at least, a slayer of bureaucratic dragons, the hot breath of which eventually would force him out of the university…

With no university electronic studio in which to work in 1977 and no teaching job to go to, I was left at home with our small studio upstairs in one of the two bedrooms at the end of a crossways hall, and the baby grand piano down-stairs, under the other upstairs bedroom, at the opposite end. What to do? I sorely needed a change of pace from the heavy electronic works I had been creating, anyway, and for the next several months worked in a daring new direction, as described in the next section.

By early winter 1978 our small home studio was again fully functional, and I returned to finishing *"Invisible Chariots"*. Movement three had only been thought about in South Bend, but I had taped enough synthesizer material to use, and built the movement around percussive sounds of pots and pans I banged together and recorded in Austin. I had been working nonstop for three years on these two large electronic works, and when I finished this piece in February 1978 I was ready for a change.

4.
"BENEATH THE HORIZON I AND III"

"Poverty Trumps at Gaudeamus Music Week"

"...Among other things, one could listen to a piece for tuba and whale-ensemble (taped): 'Beneath the Horizon III' by Priscilla McLean (USA). The bouncing rattle of the tuba—which was put forth definitely in a masterly way by Melvyn Poore, resembled mostly a hoarse pig in labor, while the whales seemed to be in heat. All of that lasts a whole quarter of an hour!"

—*Nieuwsblad Voor Het Zuiden, Tilburg,*
Maarten Brandt, reviewer, Sept. 8, 1979.

September 3, 1977 Journal: "A terrible drought this year! Trees are dying, forests are burning—just to the side of our back property two weeks ago someone threw a lighted cigarette, and our neighbor lost two juniper trees in the fire. I am trying to get Bart to take our master manuscripts and tapes to school to store, in case our house burns down, but he is not too sure of the safety of that old building, either. It must be safer than here, with our cedar-shingle roof that could go up in a minute!"

Before we moved from South Bend I listened to a recording called *"Songs of the Humpbacked Whale"*. To my astonishment, I heard these liquid melodies and deep ocean calls as a sublime music, and a strong resonance sounded in my soul.

Perhaps it was the terrible heat and drought of Austin that brought me back long-ingly to this recording. Also soon after our arrival, resident tubist Stephen Bryant gave a recital of avant-garde music at the university. I heard in my head the tuba and whale sounds combine. I approached Stephen, and we got together to record a wide variety of his experimental sounds, to spur my imagination along.

First I did not hear just one tubist, but a quartet of them with the whales. Inspired by an announcement of a contest by the Los Angeles Tuba Quartet, I began to collect whale recordings and listen intensely. From my 1977 Journal: "I consciously used the same technique of creating as I did in my electronic works: play a tape of some music I would use, usually the synth sound I was working with, and jot down random, intuitive thoughts with no sense of what-goes-where or why. As soon as an idea fragment stops generating, *Stop* and go on to some-thing else; don't try to force the sound into being (overkill by the external mind). So I did this, playing the different whale sounds and imagining what tubas would do with it…After a few days my ideas evolved into longer fragments, then sec-tions…"

As soon as I completed *"Beneath The Horizon I"* for four tubas and taped whales, I began a version for solo tuba and "whale ensemble". The tape part for the quartet version consisted of whale songs, but often somewhat altered. Begin-ning with a low whale growl which I extended to make a pedal tone, during which the tubas emerge, starting on the same low pitch, the whales then burst forth with their characteristic humpback song (I used two recordings, *"Songs of the Humpbacked Whale"* and *"Deep Voices",* both on Capitol Records). The whales and tubas then alternate their musics. In the middle of the piece I dare the hapless tubists to whistle across their mouthpieces a little tune similar to the whales. This seems innocent enough, but tubists have to put their lips in a large "O" to vibrate through the wide mouthpieces, and can't so easily skinny down to the mini-aperture of a whistle. That feature alone has probably stopped most of the possible performances of these pieces.

At the end of the thirteen-minute work, the tubists sing into the tuba, while pressing the keys for the same pitches, a really wonderful tuba-human sound that goes extremely well with the whales. The only difference between the tape parts to the two pieces is that I added ocean sounds to the solo version, to give the tubist some resting time.

In the autumn of 1978 Stephen Bryant gave the world premiere concert of *"Beneath the Horizon II"* on Bart's "Electric Sinfonia" concert series to a very cold reception from the audience. This was *not* music—these were animal noises! I felt the first chill of a coming blizzard, and was amazed. The issue here was not that the music wasn't well written or compelling, even charming. The issue was that we humans are Superior to animals, and cannot consider their bestial noises as music, and should never seriously duet between the two in a classical concert on a university stage...So I decided in the future to amplify my philosophy that humans are also animals, and must live in symbiosis with their environment, as in my composition, not dominating or destroying. This feeling I had harbored inside for many years now had a voice—a sound that no one at that time wanted to hear.

In 1979 I read on the bulletin board at UT about a competition in Holland sponsored by the Gaudeamus Foundation. Submissions that year were chamber and orchestral pieces and works for the premiere tuba virtuoso of Europe—Melvyn Poore, a young man of twenty-eight years from Birmingham, England. Tape could be included. I felt a ripple in the heavens...Paying the entrance fee, I submitted a revised version, *"Beneath the Horizon III"*, over Bart's protest of "Oh, don't pay to get your music performed! You are wasting your money and time. They'll probably not even send your score and tape back." A few weeks later my piece was accepted, and I was invited, all expenses paid except the airline's, to be an honored composer at the Gaudeamus Musiekweek, along with a dozen other composers from around the world, and two performance ensembles from Romania and Spain.

I was completely thrilled. I had never been to Europe, and would be going by myself! Bart had to teach, of course, since the Musiekweek took place Sept. 13-19. That summer Bart and I had dual residencies at The MacDowell Colony[22] in Peterborough, New Hampshire for six weeks, and I remember fondly sitting by the blazing fireplace in Kirby Studio, nestled deep in the woods of the 450-acre estate, memorizing and renewing my acquaintance of German, and planning my fantastic get-acquainted solo tour of Germany, Holland, and England. The Mac-Dowell Colony has been so instrumental in much of my writings. Right now I sit here in the MacDowell Studio composing these memoirs, my fifth time at this wonderful refuge and inspiration for American composers, writers, and artists.[23]

So on September 9 I flew to Amsterdam. My first impression when hovering over the city to land was, "It looks like old New York!" But...how...Pity the poor naive secluded American who thinks her country came first! The shock of finally being in the Old World was a bonfire, and for the next few days I gleefully explored every inch of Amsterdam, which was crawling with backpackers, drug addicts, artists, tourists from everywhere, businessmen, and lean bicycle-riding handsome blond Dutch people. On the appointed Sunday I showed up at the Amsterdam Concertgebouw for the Grupo de Musica Contemporanea de Lisboa

(Lisbon, Portugal chamber ensemble) performance for the second concert of the Gaudeamus Festival.

There I met my performer, Melvyn Poore, and an English composer, Trevor Wishart. Both young men were right out of Monty Python, and I was doubled up with laughter in the first ten minutes. After the concert a group of Gaudeamus composers, including Horia Ratsiu from Romania, Pekka Siren from Finland, the two Englishmen and I went out to dinner and then a tour of the red-light district, watching the painted ladies sitting by their open doors in the small narrow houses. Horia was so fascinated that he lagged behind, and we laughingly abandoned him while racing back to the Concertgebouw for the evening concert with the Spanish chamber ensemble. The next morning Horia related bitterly that he had wandered around Amsterdam for hours, unable to communicate and completely lost. That was not our finest hour.

"Beneath the Horizon III" was performed in a concert hall at the Hague on a Sunday afternoon, Sept. 9, 1979. The concerts for this festival were spread out over the whole country of Holland, which made for a lot of smoky driving (windows closed while all the Europeans puffed away at their interminable cigarettes). The first piece on the concert was Trevor Wishart's *"Tuba Mirum"*, a wonderful theatre piece in which the tubist is a political prisoner in an insane asylum, and he acts out through playing the tuba, each section of the piece having a different and wildly bizarre specially built mute. The last mute for the climax of the piece is a cornucopia of plastic flowers that contains a tape recorder playing in duet with the tubist, so that suddenly the tubist becomes several people. At the end the tubist dies, and the stage is left empty with only his "dead" body lying on it.

My piece was not nearly so dramatic or theatrical, but it received eight wide-eyed reviews, ranging from mildly appreciative to the one quoted earlier…The reviewers were amazed by the whale music they had never heard. The unhappy audience barely clapped—a scene I was beginning to get used to.

The whole nine days of the Musiekweek was a whirl of lectures, rehearsals, concerts, and after-hours parties. The Gaudeamus house was right out of Hansel and Gretel, with turrets and rooms going everywhere, and a large circular dining room filled with plants and flowers, with huge windows overlooking gardens and forest in this acre-long estate. We were fed tasty meals and were welcomed by Chris Walraven, the director, and Walter Maas, the German Jew who had given this house to the Foundation in gratitude for the Dutch hiding him during World War II. Maas was in his seventies, and exuded fatherly joy to all, welcoming us to this "voonderful" country.

I was overjoyed with Melvyn's performance, and invited him to perform at the University of Texas and record my piece at the same time. This happened about a year later, and *"Beneath the Horizon III"* came out on Opus One Records. The quartet version was premiered also in 1979 by the First Texas Tuba Quartet at North Texas State University, Denton, Texas, with Steve Bryant playing bass tuba. This has been the quartet version's only performance so far. While Melvyn Poore was with us, he also recorded tubas 1 and 2 of the quartet version, with Steve Bryant later recording tubas 3 and 4, thus making a really elegant *"Beneath the Horizon I"* tape (now CD), which we have used with slides on several concerts.

When I began sending the solo version around, I discovered a small group of tubists as crazy as I was. Gary Buttery was performing from his small boat off the Newfoundland Coast, leaning over the edge to jam with the humpbacks, and sent me a tape of these incredible sessions. Barton Cummings, who has performed *"Beneath the Horizon III"* many times, had been enchanted by whales who swam by his studio at San Diego State University. In Los Angeles at the Provisional Theater in 1982, Liebe Gray gave the most original recital for tuba and whales I have ever heard of. *"Beneath the Horizon III"* was performed on stage with a giant whale sculpture housed in a water-filled "aquarium", designed and built by her and a large ensemble of workers. The performance had tubist and whale together under ocean-blue light…Tuba players are a wonderful, ephemeral group of dreamers. I have had the special honor to work with them.

In 1982 we were invited to perform at the Experimental Intermedia Center in New York City. Phill Niblock, the director, warned us that there was no piano. So I began converting photos of whales and sea to slides, and put together a slide show, using two slide projectors and the university's fade & dissolve unit to accompany Melvyn's recording of *"…Horizon"*. Thus began a sea change in our McLean Mix shows. For the first time, carefully-thought out and constructed visuals were added, and I began my first steps as a visual artist.

A last incident with the whale piece must be related. Our McLean Mix tour in December of 1983 to Europe took us to Belgium, Holland, Sweden, and Norway. We ended up in Norway, and on the train from Oslo to Bergen, I picked up the newspaper to glance at the pictures. There was our photograph on the front page! We couldn't read the description, since it was in Norwegian, so we took the paper with us to the dining car, and sat with a Norwegian gentleman who knew English. After a long, friendly conversation, where he treated us to a round of drinks, I asked him to please translate the front-page article. He stared at the picture. Silence. "Is this you?" he asked warily. Uh-oh. This was beginning to seem like a bad movie. "What is it saying?" we begged.

"'All hell breaks loose in the Eldorado Theatre'" he unhappily read. The article linked my piece to the Greenpeace activist environmental organization, which was at that time boycotting the Norwegian whaling and seal-hunting industry, which had the effect of curbing their food distribution to America and other countries at the time. We were not members of Greenpeace, although I did sympathize with their efforts. "I'm sorry I bought you that drink" our ex-new friend sniffed, and we slunk away with foreboding…

The concert, sponsored by the ISCM[24] in Norway, was scheduled for downtown Bergen on Dec. 4, 1983. While we were setting up for the concert, which also featured piano & tape music of Bart's and mine, we heard that the phones were ringing all day with people trying to have the concert canceled! That night, a minuscule group of seven brave people came, accompanied by several policemen who roamed the theatre. I approached a member of the audience afterwards and asked why more people didn't come to the concert. "Because we do not want to hear beautiful music from creatures we are eating," the fellow replied, and bowed respectfully. Sing on, poor creatures. The world will change. Some day.

5.
"THE INNER UNIVERSE"

So many piano pieces in the world. So little time. And no interest for more. Why bother? When I taught piano at St. Mary's College in the early 1970s, I imagined a need for a soloist to expand the piano timbres and textures, and I would play at thoughts: What would happen if, instead of the piano echo dying away, it came back again in a crescendo? What about all the wonderful untried sounds to come out of the harp of the instrument—that great long naked body of horizontal strings, waiting to be released from punching hammers? What if the pianist struck a note and it suddenly dipped upwards, unpianistically? What if a soloist sat down and suddenly became a whole group of pianists? Truly, this would interest even the most stolid and reticent of performers…

In Austin, with more free time, I began to dream of fanciful ways to use the piano, perhaps coupled with sounds from the piano recorded on tape. I collected gadgets to place on the strings, but not jammed in-between the strings, because I wasn't interested in a John Cage-kind of African percussion sound. What I wanted was a new sound from another universe, one not yet entirely imagined. I began to jot down some ideas.

While I was working on these, I read in the *"Discover"* magazine an article about the electron microscope being able to show a magnification much smaller with vastly more detail and clarity than ordinary lens microscopes. Several photographs of the magnifications were shown, all in black and white (electrons being too small to pick up color), and the photos that attracted me most were by David Scharf. He had chosen as his subjects live flowers and insects, and the resultant images were semi-abstract and very artistic, with much interior movement. I began to feel a connection between these images and my piano & tape ideas. What if just one photo were displayed that inspired the music the pianist was playing? The black and white image complimented the piano keyboard's coloring, also. I decided to get in touch with the artist, David Scharf. I called up his publisher and found out his address, then wrote to him asking for permission to use some of his photos as inspiration for *"The Inner Universe"*. David wrote back, instructing me to buy his book *"Magnifications"* first, and then visit him in Los Angeles when I had a better idea of what I was doing. So now my thoughts had a visual focus, as well.

Many wonderful things happened to us in 1979. We received a National Endowment for the Arts Media Grant of $6,000 to produce thirteen hour-long radio programs of new American music from living composers, specifically members of the American Society of University Composers, later called the Society of Composers, Inc.. Bart and I were alternately appointed to their Executive Committee, as we had already produced thirteen radio programs in the past few years, soliciting music from the members and assembling shows, sending them off to hundreds of radio stations around the country, and recycling them one day a month. But National Public Radio had appeared, and the national programming took over all the ad hoc radio slots, forcing out any unsolicited programs (that again). We turned to the government for grant help, since they were the ones who had created this situation. With the grant money, we were able to place the new programs directly on a satellite feed, and NPR-affiliated radio stations could tune in and pick up the whole series for free, with no more tapes mailed back and forth. This sounded wonderful, but the satellite feed was broadcast only once, the stations having to be very alert to pick it up, and after a year the whole satellite feed idea was shut down, the government claiming it was too expensive. The freedom to send unsolicited tapes to radio stations never returned, either.

After lying low since our performance in the old UT electronic music studio a few weeks after we arrived in Austin in 1976, *The McLean Mix* was revived and had several engagements the spring of 1979. Touring during the winter and spring college breaks, we drove to California and around the midwest with a series of concerts, plus my interviews with composers for our *"Radiofest! New American Music"* series. By this time our concert had seriously improved. We started with Bart's *"Mysteries from the Ancient Nahuatl"* where he played prepared piano ala John Cage, we both played percussion and wooden flutes (recorders), and I narrated from Nahuatl poetry, singing only a simple folk-like tune at the end. Next came my *"Ah-Syn!"* for myself on solo autoharp (a kind of zither) processed through the synthesizer—a very virtuosic dissonant piece full of angst and giant clusters of sound. Then Bart's new electronic piece *"Song of the Nahuatl"*, finishing with my *"Invisible Chariots"*, with all three movements. This varied according to the audience and schedule.

In March my *"Variations & Mozaics on a Theme of Stravinsky"* was nominated for the Pulitzer Prize, and in April I received an NEA Composing Grant of $3400, plus our acceptance at The MacDowell Colony for a May and June residency, and the upcoming Gaudeamus Musiekweek in September…It seemed that every day a new exciting award or invitation came in the mail. I was writing about four pieces at once, in all different media. Part of the reason for all this was the Bicentennial of 1976, which established the National Endowment for the Arts grants for composers as well as other artists, orchestras, arts councils, and a host of other recipients, plus a flood of benevolent money for the arts in general from the federal government.

For a period of about ten years the arts in America flourished, until the Reagan-era, when money flowed into the military machine and away from culture, and the cutbacks began. By 1992 the NEA Composer Grants were canceled, and all the cultural organizations were seriously suffering attrition, including colleges and universities. That brief glorious bubble of government support, typical of Europe but foreign to independent, capitalistic America (spurred on because we were embarrassed to celebrate our 200th anniversary of our independence with so little support for the arts) came just at the best time for us. Bart and I flourished with the support, and even dared to dream that it was possible to compose and perform for a living, and not end up old, sick and starving in a small awful tenement room somewhere.

May 18, 1979 Journal: "'It's like being a child again!' 'It's Paradise—just Paradise!' Britt, the painter from Sweden, said the first comment. Annea Lockwood, the environmentalist composer, said the second. All nearby nodded in agreement. The MacDowell Colony. I sit by my own personal blazing fire in my own personal cabin…This is the Kirby studio, and Lukas Foss came here in 1943…also

1945, 46, 47, 48, 49, and 1950! He must have liked this cabin!" The power of the names on the wooden "tombstone" plaques, signed by the artists just before they left, focused one's mind—David Del Tredici, Aaron Copland, Vladimir Ussachevshy to name a few.

Intimidated by the plaque names and the total silence, except for the loud chorus of birds when the windows were opened to the surrounding dense forest, I circled the studio, unable to work. All my previous ideas for a series of small piano & tape pieces seemed terrible, and I immediately ditched them. After a few days, while listening to some taped piano noodlings I had done, a small fragment appealed to me. It was different from the rest, not overblown piano concerto-style or washy quasi-Impressionistic, but focusing alone on the piano texture.

So I improvised on the lovely old Steinway piano about three minutes of continuous rolling piano sound, motives and melodies and block chords inspired by the fragment, and recorded it on my Revox stereo reel-to-reel tape recorder. Then I listened. Taking two small blue high-bouncing balls called "superballs", very popular toys at the time, I bounced them delicately on the high piano strings, focusing on one, then several notes, rolling them around, etc. This live performance begins the piece, with the tape coming in after about thirty seconds, sneaking in with distant pianos. As the piece becomes more dramatic, I switch to the keyboard, and play a forceful duet with the tape, gradually going back to the superballs at the end without tape, the balls rolling carefully down the strings to the bass.

It took two weeks to compose this six-minute work, later entitled *"Landscape of a Coleus"*, from the photo in David Scharf's book *"Magnifications"*. I was in a white-hot fever the whole time, completely transported to composer/performer heaven. Afterwards I performed an excerpt of this piece on the rosewood Steinway grand piano in the MacDowell Colony library, to test it out before the other artists, who were very enthusiastic. In the summer of 1981 when I returned here, I performed the whole piece in the library. Francis Thorne, head of American Composers Orchestra, was one of the composers listening, and his comment shaped the whole set to come: "You have transported me to another universe. Thank you, thank you, thank you!!"

Colonists, as we were called, are always very kind to each other. Working at the Colony is intensely personal and powerful. A wrong comment to an artist can even result in the artist's suicide, or at the least a wild drunken spree. The ghosts of creative energy echo through the forest and swirl through the studios with insidious force. Major art works are born.

"The Inner Universe" took three years to create, resulting in eight separate works, five of which use recorded tape, and three use only on-string preparations and are interludes. Creating a completely new genre like this demands one's highest concentrated and best work, with many stillborn attempts. By 1981 I had finished four of the pieces, enough to program on a new McLean Mix concert featuring also Bart's new *"Dimensions 8"* for piano and tape.

I have to give proper credit to this idea of "new genre". In 1972 Bart wrote *"Dimensions II"* for piano and tape, stroking the strings of our home Estes baby grand piano[25], which resulted in waves of choral-like atmospheric harmonies, and recording them on our Revox. The live-performed part was solely on the keyboard. I was stunned by the tape sounds. His beautiful piece, premiered by Robert Hamilton and recorded by David Burge on CRI Records, enjoyed a wide audience, as Burge and Robert Hamilton toured with it for several years, along with other pianists. In fact, when we moved to Austin, Texas we lived for two months on the royalties from all the score sales while awaiting Bart's first paycheck from the university.

After our 1981 European Tour we returned to the MacDowell Colony, where with the proper-sized grand piano in the same Kirby studio, I composed the three interludes. That left one piece to compose. During this time I finally met David Scharf. Thin, bearded, with dark hair and eyeglasses, looking more like a composer than a photographer, he welcomed us to his hilltop Los Angeles house, giving me tea with bee pollen to combat the L.A. smog (I immediately had a severe allergy attack), and had me pick out the photographs he had used in the book, plus others, to my promise that a qualified photographer at UT would make the actual slides to David Scharf's specs for quality. A few years later I performed all five piano and tape pieces at the University of California, Dominguez Hills, and David came with his family. He loved the pieces, and said he had always envisioned them sounding this way! Music was his second love after artistic science. That was a golden moment.

In 1982, after struggling endlessly with three more works for the set, I threw them all away, disgusted. After much soul-searching I resurrected an old tape recording I had made years ago of a bass piano string bowed by a disconnected bass bow, the rosined horse hairs threaded underneath the string and rocked back and forth, resulting in a very rich long tone, almost chordal with all its overtones. Initially recorded to use in *"Invisible Chariots",* it proved too dominating, but I still loved the sound and filed the tape for possible future use.

Now listening to the tape, I could imagine muffled, brittle, percussive ostinatos and singing sweeps up the piano strings played by the pianist—what I couldn't hear was any traditional keyboard technique. So this was to be a very electronic-sounding, atmospheric piece. I picked out a photograph showing giant shards of salt crystals, and the piece became *"Salt Canyons"*, one of my favorites of the set.

Eventually I wrote some brief program notes for the five piano and tape works: "These pieces range from four to seven minutes in length, to total twenty-five minutes. *'Landscape of a Coleus'*—very dramatic interplay between piano and piano sounds on tape. There is much use of superballs on the live piano strings at the beginning and ending. The beginning focuses on delicate textures, gradually becoming contrasted with crashing chords between live and taped pianos, which build and fade in an arch form to a quiet ending. *'Sweet Alyssum/Victoria Spring'*: Melted, blurry piano chords create an impressionistic sensual wash on tape. The live piano emerges from tremolos to expanded arpeggios and fades into trills and on-string pizzicatos, as in a dream. *'Mosquitoscape'*: Block chord-by-chord antiphonal, very dramatic play between piano and surrealistically altered piano chords on tape. The mosquito-influenced chromatic melody becomes a strong structural element as the piece progresses. Some light chains are placed on the strings for change of timbre.

'Flower Power': Heavy books placed on the piano harp damp lower strings. The piece begins with solo pianist's fists knocking on the struts in rhythms, as the tape enters surreptitiously. The pianist then plays strong jazz chords on the keys to bongo-like taped rhythms, for a lively, dance-like piece. *'Salt Canyons'*: Reminiscent of Claude Debussy's *"Sunken Cathedral"*, this is a very broad, calm piece to finalize the set of five. The tape has a continuous deep pedal of string overtones, while the live piano plays bursts of ostinatos and runs. Gradually, both piano and taped piano merge into multiple ostinati and runs, until only the pedal remains."

There is a Capstone Records CD of *"The Inner Universe"*[26]. I would like to say that a famous pianist or a young virtuoso fell in love with these pieces, took them on tour and then made this recording, as happened with Bart's *"Dimensions II"*. Alas, it was not to be. Whether it was the daunting prospect of collecting the few preparations, or that feature plus working with the recorded tape which put pianists off, I do not know. By the early 80's the world was rapidly becoming more conservative, and the few adventurous souls who would have tried this faded away.

The *composer* did not fade away, however. The McLean Mix made this set a staple of our concert touring from 1981-86, and I performed it over fifty times in concerts all over the U.S. and in Europe. When I finally despaired of any pianist ever being interested in recording the pieces, I found an old radio recording of my performance at Denison University, Granville Ohio, performed in 1985 on a beautifully in-tune Steinway nine-foot grand. Unfortunately, the tape part was too distant on the radio recording, and the recording itself was running at a slightly too-slow speed, not noticeable until I tried to play the original tape part to blend in with the too-soft radio version…For years this problem flummoxed me, then along came Sound Designer software for our Mac iiCI computer, and in 1994 I placed the radio tape on my very old 1971 Revox reel-to-reel recorder with a changing speed dial, and "tuned" the music to the original tape.

However, the radio tape's speed fluctuated, as the university's tape recorder had been obviously faulty, so I took months dissecting the recording a few seconds at a time and "tuning" it through Sound Designer. Even now there are some strange "woolly" sections that I could not make more precise, and one hears two tapes slightly apart, echoey. Just at the very end of fixing all of the pieces (except *Salt Canyons*", which I had previously recorded on my own piano in my studio), my dear old Revox died, the speed dial completely worn out. Why does it feel as if one's life is followed by a *Giant Eraser?*

Interlude for a Joke (levity needed here!)

In the mountains of Germany is a high castle, and its front cavernous entryway is empty except for an ornate casket. We nervously approach the casket—there should also be a noisy thunderstorm happening—and with great trepidation lift the lid. There sits a ragged old man with long streaming white hair and huge round head erasing all his manuscripts. We see that the name on the casket is "Ludwig Von Beethoven". Oh, my! Is this really the *Master?* He pays no attention to us. Finally, I clear my knotted throat and ask him timidly, "Master, please, what are you doing?" His bloodshot fiery eyes penetrate mine, and he says testily, "What? Can't you see what I'm doing? I'm *decomposing!*"

6.
"IN WILDERNESS IS THE PRESERVATION OF THE WORLD"

When I created my *"Beneath the Horizon"* music for tubas and taped whale ensemble, I was enraptured by the combination of human and animal sounds, and struck by the similar musical organization they both had. I felt drawn closer to our animal-cousins, and thought that everyone hearing these pieces would feel the same way. I was totally shocked by the hostility of the audience. Bart and I loved the wilderness and visited it as often as we could, but this was not at all true of other musicians or audiences listening to our music. So I decided to involve the audience in the performance of this kind of music, hoping that this would dissolve the barrier of ignorance and fear. Also, I had never been happy with the audience sitting "out there" and staring at the action "up here". I knew from rock concerts that the best way for an audience to enjoy the music was to be directly involved, which often meant singing and clapping. Why couldn't this work for new classical music, as well?

In 1980, in a rare moment of enlightenment under President Jimmy Carter, the federal government passed the Alaskan Wilderness Act, which established a vast network of national parks and protected wilderness areas, the largest virgin wilderness saved at one time in America. In tribute, I decided to create a whole evening of music about the wilderness, and named it *"In Wilderness is the Preservation of the World"*, the quote being from Henry David Thoreau's essay *"The Wild"*[27]. I combed the UT music library, and found a collection of songs of Alaskan Eskimos on record, with accompanying booklet[28], which seemed perfect for what I wanted to do.

Along with sketching out some choral ideas for the Eskimos' songs, I explored a store in downtown Austin that sold out-of-print and second-hand phonograph recordings. I was looking for one with wolves howling, specifically *"The Songs and Language of the Wolf"*, with narration on the other side by Robert Redford. I was thrilled to find the only copy they had, and that it was still new! Then I made a trip with my Sony Walkman and RE-20 microphone to the local dog pound, to record a heart (and ear)-rending cacophony of mass dog barks, which happened whenever a new "customer" arrived to look at the rows of kenneled dogs. I also recorded my next-door neighbor's yappy dog, and asked him to buzz his chain saw for me, to his total mystification…Was I going to take him to court?

I was amassing everything I thought I would need for the future creation of the wilderness concert, because, sad to say, our days in Austin were numbered and nothing lay ahead…

Interlude—from Austin, TX to Petersburgh, NY, 1983

—*from Journal 1983:* "Please God—Let me live in a place
where I can go outdoors in the winter and not be sick
from the (Texas cedar) trees—where I can ski again

before I get too old and frail—where I can see and
touch snow again, see the tall evergreens with green
outstretched arms bent with white coats—where summers
are a green joy, and I can be outside and not be
sick-to-death with the heat. *PLEASE GOD*—Let me go home. "

I believe the rot set in Bart's job before he was hired as Director of the University of Texas Electronic Music Center. The department gave lip service to the idea of an electronic music studio, but had never supported it. Bart arrived, demanding money and holding the department to its promise by shutting down the old, makeshift studio until new equipment was ordered and paid for. They gave in, but many toes had been pinched. Bart is a born innovator, and over the next six years he found funding from the building and grounds department of the university, over the heads of the music department, to build one of the most sophisticated university electronic music studios in the country, with the first Fairlight Digital Electronic Music Instrument (synthesizer) delivered to the U.S. from Australia, a new analog Serge Synthesizer, and two rooms filled with processors, harmonizers, pitch shifters, noise reduction DBX units, reel-to-reel tape recorders, etc. This was all housed in two modern windowless rooms of the brand-new music building completed in 1981. Guest composers from abroad began to work in the studios.

Along with this, Bart streamlined his courses, demanding good attendance and hard work, something the students were not used to. He bypassed textbooks to involve the students in real music scores. He taught orchestration by having them write in the styles of the different composers, which required much listening and score study. He held private conferences with each student over their papers, rather than writing brief comments on their work. He tried, through the curriculum committee which he headed, to reform the outdated courses, adding more modern theory and modern textbooks, none of which happened. His composition students began winning national prizes, getting on recordings, and producing whole concerts for the school. The year the students elected Bart "Teacher of the Year" was the year he was fired.

How can this be, you ask? The Outside World looks at the University as the leader in research and innovation. However, Ladies and Gentlemen—*Not in Music.* The American university music department is built on the precarious back of old European classical music. What is revered is what was produced two centuries ago and longer. New innovations are very threatening—these might set off tremors to bring down the whole carefully constructed structure, which houses talented performers, composers, and conductors, as well as courses and ensembles controlled by professors who have made their own little fiefdoms and power structures. Without any firm government support for the arts, the university is the one sanctuary where non-commercial music can continue and be a viable voice in the community. As long as nobody "rocks the boat" too much, new music can be tolerated, but someone bent on changing (supposedly) everything—a wild card like Bart—creates a deep terror in many professorial hearts. And he was touring with *The McLean Mix* more than the performers with touring time built into their contracts (and making up each class privately with the students).

Just before Christmas of 1982 he received The Letter. He would not get tenure, and would have a "terminal year" to find another job. Although we saw it coming, it still struck like a bomb. Artist Freda Korte, one of our dear friends, took all of her dishes out of the dishwasher and hurled them against the wall when she heard about this, with us in the other room ducking. I was so upset I could hardly make eye contact with anyone, and avoided going anywhere near the university. But for Bart it was devastating. He never again wanted to teach at a university, and the system lost one of its best teachers.

All we knew by 1983 was that we wanted to get out of Texas. In March, while driving from the Experimental Intermedia Foundation concert in Manhattan to the Buffalo New Music Festival, where we were featured artists along with John Cage, Morton Feldman, Henry Brant, and Jerry Hiller, we mulled over the next step in our lives. What if we took a "year off" from seeking another university position? What if we just drove up to New York State and rented an old farmhouse in the middle of nowhere and composed, touring for our living? We longed to return to our ancestral home in the Northeast, back to cool climate, the beautiful north woods, and our own culture.

Henry Brant[29] had visited us the summer before, and recommended the area around Bennington College, Vermont, where he taught. We decided on New York State, which at that time was a big supporter of the arts, and the eastern mountainous edge was very close to Bennington as well as Williams College in Massachusetts. Also, the growing Electronic Arts program in RPI (Rensselaer Polytechnic Institute) was nearby in Troy, NY. Although we were refugees from the university, we could not scrape it off of our musical shoes—the alternative would be to move to a major city and find work outside of music, and pay twice as much for living…In July 1983 I had a four-day residency at Bard College in Red Hook, New York, and Bart took the time to drive up to Bennington to look for a location to live. Buying the local *Pennysaver* magazine, he read, "$300 a month. Large colonial historic farmhouse, four bedrooms on 300-acre estate, for rent immediately." In the middle of my class at Bard, Bart popped in suddenly and read this out loud, to the amusement of the students. The rest is history.

"In Wilderness..." *Continued*

After leaving the University of Buffalo New Music Festival, we drove to nearby Niagara Falls, where, sitting in the cafeteria dining room and gazing out the window at the Canadian Falls, I jotted down on a paper napkin my outlines of our concert-to-be. We would split up the composing—each creating two pieces, and mine would involve audience singing.

Half a year later we had moved to Petersburgh, New York in a scene reminiscent of John Steinbeck's *"Grapes of Wrath"*. I had broken my left ankle midnight jogging as we were packing, and we drove the 2,000 miles from Texas to New York in a miserable caravan. Bart drove our little Honda Civic stuffed with our electronic studio, while his mother (having just been diagnosed with angina heart trouble) and I followed behind, alternating the driving, with my leg up to the knee encased in a cast. When the pain got too great, I turned the radio to a hard rock station and blasted the music, almost driving my poor mother-in-law insane. After two major car breakdowns, we had to abandon temporarily our little (dead) Honda at my cousin's in Binghamton, New York, and crowd into the old Ford to drive all night to a furniture-less shabby farmhouse in Petersburgh, arriving about 3 a.m.. We crawled to bed on dirty mattresses lying on the floor, pulled down from the attic, and listened to mice scuttling over the bare floors before we fell dead asleep—the end of the worst four days of my life. This was truly the *End of the World,* with everything, including myself falling apart, and our house back in Austin unsold.

Nothing lasts forever. The furniture arrived, I healed, the car healed, and in November-December *The McLean Mix* toured northern Europe and Scandinavia. In January-February of 1984 we went for the third time to The MacDowell Colony, afterwards driving across country, from New York to California, for our biggest concert tour yet. Mortgage interest rates, hovering at 14%, dropped a point and our house sold. We loved living in a 1790 pioneer farmhouse with ceilings one could touch without stretching, surrounded by a sea of goldenrod and wild animals. And it was great inspiration for this new concert we started creating.

The time from 1983 to 1985 was probably the happiest composing of my life. The concert certainly was strange, beginning with *"Invocation"*, a complex fifteen-minute piece. Beginning with turkey gobbles and gongs on tape and our screeches on clariflutes, the piece proceeds with the voice of an old Eskimo sing-ing *"Shaman's Hunting Song"*[30]...Gradually I lead the audience in singing my composed tune with Eskimo words, *"Let me sing a song of thanks"*, while banging large suspended pots and Bart playing clariflute. Gradually the Eskimo voice is joined by wolves howling, and a singing chorus (live, if possible). The piece ends with us playing clariflutes and taped Australian black swans bleating.

In the attic of our old farmhouse, Bart came upon a lone bicycle wheel resting against a beam. He struck a spoke with his thumbnail. It gave off a beautiful ring-ing clear tone. In subsequent years our landlady's son, Tim Congdon, who lived a half mile down the dirt road in another ancient farmhouse, would ask us askance, "Is that *my* bicycle wheel you are using?" "Who? *Us?*" Tim housed several mala-mute huskies, and we recorded one, who howled on cue while searching the sur-rounding mountains when we played a nearby cassette tape of wolves. Neighbors passing our house began to wonder why we were keeping geese in a second floor bedroom...

For our second piece, Bart wrote the poignant, mystical *"Voices of the Water"*, where he bowed the amplified bicycle wheel with bass viol and violin bows, and I narrated and sang a text from Steward Edward White's book *"The Forest"*[31] about hearing voices in bubbling mountain streams.

The third piece almost ended our concert career forever, and was probably the most dangerous music I have ever written! During our 1984 nationwide tour, we stopped off at Bowling Green, Ohio to negotiate a commission for their 6th Annual New Music Festival (1985). We were to be the guest ensemble, with someone else as the commissioned composer, but we convinced the festival com-mittee to give us a commission to premiere our new wilderness music. This was dicey, but they agreed to add it to the performer fee. These wonderful innocent people had no idea what we were up to, and took us on faith.

That summer I finished *"O Beautiful Suburbia!"*, a black humor piece where I and the audience and chorus sweetly sing *"America the Beautiful"* to an increasing din of bug zappers (the first sound heard on tape), chainsaws, fire sirens, and a crescendo of dog barks, becoming increasingly hysterical. Just then a group of the ugliest, noisiest, crass television commercials I could find come blaringly in, yell-ing, "Lemony Ajax! Squeaky clean!", "Dynamo Action Plus!", "Pets add so much to our lives, and Purina wants to add as much to theirs", "Good time! Great Taste!" etc., etc.. Just at the point when the audience has been completely drowned out by our "civilization", all the noise stops and we are in the wilderness forest with Thoreau. A plaintive chorus of wolves sings in harmony, and inspiring narration by writer Ewan Clarkson[32] ends the piece.

The concert ends with Bart's *"Passages of the Night"*. Bart as Ancient Forest Voice quietly sits alone on stage lit only by one standing lamp and recites several excerpts about the beauty of the wilderness night, from great poets and writers, while altering his voice through our analog harmonizer to that of an old, wise sage. His composed tape music plays underneath, with drones and night bird calls.

The summer of 1985 was frantic, as I was completing several works, we were rehearsing our *"Wilderness"* concert in the above-ground basement room with wood floor—a large empty space, and I was preparing to fly to Hawaii for a guest professorship at the University of Hawaii for the fall semester. Just as I left for Hawaii, I was awarded a third NEA Composing Grant—for $9500, and I flew away, my head already in the clouds.

Never having taught full-time at any college, and never any of the subjects assigned to me this time, I spent six days a week preparing my courses, plus teaching, and practicing two completely different concerts—one for an early September recital at the University of Hawaii of my works, and the other our *"Wilderness"* premiere for Ohio in November.

My voice was giving me a lot of trouble, and, indeed, I had sung very little for fifteen years, but the November concert demanded my singing. Trained as an alto in early youth, I had only the weakest of upper ranges unless I forced the tone. Although I had studied two years of voice (and violin) at Indiana University, and voice was my major instrument, no teacher had been able to solve my problem. But on the faculty at the U. of Hawaii, in the Musicology department, was a Delivering Angel: Leslie Wright, a beautiful young associate professor who befriended me and gave me *one* lesson in singing. In five minutes she released my voice from its prison, and I was able to sing up to a high G, and after a few years up to a high C, where my voice has been for the last several years. Here is what she said: "Think of your voice as sitting in an elevator. As you go higher, the string pulling up the elevator gets lighter and lighter as your voice ascends in your head. At the top, it is as light as a bird, and should float out through your skull like the bell-tower of a cathedral." Ever since, when I vocalize I move my hand as the "elevator" and focus my voice to come up in my head. It works!

On November 5 I flew to Toledo, Ohio on a torturous 20-hour flight from Honolulu that had me sitting in the Denver airport for hours. Bart drove me to Bowling Green, and for the next few days we rehearsed non-stop for our premiere. Bart, having had too much time alone to think, had decided that *"O Beautiful Suburbia!"* was too tame, and wouldn't get the sardonic point across(!), so he decided to "doctor" the piece in my absence. He arranged for a few "additions" during the concert...

Bowling Green University's 6th Annual Festival of New Music went familiarly well, everyone being content, the audience full of students and composers from the Midwest. Then we had our premiere.

The concert started out quite nicely. A freshman chorus had been gathered, conducted by composer and faculty member Marilyn Shrude, and they gave a hearty folk-like rendition of the music in *"Invocation"*. The audience sang hesitantly, but at least audibly with me, and everyone seemed to accept the wolf howling as well. *"Voices of the Water"* went well. Then, for some perverted reason, we scheduled *"Beneath the Horizon"*—the totally recorded quartet version, plus multiple slide projections on a far-away screen in back of the stage. The blue-green of the whale slides were very dark and murky from the position of the audience. There was a glitch, and I had to start everything over at one point. The audience's tolerance was fraying...

Then came *"O Beautiful Suburbia!"*. Behind the curtain Bart had amassed a huge pile of pots, pans, metal construction materials, boxes, and anything else he could find or borrow, held behind a rope that ended by his chair on stage. I vaguely knew he had done this, but hadn't paid much attention, being very busy in rehearsals with the chorus and ourselves. The audience, chorus, and I started singing. The taped dog and chainsaw cacophony built, and just at the loudest spot, the curtain was dramatically thrust aside, and three motorcyclists roared onto stage, wheeling around as fast as they could, revving their engines (and sending clouds of fumes into the audience), and as they roared offstage, Bart pulled the rope, and down came a deafening blast of the pile of metal onto the stage. The audience literally jumped out of their seats. Burton Beerman, the director of the festival (and our good friend who had performed with us as *The Mix* a decade earlier), said afterwards, "It scared me to death!" This was pure Vaudeville, and sealed our doom for performing in Ohio for about ten years afterwards...

At this point the audience was supposed to stop singing, as the music settled down to soft wind blowing and narration by Thoreau, but composer Syd Hodkinson was so incensed with rage at this performance by this time that he continued singing *"America the Beautiful"* in a very loud voice, then when I begged the audience to stop, he stormed out of the hall, slamming the door as loud as he could. This did nothing for the contemplative mood or Thoreau, and the piece ended in devastation.

Bart's *"Passages of the Night"* ended the concert, but everyone was so shell-shocked that they hardly heard. Afterwards, the composers avoided us. At the party-reception they turned their backs…I got up the courage to ask one of them, a fellow colleague, what he thought, and he said (having had the comfort of a few drinks by then), "Priscilla, I like you. But (sigh), I *hate* your music!!"

My return trip to Honolulu was very depressed. I took to drinking martinis, and I blearily remember sitting next to a snake charmer who cheered me with pictures of herself scantily clad, wrapped in snakes. Due to fog and interminable delays, the flights took twenty-two hours, ten-and-a-half hours late! I canceled my classes, and sank into a deep funk, rethinking the whole concert. I don't know why premieres are so popular. The premiere is surely the worst performance ever of the new music, unless it is performed by a special group for just that one event. Almost always, major revisions are made, and the next performance is light-years better. Such is the perversity of the human soul that experiencing something for the first time is more important than the quality of the experience.

In the summer of 1985 I wrote a five-minute introductory piece to the concert, because it needed something more (and not *"Beneath the Horizon"*). I decided to feature the queen of the forest, the lowly mosquito, and captured one in a mayonnaise jar with the large RE-20 microphone sticking through the lid. The jar amplified the mosquito sound, and in trying to escape, the mosquito flew all around the microphone, resulting in a very wonderful recording. I used two mosquitoes and some honeybees I had recorded earlier (the honeybees reveling in a pile of old bird seed under our backyard feeder on a warm May morning). I sang in duet with myself on tape, a series of diatribes against insects and the mosquito, from Stewart Edward White"s book *"The Forest"*, in a squeaky wavering mosquito-like voice. All this was accompanied by Bart's striking the bicycle wheel spokes with soft percussion mallets, and bowing them. The piece was called *"On Wings of Song"* (similar in name only to Felix Mendelssohn's version), and became the most popular number on the concert.

We performed *"In Wilderness is the Preservation of the World"* for five years. In that period the world changed. People became much more aware of wilderness and the idea of preserving it. The audiences changed as well, from hesitant singers and non-singers, to the last performance we gave at Ohio University in 1990, with the audience singing so strongly that they could have been a chorus themselves! And everyone loved the music. I loved being Shaman on stage, banging my pots and conducting the audience and singing. It was pure theater, and we became dramatic performance artists as well as musicians.

7.
"A Magic Dwells"

"The breath of life moves through a deathless valley
of mysterious motherhood
Which conceives and bears the universal seed.
The seeming of a world never to end.
Breath for men to draw from as they will:
And the more they take of it, the more remains."

Lao Tsu, from The Tao te Ching, 604 BC

For many years I was intrigued by the sound of orchestra mingled with stereo tape music, which I heard in rare opportunities at composer conventions and student orchestra concerts. I was also inspired by the 1965 recording of *"Ricordia cosa ti hanno fatto in Auschwitz"* by Luigi Nono, a bleak but haunting stereo tape piece which blended special sounds and voices to recorded brass and percussion, all blurred electronically to chilling effect.

In Bart's new University of Texas Electronic Music Center, housed in two rooms in the just-completed multi-story music building in 1982, there was a device called the Bode Vocoder. It had the special ability to take a regular recorded sound, such as a flute, and mix it with another sound, such as someone singing words. One recorded sound would "follow" the shape of the other, so, for instance, the flute could sound like a flute singing words. Of course, the television industry had already potentially ruined this effect by using it in the crassest commercial way, but it still intrigued me.

One day in my Austin home, I stopped, looked out of the window and wondered, "What if the orchestra were performing and suddenly the chords the instruments were playing turned into voices singing words one could clearly understand?" This effect might be very stunning, and I immediately began writing out chords in various instrumental combinations that could be recorded for the Vocoder.

I was pushed along with this effort, because in late 1981 I had received another NEA Composer Grant to write a piece for orchestra and tape, and had proposed the Houston Symphony as a possibly interested orchestra (which never came to pass). If the orchestra "spoke" words, the words should be very important and meaningful. Only short phrases would do, or the effect would be too long and become obvious.

I had started a collection of creation myths, which had fascinated me for a long time, and from these began picking out words and phrases that would be revelatory. "The breath of life" is a phrase that has always fascinated me, and I found several others, from Lao Tsu (*The Tau*) to the Ankh (Egyptian), to American Wintu Indian myth, to the Bible.[33]

Bart set up a recording session with the University of Texas Symphony Orchestra for May 5,1982, its last meeting, and I recorded various sections of the orchestra playing the chords, plus the whole ensemble. Each chord-group lasted from seven to twenty or thirty seconds, fading in and out. I also recorded some sketches I might use for the live orchestra, as well.

During the summer session our English composer friend Trevor Wishart visited us and worked in the UT Electronic Music Center. He resided with us for a few days before moving to a dorm room at the university, and between uproarious times of laughing and reminiscing on Europe, we three composers got together and sang trios, duets and solos using the same orchestral chords, with the creation phrases. Trevor's voice alone eventually ended the piece with: "It was not born; it sees not and is not seen"[34], which he whispered in his thick Yorkshire accent, giving the exotic touch I wanted.

I borrowed the unused Vocoder from the university, and combined the two recording sessions, orchestra and voices. But this was not enough. I needed a low pedal tone.

Writing an orchestral piece has always been terribly hard for me, and after spending months filling up wastebaskets with sketches, I literally gave up. I couldn't do it. It was impossible! However, late one night when half-dozing on the couch I heard it: the orchestral voices rising out of a pedal of bowed bass piano strings...Oh! *"Salt Canyons"* that I had just completed...and the orchestra could be the little ostinati that race around the keyboard, like frenetic humans, while the cosmic Voices of Creation would appear and disappear, like messages only very psychically attuned people can hear, and the Pedal of Eternity plays on forever. Sort-of *"The Unanswered Question"* answered...[35]

Expanding *"Salt Canyons"* into an orchestral version, and extending the space between the frantic sections to add the ethereal voice-chords was surprisingly easy. It is as if the piece was just waiting for this treatment.

Bart's last year at the university was extremely busy, but not with schoolwork. He had become "persona non grata", and was given the minimum amount of course work, his teaching assistant was taken away, and there was now a co-director to the Electronic Music Center, to make sure that Bart didn't abscond with any of the goods...He took it as a golden opportunity to hole up and compose extensively, resulting in seven compositions that year, all in different media. Piano and tape, symphonic winds, chamber ensemble, electronic, choral. It seemed that at every concert there was a new premiere by Barton McLean! I was frantically busy, copying several of my works, practicing the piano & tape pieces for tours every few months, and working on *"A Magic Dwells"*. By the time we moved to New York State, I had a penciled version, mostly orchestrated, of the whole one-movement, fifteen-minute piece.

The one sticky element was how to conduct a score that switched between meters and stopwatch seconds, between tightly written down and more improvisatory notations. I took the piece to Louis Calabro, the conductor of a remarkable amateur orchestra, the Sage City Symphony of Bennington, Vermont, who in the year 1985 had commissioned music from more composers than any other U.S. orchestra, amateur or professional. Lou and I worked out a system of hand gestures for the conductor, to change from meter to seconds, and freer timings. In January Bart and I were back at The MacDowell Colony for the third time, and I finished the orchestration and copying of the whole score, working every day without stopping. The day after our residency was up in early February, we were driving to Ohio for our first performance of our tour. So for a few months I didn't have to face the next burning question: Who in God's name will play this piece?

In the orchestral world, the doors open and close rapidly. After sending the piece to conductors I had met—directors of the Albany Symphony, Houston, San Antonio, Louisville, Indianapolis—I waited in vain for any reaction. Totally engrossed in our new wilderness concert, I shelved the orchestral piece until I could see any hope of a performance. In 1986 one contest advertised in the American Music Center Newsletter stood out that attracted my attention: The Sigvald Thompson National Orchestral Composition Competition of the Fargo-Moorhead Symphony, held every two years. The winner would receive a $2,000 award check and a premiere of the chosen work, which could be for orchestra or *orchestra & tape*. The magic words! I sent in my piece.

Such is the perverse nature of the composer that if (s)he is stranded on a desert island with one piece of paper, surrounded by oceans of indifference in the medium (s)he wants to work in, the hapless artist will sit down and begin *another* unwanted piece in the same medium. So, due to the prodding of another NEA Composer Grant, in February 1987 I was in the middle of composing *"Voices of the Wild"* for—get this—*electronic music soloist* and orchestra (this time with the guarantee of the premiere from Peter Kermani, the president of the Albany Symphony), when I received news that I had won the Fargo-Moorhead contest for a premiere in January of 1988! From zero chances of any orchestral interest, to two premieres in a row coming up—I found it hard to breathe…

Over the months of touring and orchestral writing, being a guest at the Leighton Artists Colony and the Banff (Alberta) Arts Centre in the summer of 1987, exploring with Bart the Canadian Rockies for weeks afterwards, and involved with premieres of other pieces, I didn't have the chance to think about what was coming up. Only when I was in the midst of a blizzard out of Sioux Falls, South Dakota on January 19, bound for the wilds of North Dakota in a tiny commuter plane bumping around in the wind (with only ten other passengers), did I actually focus on the situation: Fargo, ND, often listed as the coldest place in the U.S., in January…

They closed down the Moorhead, Minnesota (sister city to Fargo) airport just after my plane arrived at midnight. I reeled airsick off the plane, and no one came to greet me and transport me to my guest residence. After an hour of waiting in the airport packed with stranded travelers, I called the orchestra manager's home phone. *"What?"* he answered, sleepily. "All flights were canceled, and the airport shut down! How did you get here?" That was my first indication that this was not going to be a flawless adventure…

Eventually I was brought to the house of Ed and Jane Stern, patrons of the orchestra who lived in a tall brown very modern house in a neighborhood of palatial homes. The inside of the house was colossal—a *true* cathedral ceiling with a balcony running around the entire second floor, where my bedroom was in the back. The house was filled with art works, and a two-story picture window looked onto a golf course with picturesque river and trees in the distance, which I saw the next day. I felt like a celebrity, especially when Ed loaned me his new Buick, with automatic steering, for my personal use. Isn't this the way *every* orchestral composer should be treated?

The next few days were difficult, but very satisfying. I struggled with the large car and all its automatic features, slipping on the icy roads (a permanent condition the whole winter up here), and almost missed the first rehearsal-with-composer-present by getting totally lost. There were three rehearsals that week, and I had the pleasure of hearing the orchestra go from playing extremely timidly, and the tape part barely audible (and the English horn part written wrong, which I corrected in the wee hours of the next morning), to, by dress rehearsal, a forceful sound of excellent players, with the tape at equal volume level to the orchestra.

What was amazing was the superior level of musicianship of this group, whose young players were earning $3.45 an hour! And they had never even heard music of the famous European orchestral composers who had influenced me: Gyorgi Ligeti, Luciano Berio, Krzysztof Penderecki—the new music contest was generally all the new music they played for the year—so I had to teach them how to listen and understand the style in *"A Magic Dwells"*. Only the winner of a contest would have the privilege of doing this with a professional orchestra, the conductor looking on benevolently. Robert Hanson, the conductor (and also composer) had just about memorized the score. It was a joy working with him, our heads bent over the often-confusing manuscript, which he helped to straighten out.

During that week the manager, Mark Madson, had a celebratory dinner at his house for the directors and winning composer. Not only did I gather much inside information about the contest, other composers chosen, the world of the artist in North Dakota, but I was able to experience the true Scandinavian midwestern people. Both manager and conductor were of Norwegian heritage, as were most of the other people there. Modest, self-effacing, but very focused and artistic, and conservative. I felt myself reining in my wilder gestures and comments…

I learned that Lukas Foss had been one of the two final judges, and that he had loved my piece so much he voted mine the highest score and gave zeros to the others! I was so flattered that, years later, when Mr. Foss was a guest composer of The Albany Symphony, I mentioned the contest and his judging. "Oh, yes, a very intriguing piece. I didn't understand it at all! That's why I chose it." Oh. Do you think the Brooklyn Philharmonic would play it sometime (he was the conductor at the time)? "No, no. It's too far out for such a public orchestra that needs so much financial support. This is where contests like Fargo-Moorhead are most useful, in allowing this music to be heard." Oh. But I can only win this contest once (and they all have to be premieres)…

The first inklings of disaster came on Saturday, when a brutal snowstorm raged all day. To my utter surprise, the dress rehearsal went as planned. This was extremely fortunate, because the orchestra played in a large gymnasium, surrounded by a portable acoustic shell, and the tape part was lost in the extended echoes of the space. It took a long time to "tune" and balance the tape sounds to account for this, and achieve a decent balance with the orchestra, who had to play much harder to overcome the reverberant basketball space. Dvorak, Wagner, and Handel were run through quickly, and all the time was devoted to McLean—again, a major problem of scheduling any new music and especially *this* style of music. After the rehearsal, many orchestral performers, Mark Madson, and I went to the best Chinese restaurant I have ever experienced, and had a celebratory feast. It was wonderful, and I was lulled into complete happiness and warm feeling toward Fargo, Moorhead, and orchestras everywhere...

Sunday, January 24. From my 1988 Journal: "*Raging Blizzard* wiped out my premiere...my baby...my life...! I sat "crying" over an imported bottle of Rhine wine with my philanthropic hosts by their twenty two-foot-high fireplace, while 50 mph winds blew over the golf course evergreens. (felt like crying, but did "stiff upper lip" routine—)" My non-refundable flight was scheduled to leave the next day. It was canceled due to snow, but rescheduled promptly the next day. The premiere took place on January 31, the composer long gone, never to hear this first performance except on the tape recording sent later. I hear the audience clapped politely. I feel this is the best orchestral work I have ever written, and like Charles Ives, I look to the future for an angel to float by with a willing orchestra...

> "A magic dwells at each beginning, and
> protecting us it tells us how to live."
> —Hermann Hesse: excerpt from *"Magister Ludi"*

8.
"THE DANCE OF SHIVA"

> "The full moon
> The flying bird
>   The peaks of high mountains
>   The lotus leaf wet with rain
>   The roaming bee, the woodland mire—
>   All these things are beautiful."
>   from Buddhist prayer book

Towards summer 1988 Bart and I planned to do something of which I had dreamt for many years. We signed up with some other members of the Adirondack Mountain Club for a trek through the Himalayan Mountains to the base of Mt. Everest. This was to be a very adventurous trip—flying to India, then Katmandu, Nepal, and finally to Lukla, where the group would hike with sherpas a seventeen-day round-trip to the Mt. Everest base camp and back. The guidelines suggested the qualifying test for being in appropriate physical condition for this arduous journey was to climb to the top of Mt. Washington in New Hampshire, the highest mountain in the Northeast, and then climb it again the next day. I had climbed to its summit five times since the age of twenty, but never two days in a row!

Music composing and touring involves a great deal of sitting. To be in the condition needed was a tall order for us, so we decided to begin by hiking one of the peaks in the Adirondacks every week, starting in early June. On the third week of climbing, we became so ambitious as to climb three mountains in one day, a nefarious group of no-peek peaks (no views from the tops) of Bear Den, Dial, and Nippletop, a fruitless fourteen-mile hike, which had us down at nine o'clock at night. The next day I couldn't walk—my ex-broken left ankle had an overuse injury.

We were still hopeful we could be in shape by September, when the trek was planned. After a month of resting the ankle, I felt I was ready to climb again. We drove to Mt. Katahdin in Maine, which I consider the hardest mountain in the Northeast. On a very hot day we climbed to the top and down, and the next day climbed a peak nearby. No pain. I was ready to go!

In August we began to acquire the multitude of immunization shots necessary to travel to these places in Asia. Because of my ankle problems, we were late in beginning the shots, and doubled up on a few, to finish in time. Meanwhile, in my family, my parents were having a hard time. Also in August, my father was put in the hospital for collapsing in exhaustion caring for my mother, who suffered from both metastatic breast cancer and Alzheimer's disease. I went to Fitchburg regularly to help out, and was quite distraught about both of them, Dad also having had several strokes by that time. One day I noticed a strange spot on my face...

The last series of immunization shots were cholera-typhus and meningitis, administered together to save money, and we shared the meningitis serum with several other people, reducing the cost (from 1983 through 2003 we had no health insurance). As we left the hospital, I felt dizzy. "My face feels funny," I said. So during the next two days came on a virulent attack of facial shingles (herpes zoster), which had been waiting in the wings for my immune system to be compromised. Instead of hiking triumphantly to Mt. Everest, I lay for a month unmoving on the couch in excruciating pain. Such are the turns and twists of life...

Out of this came a vital interest in the Far East. I had bought several books to learn about Nepal, Hinduism, and the people, and found myself fascinated by the god/goddess Shiva, Lord of the Beasts, Lord of the Dance (of life and death), and god of destruction and creation. Shiva whirls around in his/her mad dance, holding in four arms the drum(beat) of life, fire, the other two arms in symbolic gestures, and trampling on the beast representing the illusions of the world.

Late in 1989 I began my first large electronic work since *"Invisible Chariots"* twelve years before. This would be my first piece in the new medium of the computer, although it was a "half-breed", as I still recorded on the old reel-to-reel tape recorders and used them in my mix-downs. I heard the dancing whirl through glissandi on my autoharp, sampled and played back at several pitch levels all at the same time. I elongated a recorded Buddhist chant to act as a pedal tone, and spoke in many voices the Buddhist words already quoted.

On January 1990, Mom died, having valiantly struggled against her diseases for fifteen years. Near the end, she was in a nursing home, and to keep her from wandering away, she was tied to a chair. I was so shattered by this experience, seeing my beloved mother suffering like this, that I wrote the following poem shortly after her death:

Elegy

As you sat slumped and tied to your chair,
Mom,
I asked: if you could be granted any wish
What would be your happiest thought.
Your blurred aged eyes and mind
Carefully focused on mine and said,
"To fly."

As we sadly gather around your coffin,
Mom,
Amid the droning of unwanted organ hymns
Amid forced ungay flower clusters and faces
My eyes behold your discarded shell.
My heart hears laughter, and the beating of
Wings.

After I had begun *"The Dance of Shiva"*, with its eastern philosophy of the dancing cyclical whirl of life and death, I realized that my mother had been in the back of my mind the whole time. I felt a deep need to include the faith of our own Christian culture in this piece that I planned to dedicate to the memory of my mother. Back in 1985 when teaching a course on the history of women in music, I was given a recording of the music of Hildegarde von Bingen. My first connection with this very famous abbess of the Twelfth Century had been when I had inadvertently wandered into a castle dedicated to her and housing her works in a museum on the top floor in Bingen, Germany in 1979, after the Gaudeamus Festival had ended, and I had explored Germany and England on my own.

I loved Hildegarde's music, and discovered to my exultation that her liturgical songs fit beautifully with the recorded Buddhist chants, even to being in the same key with no alteration! The effect of the two together gave an overwhelming feeling of the yearning in a human soul, and the mood of deep prayer. In *"The Dance of Shiva"*, towards the middle of the sixteen-minute piece, I created a long fiery section of the "destruction of the world" played with drums, violins (all performed by myself) attacked with bouncing steak knives, violins bowed in a gritty frenzy, along with other wild sounds. This all dies down to a chorus of my sampled voice speaking bits of nonsense backwards in painful screech-sob tone, dwindling, finally, to silence. The void of the ineffable. Then, through a gentle haze of sitars and gliding (altered) autoharp pitches, the clear tones of Hildegarde's music float forth, as solo and then duet using two different songs, eventually mingling with the Buddhist chant, which continues and ends the piece as it began, completing the cycle of life.

At this point in the career of *The McLean Mix*, visuals were expected for each piece on the concert, unless it was live-performed. In the summer of 1990 this meant multiple slide projections, and I raided the Petersburgh library's collection of National Geographic magazines, which dated back to 1969. Along with some other books, I laid the magazines on the back porch out of direct sun, but lit with natural light. There I photographed erupting volcanoes, masses of people in India, flocks of birds—many pictures to symbolize the abundance of life before the destructive cycle, then pictures of enormous volcanic eruptions leading to a barren volcanic charred "dead" landscape in Hawaii, and a lone flower of hope emerging between two rocks (the columbine flower in the Colorado Rockies), from my own collection.

The Williams College Art Museum had allowed me to copy their extensive slide collection of Shiva dancing in different sculptures, and a sculpture of the Virgin Mary and child to complete my set. Filling two carousels with my created slides, I programmed our fade-and-dissolve unit to mix the slides at different speeds with each other, creating abstract mixtures and multiple "double-expo-sure" images, in time to the music. This made a very powerful multi-media show.

Almost immediately afterward, we flew to Melbourne, Australia for a nine-week tour of Australia, New Zealand, and Hawaii, in August of 1990. After the numbingly long flight of two days (more or less) and the sixteen-hour time differ-ence, we reported to La Trobe University in Bundoora, twelve miles from Mel-bourne, in a zombie-like state, to hear from the music department secretary that Dad had collapsed in his hallway in Fitchburg from a small stroke and had lain there two days before the landlady heard his cries and moans. Right then he was in the hospital, but soon would be transferred to the same nursing home that Mom had recently died in. The end of life is hard, very hard. My brother Conrad was looking after him.

Along with the pain and exhaustion was the complete delight of being in Aus-tralia for a month! We are always very careful to program free time into our schedules, to become familiar with the places we are performing. Otherwise, it is just a "This is Tuesday, are we in Brussels or Melbourne?" experience, which can-not enrich the life of an artist much, and just makes for world-weary dreariness after awhile.

While in residence at La Trobe, we were invited guests of Jim Sosnin, the tech director and his girlfriend Cindy, who with her two teenaged children lived in a nearby affluent suburb, in a huge square house with garden and outbuildings. The area resembled San Diego's landscape, and again I had one of those weird jolts. "Gee, did they import all these eucalyptus trees from California?" Nooooo, again. The more we saw of Australia, the more we learned that eucalyptus trees there are like pines here—they are everywhere, as are black swans.

Jim generously took the next day off and drove us to the Dandelong Range of mountains, past Healesville north of Melbourne, for a famous Australian "bush-walk". Although it was winter there and pouring rain and chilly, we were extremely eager to see the wilderness in this large nature park. We were amazed at the birds, ones completely new to us and to anyone in the northern hemi-sphere—red rosellas with blue wings (small parrots), green parrots, galahs–which are pigeon-like, large pink and gray birds with whistle-squeak voices, kookabur-ras–very large white and gray birds with topknot and large ominous beak (carniv-orous), having the most incredible squawks and calls, black and white magpies which sounded like their songs were going through electronic processing, etc.

As we slogged down the muddy trail after eight miles or so, I saw a strange sight—something running across the road in front of me with long skinny legs that resemble a road runner but feet moving like bicycle wheels, and the head and body of an ancient pterodactyl! "What is *that?*" I barked. It was also emitting very strange sounds. Jim exclaimed in amazement, "Oh my God—it's a lyrebird!" We had been in Australia one day and I had just seen a very rare bird hardly ever seen in the wild. I knew this was going to be an excellent tour.

La Trobe University is a beautiful campus, large and sprawling, with sandstone buildings amid vast nature areas, ponds and streams. On August 22 to a roundtable of invited guests at the music department, I gave a lecture on women composers, playing excerpts of music by Lois Vierck, Amina Claudine Myers, Joan LaBarbara, and Pauline Oliveros. From my journal: "Afterwards, the questions were surprisingly hostile. 'Why did you pick an uninteresting topic like women composers?' (this from a woman!), "Why did you avoid the *real* issue of the subjugation of women by men just to play music and talk about general problems?'. A group of these women, Jeff Pressing who headed the music department, Bart, and I went for tea to the cafeteria and continued the discussion. The hostility was only skin-deep, and the pervading Australian friendliness and desire to please rose again quickly."

The next day we not only set up our "Rainforest" installation, using many found and made instruments from their improvisation lab plus our own synthesizers and microphones, and had people wandering in to perform for several hours, but we met a very fascinating individual–Warren Burt.

From my journal: "Warren is a human encyclopedia, talk show host, song and dance man all rolled into one! Living here for fifteen years, he originally is from Waterford, New York (near us). He is six feet tall, large, black bearded, wears a rippled patterned black and green cardigan, heavy wool sweater and jeans (heavy wool sweaters and jeans seem to be a national code of dress here), and walks hunched over, like a philosophy professor." But the most amazing feature of Warren Burt was not in the journal—he lives off of composing avant-garde music. He resides in Australia, because the arts there are much more supported by the government, and he can survive, unlike in the States…Warren also does some teaching, as we all do at times. He interviewed us for the ABC (Australian) Radio Network after the installation.

The concert on Friday, August 24 featured the World Premieres of *"The Dance of Shiva"* and Bart's *"Earth Music"*. My voice was beginning to fuzz up, just as it had at home with the sea of goldenrod around our house. But there was no goldenrod here, only those beautiful yellow-flowering trees all over campus called wattle trees…(oh—*they are related?*)…One can run—to the other side of the world yet—but not hide.

I would like to report that these premieres went flawlessly, the audience was enchanted, and there were no gremlins lurking and smiling maliciously. I would *like* to report that. Perhaps in the next life…

After struggling all day with the foreign slide projectors and different electric current influencing the speed of the fade and dissolve unit, I had everything timed correctly for the concert, which began satisfactorily. After a few minor glitches in *"Earth Music"* (glacial rocks with no reverberation/delay, since it wasn't plugged in, etc.), we came to the final piece, *"The Dance of Shiva"*. I took my place behind a high glass wall in the projection booth in back of the recital hall.

From my Journal: "Two-thirds of the way through *"The Dance of Shiva"* at the big climax, the last continuous slide, a raging volcano, fades and goes dark just as the music fades and pauses, as planned. Unwarned by me beforehand, the audience clapped. Then Bart turned on the lights! A mad woman (myself) in the lighting booth working the projector waved and pointed—finally he got the hint and darkened the room so the piece could continue. Lordy—Lordy—what a disaster!" Music that dies down to a silence, and then builds again is a perilous situation in a concert…

I will relate one more adventure in Melbourne, which occurred the day after our concert. Warren Burt showed us around the "Greenwich Village" of Melbourne, St. Kilda, where all the artists live and hang out. After stopping at his small neat apartment (dominated by electronic equipment), we all took a cab to a loft space just outside of town. Here occurred the strangest "avant-garde" improvisation event I ever had privilege to see.

About thirty people in small groups performed short improvisations, often having nothing to do with music. Warren Burt and Jane Refshauge, a modern dancer, each had accordions, hers little and his large. They rolled over each other on the floor, and as they rolled their accordions, accidental sounds or cluster chords would emerge. Another "skit" involved another American man pulling little objects out of Warren's duffel bag, playing them or sticking them in the audience's ears. At one point, Warren inflated an umbrella and danced around the room singing *"Chim chiminee"* (from *"Mary Poppins"*).

Journal entry: "One very funny trio of Australians did a Monty Pythonesque skit. One man scrabbled across the floor like a dog while the woman kept repositioning him when he would run into a wall. At the end a second woman, also on all fours, was led to be head-to-head with the man while they kept trying to advance against each other. The woman said, "It's hard to advance when you're against someone else's head!" The skit ended when the first woman came out like a beggar, the man offered her a "small serious thing", and she refused, saying, "Sorry—I've got one of those already!"

As part of a 1 1/2 hour profile on *The McLean Mix*, we performed *"Earth Music"* and *"Wilderness"* live over the ABC Radio Network the next day, and actually were paid for it, just as in Europe. Australia is a much more sparsely populated country than the U.S. Yet their support for the arts makes us embarrassed to be called Americans...

"The Dance of Shiva" remained in our repertoire for several successful years. Now it sits quietly in my CD case, waiting for me to transcribe the slide show to video, and make this multimedia work performable again.[36]

9.
"RAINFOREST IMAGES"
Our First Collaboration

"Olelbis, the Creator, built a great and awesome sweathouse,
its middle support being a huge young white oak,
with various kinds of oak trees being side supports,
various flowering plants serving as binding and as sides..."
—Creation myth of the Wintu tribe, northwest America

In December of 1988 we embarked on a four-day vacation to Puerto Rico, as a "celebration" of my recent recovery from the facial shingles. While there, we hiked for a day in the El Yunque National Forest, our first experience of any tropical rainforest outside of Hawaii. That night, as we headed back to our car, a chorus of coquis–tiny frogs–started a symphony of squeaks and chirps, until the whole forest was ringing with them, in various pitch levels. We stood in the middle of the road and rotated our bodies, transfixed with all the combinations and becoming more and more excited about the musical possibilities...Bart was especially inspired.

Back home, he began to realize an idea he had had for several years—to create a musical setting that people could walk through and interact with, improvising and "jamming" in the style offered, and have a deep, personal artistic experience. The rainforest, so rich in sounds, gave him the impetus to create a portable installation with which we could tour, that would be a musical experience, but would involve bird and animal sounds of the rainforest, creating an atmosphere similar to the one we had heard in Puerto Rico.

First he composed a tape using a crowbar jammed under the bass strings of the piano harp and gently rocked for a wave of ethereal harmonies (please note that he used only *our* piano!). He added a synthesized low pedal, and recorded birds. The tape alone could be heard as "new age music", very soothing and contemplative.

Later I joined Bart in creating discs on our Prophet 2000 Sampling Synthesizer featuring a variety of sounds, some by musical instruments, some of birds, frogs, animals—anything that would fit and be flexible enough to play around with on the keyboards. Bart created electronic sounds on our WaveStation (digital synthesizer) to add to these, and I gathered, after much trial and error in our garage, a group of found objects one could bow, scrape, and strike (nothing blown, because of spreading germs) into a microphone. So was born our *"Rainforest"* installation. It took a year of creating.

"Rainforest" has been a tremendously successful musical venture. We have literally financed our lives since 1989 on its performances, all over the world and even into the deepest rainforest of all–Borneo. It had its birth at the University of Wyoming music library in April 1989, with the president of the university and his guests participating, to his amazement and our delight.

The music held people's attention, but it wasn't enough. We needed fade-and-dissolve slides of the rainforest as a focus for the participants, and to add the dimension of art. This meant enough slides to run continuously for eight hours, or a collection recycling each hour or so, because an installation like this is not a concert. It is a special mixture of music making and exploration that can be a revelation (or revolution) to the person interacting, who can return or stay for days and be fundamentally changed by the experience.

We needed our own photographs, which meant we had to travel to tropical rainforests. After our failed attempt to hike in Nepal, we decided to try the musical route, and applied for a Fulbright Faculty Fellowship for teaching in Australia. Joel Chadabe, a good friend and later, the founder and director of The Electronic Music Foundation, helped us contact Australian universities who would be willing to have a Fulbright Fellow on their faculty. Also, he gave us the name of Warren Burt, an American composer freelancing and teaching over there. So I set about lining up not only possible teaching situations for the grant, but McLean Mix engagements, as well. The Aussies seemed amazingly open to all ideas—an unheard-of situation in the U.S.. So we were ready to fly—as soon as we heard from the Fulbright committee.

Of course we were turned down. No grants that year were handed out for music, but rather political history and science. Much to our surprise, however, the Aussies were far more interested in having the McLean Mix perform rather than teach, anyway, so we organized a tour, which with our other contacts spread to New Zealand and Hawaii as well.

So a very exciting adventure started for us. We "penniless" freelancers had never expected to see the other side of the world, and to do it for a month while performing our music…! Australia is, as everyone knows, a country/continent comprised mainly of desert. But up the east coast there is a dense rainforest, more tropical as one heads north. After Melbourne, we spent time with friends near the Blue Mountains west of Sydney, photographing whenever there was a chance, but the surprise came in Canberra, the country's capitol and a bit inland.

This was not rainforest country, so we were prepared to set up *"Rainforest"*, perform, view the large numbers of kangaroos freely roaming the parks and suburbs, and travel on. The shock came at 9 a.m. the opening day of the installation at the Canberra School of Art and Drama. Waiting patiently for us to unlock the classroom door were two young men with didgeridoo and clapsticks.

The didgeridoo is an Australian aboriginal instrument made from a hollowed-out eucalyptus log with beeswax mouthpiece. Usually three or four feet in length, the didgeridoo can produce a very low pitch that the player holds for as long as he can, sometimes continuing for twenty minutes at a time. This is done by circular breathing, which Brendan Dickie, the fellow in the hall, could do, and is excruciatingly difficult. The aborigines also make a series of animal and birdcalls through the didgeridoo as well, but the pulsing low furry-hollow sound of the held pitch I think is the most satisfying.

After an hour or so of these two men performing, two art students came in—Kerrie Ryan and Ivana Troselj, who also sang professionally in night clubs at night. They immediately began improvising a combination of quasi-jazz, avant-garde new music, and speech that was totally mesmerizing, while the didgeridoo and clapsticks underlay and punctuated their songs. We barred other people from playing, and made them sit as an audience, and we recorded this ad hoc ensemble for at least an hour. At this moment, in a haze of rapturous joy for us, was born "Rainforest Images".

David Worrall, our host and at whose house we stayed, was an eccentric himself, having developed an electronic music center (not totally accepted by the university), which was housed in a connected group of trailers at the very north end of the campus from the Music Department. Looking like a lonely army barracks, these rooms housed state-of-the-art computers and music synthesizers, and he and his staff invented music software daily.

David had created a portable geodesic-domed concert hall from inflatable plastic, which could be placed on a raft and floated down a river to the next performance! It was extremely successful, creating a cloud-like visual atmosphere with great acoustics, and had been used for several concerts already. His dream was to float down from Albany to New York City on a raft with this dome and perform all along the way. I am not sure this ever came to pass, however.

By 1993 we had slides from our expeditions to rainforests in Australia, New Zealand, Hawaii, Puerto Rico, Peru, and cooler wet forests in coasts of the U.S. and Alaska. The slides, slowly melting into each other and shown on a wall in front of the audience-performers, added immeasurably to the installation. Sometimes when no one was performing, people would come and lie on the floor, propping their heads up to see the slides, and just watch and listen to the continuously playing "new age" tape for hours.

"Rainforest" has been set up in college classrooms, concert halls, libraries, museums, nature centers, convention centers, alternate music performance spaces, science centers, art galleries, churches, hotels—hundreds of times and still counting. School children are also sometimes employed, but we try not to encourage large classes, since only five can perform at one time. We have had young children to 90-year-olds…Amish families next to a turbaned gentleman from India next to a five-year-old black boy and his white guardian mother next to a handicapped boy gleefully singing into the microphone next to an art student creating a painting of the installation—we've had them all! The university, however—that great patron of new music, has been the principal venue.

By January 1992 we were ready to make an organized piece of music out of our "Rainforest" experiences. This was helped along by a young man with a wonderful tenor voice, who worked with Pauline Oliveros. Paneotis, as he wanted to be called, was one of her main vocalists plus a highly gifted programmer on Pauline's analog Lexicon effects processors. Pauline was recording her "Deep Listening" album at the time, and generously allowed us to record with her seven processors. Paneotis invited us to spend a few days with him at his home, where the Lexicons were, and improvise with him while he tweaked the processors. Before we went to Kingston, New York, we outlined what kind of sounds would work best with the "Rainforest" tape.

I can manage my way around a violin enough to produce effects, simple melodies, and drones, so between the three of us we sang, entoned drones and overtones, played violin, recorder, and our clariflutes and processed everything—it was an exhilarating time for all and launched our new piece.

Now came the rub. How do we create this piece? Who actually will create it? The other duo-electronic music composers who collaborated on pieces–Vladimir Ussachevsky and Otto Luening–had had a method where each took a section and created the music. Then they had linked the sections together. No arguments, no fussing with each other's styles, very sane. This route we did not take.

No, we took the one that directly leads to divorce. First, Bart started the work because he had created the drone tape, which begins the piece. Then I continued it…We had basically lined up sections that fit our personal preferences, and I created all the vocal group sections, while Bart organized the rest, but we also altered and revised each other's as we saw fit…

Uh-oh. Not a good idea. I would work nonstop in the studio–seven days–creating my section. Bart would come in the next week and, thinking it was too thin and boring, add a huge amount of note-filigree around the vocal material, and continue into his section. The third week I would come in, cry out in horror for the total obliteration of my music. We would have a "conference" of high decibel range, after which I would erase everything he had added to my section and thin out his section, as well. Then he would come in, be appalled by what I had done, we would have another "conference", etc. etc. for a whole year!

Shockingly, at the end of the time we were *still* married and had produced together one of the best pieces in our repertoire. My wild simplicity and his more cerebral complexity worked together beautifully in the end—I wrote in my journal of January 17, 1994: "*Rainforest Images*' is the signature piece of our marriage, a reflection of its soul.

"Our working together, our being able to quash our egos for the whole, our equal love of creating something special and memorable, our love of nature, our experiences with other musicians, traveling around the world, our respect for the Wintu Indian creation myth stemming from the 'Tree of Life', our transcending the limitations of each of our styles for a deeper, farther reaching musical experience that is the combination—our respect and love for each other. All in a little CD! What a wonderful capsule of our life together!"[37]

"Rainforest Images II"

"*Rainforest Images*" is a tightly knit mesmerizing work of forty-eight minutes. This is a good length for a CD, but not for a concert. We enjoy making CDs, but our "bread and butter" comes from our performances. What to do next?

The obvious answer was video. We needed *"Rainforest Images"* to have its own life separate from the installation, and slides were becoming passe as a visual medium—hard to set up, cumbersome with expensive light bulbs which always burned out at the worst times, heavy projectors, and aging, ailing slide equipment furnished by universities, because they were investing heavily in video equipment by 1993.

I knew nothing about video. We owned no equipment, and had spent a fortune with music electronics. We were *not* going to get involved in video—! But we needed to have a video made.

Near to our home in Rensselaer County is a state-of-the-art facility called Rensselaer Polytechnic Institute, the oldest engineering school in the country. Since we had moved to Petersburgh in 1983, the Institute's electronic music center had grown to become the iEAR Electronic Arts Center, melding music, art, and literature together into their electronic counterparts, including sophisticated video techniques. We had close connections with RPI, having performed there and with Bart teaching there on occasion.

While attending the video events, we were especially taken with the work of a young painter-turned video artist from Malaysia, Hasnul Jamal Saidon. He liked to use nature in his work…After talking with Hasnul about creating a video for our *"Rainforest Images"*, which he agreed to eagerly, we approached Neil Rolnick and the other directors of the Center. They agreed to allow him to adopt this video project as one of his courses, and we would become extra advisors for his degree. Ah, the joy of working with a private university!

Hasnul Saidon spent the next six months in 1993 working on this project, in close communication with us. One week before he was to graduate and fly back to Malaysia, he handed us the finished video. He had created two, the second a shorter version of twenty-three minutes, which became the video we have toured with since 1994, to fascinated audiences everywhere.

Behind this story lies the original source video. We decided in January of 1993 to take a two-week eco-tour of Peru's Amazon region and the Machu Piccu area, primarily to film the rainforest. Having nothing of our own, we rented a video camera from a store in Albany, did the unthinkable of taking it out of the country, and promptly losing it on the bus after landing in Iquitos, Peru. I knew I loved the country when the bus driver came to our hotel room with our video camera in his hand. "I believe you left this on the bus, Senora," he said smiling. And this in a city with no panes of glass in the windows!

Videotaping in the jungle can be a futile experience. The batteries run down after about four hours; the camera lens can fog up from plastic-eating fungi; the videographer can be holding a shot while ants run up his legs, stinging as they go; the cameraman perspires in the unrelenting moist heat, dripping onto the lens and, of course, the animals or birds always decide to leave just as the camera is ready to shoot. One toucan would aim and let fire with his scat, usually on the camera itself. Plus we were newborn babes without a tripod or any idea on video techniques or even just holding the camera steady. It was amazing to me that Bart, who did all of the shooting because I wanted nothing to do with video at the time, got enough footage from four videotapes for Hasnul Saidon to make forty-eight and twenty-three minute artworks! While Bart shot video, I shot slides for our installation. Teamwork.

We were so grateful to Hasnul Jamal Saidon for his wonderful video work, that we planned a dinner party with his faculty advisors as guests, jointly with Karl and Freda Korte at their elegant home in Cambridge, New York, where they now lived, as Karl was retiring from the University of Texas. Prior to working with us, Hasnul had created a shorter video work for Karl Korte's (Texas) *"Hill Country Birds"*, so Freda and I jointly prepared food as close to Malaysian recipes as we could find. After a successful dinner we all assembled in the Korte's comfortable living room and played Hasnul's new videos for everyone, including Hasnul's wife Ana, who is also an artist, and their frisky one year old daughter Avila. The party was a huge success; everyone loved his videos, and Hasnul vowed to have Bart and me work with him again, this time in Malaysia at his invitation.

Fast forward to February 24, 1994: The University of West Virginia, Morgantown, the World Premiere of the music-and-video *"Rainforest Images II"*. RPI had already paid us for our premiere to take place on February 6 on our McLean Mix concert, but the concert had been canceled due to a heavy snowstorm (we prefer not to tour in January or early February for obvious reasons). So the premiere in West Virginia took place on a television monitor with 18-inch screen. Afterwards, I wrote:

"Feb. 24. Thurs. Lecture/Concert day. Today we learned what not to do: 1. Don't give an hour-long class at 5 p.m., not giving yourself enough time to set up and rehearse...2. Don't play a 23-minute complex new (world premiere) video—*"Rainforest Images II"*—on an eighteen-inch screen in a good-sized hall for one hundred people. It's like looking at somebody's key ring from a cereal box of the '40s! 3. Don't let a janitor meander through, trying to throw away your large cardboard arrow (for long-distance volume setting with Bart on the stage) because he thinks it's litter—plus your insulation, equipment boxes, padding, etc. ('What? Oh—I thought it 'twer junk, sorry!'). 4. After the video, during the long credits and before *"Wilderness"*, as several members of the squinting audience are preparing to go, don't run up to the front of the stage (me) and yell, "Don't leave—the next piece has live performers!" 5. Don't forget your flashlight, and both of you, nose to cold-filled nose (between sneezes) have to fumble myopically with the black-on black "play" and "stop" buttons of the brand-new three-inch DAT (digital audio tape) player while the audience titters in the dark…"

On March 4, *"Rainforest Images II"* finally got the performance it needed—at the University of Texas, San Antonio. Reed Holmes, the director of a three-day festival of electronic music–Bart's ex-graduate student from UT and a good friend–set up a large slide screen, and with a video projector. The performance went beautifully. To our happy surprise, a stunning review of our concert appeared the next day in the San Antonio Express. Our first music video was launched.

10.
"IN THE BEGINNING"

"The Ungambikula, the Self-existent Spirits,
came down from the sky with long stone knives.
They caught embryonic forms of life, which
swam in the salt water, in the sea shallows of the
shore, and with the knives shaped them into
complete human forms."

Arunta Creation Myth

In 1982, when I was collecting photographs of whales to make into a slide show for *"Beneath the Horizon"*, I became fascinated by whale mythology. I found that there are many myths from all over the world about the birth of the world from the ocean. In these myths, the Ocean Mother harbors life-forms of all kinds in a kind of creative stew, until a male god or group of beings rush down and cut open the ocean with light or knives to produce a world of living creatures. Often, the ocean womb is described as a dolphin or whale, penetrated by the male force, like Jonah and the whale, resulting in an explosion of living beings, and a separation of earth and sky.

Twelve years later, after touring full-time for over a decade, my voice had expanded from a weak non-soprano to a strong mezzo, with quality high notes. In 1994 I was already 52 years old. The past few years had been difficult, with the deaths of my mother in 1990, my father in 1993, and Bart's mother in the summer of 1994. I had reacted by composing *"The Dance of Shiva"*, the dancing god of destruction and creation, the life cycles of the world constantly swirling round and round. I also wrote a set of songs for voice and piano about life and death (*"Sage Songs of Life and Thyme"*) around the same time.

We were touring extremely heavily all of 1994, and as my voice grew stronger singing *"Wilderness"*, I began to want a piece that would really tax me and challenge my vocal abilities before I grew too much older. I decided to write the wildest· piece I could manage, using only my voice for all the sounds, sampled and processed through our electronics.

I decided to write a piece about the beginning of life. The idea of all forms being possible at the beginning had fascinated me for years, and the ocean myth would allow for a variety of extended vocal techniques.

First, I went to friends nearby who were extending their home cellar. The cement walls were in place but had no roof yet, and it made for a very reverberant echo chamber. I spent the morning singing, speaking, howling, and playing instruments in the cellar hole, to the puzzlement of the local coyotes, and having a wonderful time. Nothing came of it, but it gave me many ideas…

I made my voice into many different qualities—percussion sounds, choral voices, singing on one tone while shaping my mouth in many ways to produce overtones, then recording and playing the sound across the keyboard—electronic but strangely human (one of my favorite sonorities), cries, and the myths spoken in a variety of styles. Some of these were sampled and some were recorded directly onto the Macintosh "Studio Vision" computer program.

As I composed the taped part, I also wrote out the live performance, which would be altered slightly through effects processors. This involved hours of singing at the top of my range, which expanded to a high D (by singing while breathing in—the beginning "birth cry" of the piece). I also wrote a section for singing in the bass range, which strengthened my voice, but got cut out eventually.

The sound of a soprano experimenting at the top of her lungs for hours every day has an unsettling effect on a marriage…*Journal, Nov. 17, 1994:* "Composed in studio. Boy—it gets tiring holding a low D for hours! Am building the piece into another rousing percussion section. God knows who will listen to this thing (not Bart—he's hiding under the bed with earplugs)!

"Jan. 23-26, 1995. I can see the end of my piece just ahead! I'll be sad to finish, it's been such fun, but a four-month hiatus of touring would kill any ideas if not yet realized. It ends with a quiet choral chord shimmering while the solo sings low melodies with delay effects (sounding like a departing whale)".[38] But the oncoming long cross-country tour was only the beginning of distractions.

A composer should be able to split herself into two people—one who composes undisturbed, and one who has a life. Sometimes a piece takes years to complete, because the living takes up all the time. After we arrived home from our tour on May 2, there was a message on our answering machine: the landlords wanted to sell our rental house, and we had to buy it or move. We knew, of course, that this would happen someday. We couldn't afford to buy this house, with its huge acreage, and the house limitations were wearing on our nerves—no bathtub, no insulation in the walls, tiny dark windows, dirt blowing in from the cracks in the floorboards, the attic separating from itself as the house slowly slid down the clay hill it had been sitting on for 204 years, etc. etc. So we had to find another home very quickly. We decided it was time to buy.

We went to a local realtor, Nancy Hewitt, whose ancestors had built the Hill Hollow farmhouse we lived in for twelve years. We told her what we needed: privacy, at least an acre of land, big rooms—especially in the bedroom area for our electronic studio, a steep hill nearby to climb for exercise, woods surrounding the home, nice neighbors—oh, and if you could also throw in a fireplace and some wood beams, that would be nice…Of course, we couldn't afford anything over $90,000 (in 1995). "What do you have available?" we asked. "Well, there's a lovely house on Coon Brook Road, just a mile from the center of town." Great! What else is available? She looked at us severely. "For that price range, with those qualifications? Nothing. That's it. Take it or leave it!"

By May 30 our tour was completely finished, and we went to see the house on Coon Brook Road. Not only did it have the fireplace, but the fireplace was in an 1834 dining room with wooden beams and ceramic tile floor, plus an in-ground swimming pool right off the front porch area, a huge Jacuzzi in an attached motel room, with a long porch leading to the second motel room which was a summer guest room…There were fourteen rooms in all, with huge bedrooms, giant windows throughout the house, well-insulated, with walk-in closets and shelf space everywhere (except the kitchen—the kitchen basically didn't exist), plus two modern bathrooms, glass-enclosed converted side porch large enough for a full office, garage with workshop, myriad perennial flower gardens on one-and-a-third acres of land, and nearby steep wooded hill!

When we walked in the front door to the dining room, the house smelled like The MacDowell Colony. Bart smiled and said, "I love this house!" But as I walked in, the broken ceramic tiled floor tinkled like those glacial rocks in the Canadian Rockies. Hmmm. And none of the doors shut. The front "porch" was an indoor floor with pieces of walls on one end. The electricity wouldn't turn on. The upstairs bathroom tub/shower tiles looked like an earthquake had redistributed them. The ceilings upstairs were all pregnant and due very soon. Ancient wallpaper hung in shards from our future studio. Uh-oh...

Yes, we bought the house. For $78,500. Then spent the rest of the year working on it twelve hours a day, seven days a week, with two assistants, Asa and Jean Zossman–electricians, Brian O'Dell—the handyman, who was at our elbow for six weeks, Rich Midwood–the professional tiler, the well-drilling company, the plumber...Everything that could be wrong with a house was! We changed from aging touring artists, a bit soft around the edges, to pretend-young, hard-bitten, sunburnt, slender, muscled work people with perpetual plaster in our hair and grout under our fingernails, squinting eyes and a bit of a twang in our voices...

As anyone who owns an old farmhouse will attest, one never finishes working on it. It took years longer, working in the summers, to make it into a wonderful, comfortable old genteel home that we will probably live in until we can't manage the fourteen rooms and dozen flower gardens, or decide that maybe owning a house like this, plus composing music, making videos, preparing and performing annual tours, and writing autobiographies is maybe too much to do when one is eighty...

"In the Beginning" was finished in January of 1996, in our new roomy studio painted a bright peach color with antique wide-board Vermont spruce floors newly sanded and shined, and my hand-stenciled wall designs. *"In the Beginning"* is definitely the most difficult piece I have ever performed, and it took months to prepare, also for Bart, who had a complex set of live processing instructions to follow. Invited back to the University of Akron, Ohio for the seventh time, we premiered the piece on our tour on March 15, 1997 in their black box theater. The audience loved it.

During my years of working on this piece, I saw a stunning Masters degree recital performed by composer/video artist Svetlana Bukvic, at the RPI chapel in Troy. This was the time of the bombing of Sarajevo, Bosnia, and during one piece, Svetlana wore a large white sheet as a skirt, and sang as video scenes of a once-peaceful Sarajevo projected onto the skirt-"screen". I was fascinated by this image of a person wearing a video as she performed. What if I performed *"In the Beginning"* with (video) waves of ocean water pouring over me? This would have to be a compelling addition.

In June 1996 I drove to York Beach, Maine with a rented video camera and a newly-bought tripod. By the cliffs near Nubble Lighthouse, I videotaped the motion of the ocean over the rocks for several hours, until darkness fell. This was the first video work I had ever created, and I felt an exhilaration beyond anything, except composing.

A classmate of Hasnul Saidon's was now assistant tech director at RPI—A.J. Jannone, whose video work I also admired. Over the summer I contacted A.J., and we got together to plan how to make an art video from my ocean coverage, to coincide with the three main sections of *"In the Beginning"*. It took several months, as he was extremely busy, but the end result was wonderful. He began and ended with the ocean waves, turning them red after awhile. He mirror-imaged the waves crashing into each other, and in the middle of the piece, spun the whole scene until it became a mandala, with the rocks skimming out like thrown knives! How better to show the birth of the world?

The next job was to process me into the video. Bart and I decided to project only my head into the ocean waves, as the ocean "goddess" telling the story. With our new Videonics analog video mixer, my head was under the waves, peaking out at times, then inside the waves, and finally the waves were contained inside my head. So the audience could look at me performing to the side with my black-painted microphone, and also watch the center screen (hopefully large) to see the ocean goddess and waves.

Every few years we completely change our main concert. So from our *"Gods, Demons, and the Earth"* concert which ran from 1990 to 1997, we began a new concert called *"Inside the Time Machine"* in 1998, featuring my oldest electronic work, *"Night Images"* as well as my newest—*"In the Beginning"*, premiered at Roosevelt University's Chicago Musical College, April 15, 1998. Also on the bill was Bart's *"Happy Days"*—a live-electronic theater piece with me as clown playing copper music boxes and many gadgets, while Bart performed sampled and altered music boxes and gadgets. The last piece was *"Jambori Rimba"*…

The best performance of *"In the Beginning"* came a year later at Living Arts Space in Tulsa, Oklahoma. From my *Journal*: "'In the B.' came off stunningly. Bart made a mistake and ended up with the video of the ocean mandala in the middle of the piece spinning around my face, creating a goddess image with a headdress! Steve (Liggett, the director of Living Arts) said later that he had just returned from an international experimental video festival in Dallas, and *"In the Beginning"* was by far the most innovative video of the lot!"

Continuing on in the *Journal*, I describe the artist's life packing up from a downtown city arts space: "We broke it all down and packed up. As Bart was stuffing everything into the Honda, amid groups of jolly drunks rolling by, trains, a stuck car alarm and the across-street boisterous bar music, Steve and I were riding gleefully around the now-empty Living Arts space on a dolly, I shrieking and he pulling the 'cart' every which way. A crowd appeared at the door, and one of them asked if he could ride for fifty cents! Ah—what a life!"

11.
"JAMBORI RIMBA"

Journal, Oct. 9, 1996: "Oct. 9, or is it 8? at 8:55 EDT (any relation to reality is existential)...My head and stomach are upside down, and I sit in the beautiful, whisper-quiet Singapore carpeted airport awaiting 9:30..."

Our residence at the Universitii Malaysia, from same journal entry: "The guest house has four (furnished air-conditioned) rooms and a bath. Fluorescent lights on the ceilings are the only "lamps"—it really does resemble a camp. The bathroom is un-air-conditioned, with high small open windows (and screens) facing the noisy dorms and street, and a cold water shower and sink. Basic. & toilet with large bucket and dripping hose to wash—? *your feet?* & plastic dipper. It ain't New York! The place is decorated in early bachelorhood, and I groggily picked up while Bart put food away in the kitchen. Then—It Happened. A 5,000 watt close-encounter edition of *Call To Prayer*, the (one of four) megaphone pointed directly at our guesthouse (from the mosque across the street—really a *different* experience!"

Hasnul Jamal Saidon had accomplished the impossible. He had gotten the University of Malaysia at Sarawak (UNIMAS), outside of Kuching on the island of Borneo, where he was the Director of Video in the Arts and Culture Department, to hire Bart as the guest tech director of the brand-new fledgling electronic music studio, and to hire me as a "guest researcher"—all this with the enthusiastic help of his good friend Mohammed Abdul Fadzil Rahman, the young composer in the Music Department. Both had graduate degrees from the U.S., Fadzil's being from the University of Kansas, had worked together before, and both were highly respected in the University.

I had been reluctant to fly to Malaysia for a semester, because we were so deeply involved in renovating our home (beware the giant sucking sound of a needy house), but Bart realized that this opportunity comes once in one's life, if at all. He went in September to put the new studio together, which was piled in boxes awaiting his arrival. I came a month, or a few very frantic leaf-raking, music-organizing, storm window on-putting, settling all services—all the work of leaving a big house and business just before winter—weeks later. I was afraid of everything—the intense heat, the legendary leeches, the mosque calls, the Muslim people, the idea of creating a collaborative work of music in a strange place, the inability to sleep in a noisy environment, monumental jet lag, the three-day plane flight, the strange hot food, the oldest jungle in the world—all of it!

Universitii Malaysia at Sarawak was a campus of dark brown wooden buildings and large concrete complexes, interlaced with stone paths amid lovingly tended gardens of tropical plants and trees. Completely surrounding the campus was the impenetrable jungle, stretching for miles, ringed by a winding river with rare giant crocodiles lounging on its banks. The students and faculty seemed oblivious to the ominous surroundings, except one morning when I walked by a huge black scorpion sunning itself in the middle of the street, and a student came merrily barreling forth on his motorbike and squashed it beyond recognition, singing all the way…The grounds workers were very afraid of the jungle, and when I attempted to explore a bit, they screeched, "No! Bad! *SNAKE!!*" The one afternoon I walked into the jungle in back of the music building, I was instantly lost, and became almost panic-stricken before I could retrace my steps.

The campus was fifteen miles from Kuching, an exploding city which had grown from 25,000 people to 400,000 in just a few years, mowing down the rainforest as fast as possible, which is an endemic condition in most of Southeast Asia. The government of Malaysia, who built and funded this two-year-old university, the only one in Sarawak (a state in Malaysian Borneo about the size of Texas) had hired researchers from all over the world to document the native peoples and cultures before they were lost or forever changed. The Malays themselves were abroad, earning doctorates in major universities, and for now the home shortage of teachers was made up with visiting faculty from all over the world.

Malaysia is a gold mine of beautiful, huge rainforest trees, and was harvesting these to finance its education system, electricity, and to upgrade its people to modern living. It is so easy to sit in one's armchair in America and complain about the destruction of the rainforest, while one's arm reaches to turn on a light and the other arm is poised over the computer keyboard…Try sitting in a baking, steaming hot (leech-filled) jungle on a wet rock, and reach for a crumbling leaf to write on…How does one condemn another culture to a life without electricity, toilets, cooling fans, books, a variety of foods?

The argument is that if undisturbed, the native people have their own food sources, rich culture, ways of cooling down, etc., which is true. We lived with an ancient Iban tribe for a few days, experiencing this, while in Borneo. The rub comes when this system is altered. The consuming world takes from the native world, stripping them of their resources. Yet, can we all go back to living a much simpler life in the jungles? Even this tribe, which I loved, had one third of its members die from malaria the previous summer. Had this not have happened, they would have multiplied so much as to endanger the whole community. Somehow we must all find a balance that everyone can live with. And this must be done soon—very, very soon.

Although the video wing of the art department had many students and a double roomful of computers and monitors, the music department had four students and one practice room. The brand new electronic music studio was in a tiny room, filled with a digital 32-channel mixer, the latest sound designing programs on the Macintosh color computer with four hard drives, and a small synthesizer. No one but Bart knew the slightest thing about how to work any of it. However, a Malaysian director arrived just as we left in December, who with his new doctorate would be running the studio. So for this semester, Bart's and my only job was to research, record, and create a composite work profiling the music of Borneo, along with the video being created by Hasnul Saidon.

So a series of adventures was set up for the three of us plus Fadzil, who had been the chief organizer. It was probably the most thrilling three months of my life. Imagine visiting native peoples, recording rainforest sounds and tribal performances, traveling to wild places all over Malaysia, with the (Muslim) government paying for every expense and giving you a salary…! And we were escorted everywhere, and treated like royalty. In-between our short forays, limited because Hasnul and Fadzil still had to teach their courses, we constructed our new installation, entitled *"Jambori Rimba"*. The title translated from the Bahasa language means, literally, "Jungle Jamboree".

Bart took over creating the synthesizer ground tape, which, as in *"Rainforest"*, would play all the time as the audience participated. By some miracle, he constructed a rich, harmonious, plaintive sound, slightly bubbly, which not only fit with all the sampled sounds I recorded plus the live improvised microphone sounds, but harmonically was in the same "key" as all the insects and birds he recorded later. Nothing needed to be altered! There is a tonal center in the rainforest, which came as a complete surprise to us. Maybe Olelbus[39] was with us on this adventure, shaping our minds.

We visited national parks, nature preserves, and native cultural centers, as well as bird and butterfly parks later on the mainland. Our one major foray into the heart of the jungle was a four-day visit with the Iban people who lived along the Ai River, beyond roads, five hours from Kuching. Taken up the river by motorized canoes, while the guides stood and fought off the rocks with long poles, we all were frightened and wary. Doris, a worker in the music office and a native Iban, was appointed to accompany us for my sake, as I was the lone woman in a group of men (It is curious that, although the government is run by Muslims, all native tribes are Christians, and have Christian names, converted by missionaries decades ago).

We lived in a guesthouse across the narrow river from the Iban longhouse, which kept visitors apart from the tribe and their culture intact, at least for a while longer. The longhouse and people were so alluring, that, after I cajoled a reluctant Hasnul to videotape them, he became so enthralled he recorded four hours continuously and used up all his batteries! Then he suffered severe head and neck aches from holding the heavy camera up over his shoulder all that time, and had to spend most of the next day in the cabin cot, on our next sojourn further up the river with the Ibans.

Hasnul Jamal Saidon is a fascinating artist. He was my mentor, teacher, and catalyst for becoming a video artist myself. Known for his paintings, he sketched furiously on all our trips, late at night, and by the day of our performance had produced a gallery's amount of wonderful drawings, most by hand and a few using video. He carried a mirror around with him to videotape odd angles and sun reflections. He worked constantly, long after we were all exhausted and lounging around. He overlaid images of several videos, and created layers of composites—richly dense and sometimes abstract. I hope he continues his wonderful video art. He creates against all odds, as we all do.

Armed with a vast array of sounds and images, we had two weeks of uninterrupted quietude during semester break to put this show together and try to create a viable musical work. Bart took to staying up all night. The electricity was intermittent. Every day there would be a huge thunderstorm to cool off the 100-degree heat, and invariably the lights and computers would be off for up to a half hour, usually right in the middle of one's best work...One day Bart arrived in the studio to find a giant spider had taken over the keyboard. It *is* the jungle, after all!

By the end of November we had finished the *"Jambori Rimba"* installation and a rough sketch of a future concert piece. Hasnul had four full videotapes, which he played simultaneously and mixed during the event. Having already set up the *"Rainforest"* installation a few weeks earlier and having only Japanese, Chinese and a handful of Caucasian students and faculty participate, I knew the way to involve the main body of people was to make the event a concert, with required attendance, and special seats for the (Muslim) heads of the department.

November 26 was concert day, at the accustomed hour of noon. I was incredibly nervous—our first Asian audience, and mostly Muslims at that...To a packed house, we improvised on the *"Jambori Rimba"* tapes created by Bart, using voice, clariflute, soprano recorders, and synthesizer for about a half hour, while Hasnul played the videotapes onto a wall-sized screen in back of us. Half-way through the improvisation, Fadzil and his friend performed on a beautiful set of gamelan instruments a piece he had written for the event, with student and faculty dancers as hunter and bird in the forest. A crew from Malaysian national television recorded the event, and it became part of a documentary about the new university, broadcast over the whole country the next week.

Immediately after the performance, we bowed to the faculty heads and asked them to honor us with their participation in the installation. This allowed the rest of the audience to come up and try the microphone, sampling synthesizer, array of rainforest sounds we had assembled, a table of taped music from different tribes they could mix and listen to, and a new station—ceramic construction pipes decorated by the art students and placed in an inviting circle, with wood art-stick "mallets" on which to play rhythms, in the middle of the auditorium floor (no stage area—the floor went out to the padded audience seats, which rose in bleacher-style surrounding the open area).

To our delight and amazement, while people were making rhythms on the pipes (the most favorite station), singing softly through the microphone and playing the sampler and tapes, some students started dancing in tribal style—many, of course, were from the nearby local tribes. Their images were projected onto the huge screen, mixed in with the videos playing, the camera projecting from the high recording booth in back. This is the best cross-cultural experience I have ever participated in!

It is hard not to write a whole book about these months in Malaysia. After a wonderful celebratory music department lunch in our honor, with "American-style" steak and mashed potatoes (boiled steak in ginger, with ginger potatoes), and a week spent on the Malaysian mainland with Hasnul and at times his family, we sadly left, flying back on December 4 and arriving Dec. 6 in Albany.

Three weeks later we were flying to the Philippines, to perform in the Asian Composers League festival named *"Tunugan"* ("festival" in ancient Filipino) held this year in Manila and nearby areas. It was ironic that although the Philippines and Borneo are near to each other, no composer from Malaysia had been invited to the festival. We were the sole contributors of Malaysian culture there, from distant New York! We performed an earlier concert[40], but gave a seminar on our new work in Borneo. The Philippine festival, six days long, had wonderful performances by the best artists from Manila, Taiwan, Japan, Korea, Vietnam, Indonesia—a special gamelan ensemble who played traditional and experimental music as well—as well as Australia and New Zealand.

I carried our newly bought video camera (also used at times by Hasnul Saidon in Borneo), and was able to record traditional Asian music and dance I had never experienced before, which I used later in *"The Ultimate Symphonius 2000"*. One opportunity feeds another…The most surprising and pleasing impression we both had of the festival was the quality of compositions presented, often in the western contemporary classical style. Almost *all* were excellent! The standard of composition and performance in this organization is to be admired and envied. These people are very serious about their art, and, like Hasnul, often work harder than we do. And the quality of inventiveness is a revelation. I find working and being with Asians a wonderfully enriching experience, and humbling.

The director of the festival, Ramon Santos, was an old school chum of ours, back in the '60s in Indiana University. He returned to his country after receiving his doctorate from the Eastman School of Music, and resurrected the traditional native music, as well as forming children's ensembles all over the country to revive the languishing musical talent, which had been so rich before the American occupation. After twenty years, these children are now the leaders of the Philippine musical world, with first-class orchestras, choirs, and native ensembles. If anyone deserves a musical Nobel Prize, it is this humble man of Chinese/Filipino descent who cared enough to bring his country back from its existential cultural despair. Ramon Santos is also a fine composer.

During 1997 Bart carefully constructed an autumn McLean Mix U.S. tour with Hasnul Saidon as the guest video artist. Southeastern Louisiana University was the key venue, with a two-week residency with the Art Department, and a linking concert with the Music Department during its autumn music festival. The premiere of the *"Jambori Rimba"* installation would take place a week earlier, at Siena College in Albany, New York, along with several lectures on video techniques Hasnul would give at local colleges, including his alma mater RPI. Hasnul received a grant from his government, which paid for his transportation and expenses and a stipend. We were all very excited about this.

Then El Nino happened. The forests of Indonesian Borneo burned, twenty miles from Kuching. There was fear that the inhabitants of the island would have to be evacuated to the mainland, because the smoke was horrendous. The university was temporarily shut down. Hasnul's wife Ana and their two small children would be left alone, while he was safely touring the U.S.. He, a good caring Muslim, wouldn't abandon them. Already in Kuala Lumpur, ready to fly here, he canceled. We were distraught. How could we handle the tour without him and his video expertise?

Bart had to cancel all of the video lectures, while we figured how to work the visual part of the installation, which included Hasnul's hour-long composite video he had sent us. But I had no idea how he was able to project live participants onto the video screen and mix them with the film…

I had prepared a multiple fade-and-dissolve slide show of Borneo, from my filming during our residency, and we decided to leave the fascinating video alone, and project the dancing people onto the moving slides via a video camera. There was no way to suspend it overhead, even if we knew how, so the camera stood to the side, and we constructed a curtained-off area the dancers could move in, and the camera projected all but the lower part of the body. Bart had the idea of putting the projected image through our Videonics (video) Mixer, and manipulating the dancer's image through the settings.

The trouble with producing a new and expanded installation is—room. Where can our host place two synthesizers, two microphone stations, a bicycle wheel to bow and strike, a large area of clay construction pipes painted Borneo-style by artist Anne Lindsay, a video screen and chairs, and now a slide screen with booth to dance in? The premiere took place in a faculty lounge at Siena College in Albany, New York on Sept. 29, 1997—a set of two small rooms, which canceled out the dancing part, but allowed for the rest. We made a large display of Borneo folk art we had bought in Kuching in an adjoining anteroom, along with a testimonial to Hasnul and the terrible fire in Borneo. Although the premiere was well-attended and successful, we felt very disturbed about Hasnul's absence.

The premiere of the whole set-up came the next week at Southeastern Louisiana University, in the large gallery of the Art Department, and was hugely successful. It ran for a whole week, eight hours a day, attended by over a thousand people. The music with the native sounds made people very contemplative and subdued. I can still hear the hauntingly beautiful Iban melodies and sape (east Asian lute) playing of Minggu—the premier virtuosic performer of the Kenyah tribe–riding over Bart's ground music. We teamed up with a graduate student dancer and improvised one afternoon to a delighted audience. We had gone ahead without our video artist, but with heavy hearts. To this day, we have not seen Hasnul again. We hope that in future, if the world ever calms down to the point of sanity, that we three once more will be making music and art together.

In 1998 Bart and I collaborated again on a concert version of *"Jambori Rimba"*, and Hasnul sent a shortened video to go with the twenty-six minutes of music. Instead of alternating the composing of musical sections, and creating a work that was not live-performed as had been done in *"Rainforest Images"*, this time we chose a different method. Bart recomposed the *"Jambori Rimba"* installation ground tape, adding the Iban and Kenyah musics and Iban children playing, plus cicada and bird calls. I then composed the live performance music for recorder, clariflute, bicycle wheel for Bart, and for myself—pitched suspended sawblades struck with mallets, and straight soprano singing with slight digital processing. The idea was to blend and alternate our composed music with the native music and sounds in a serendipitous whole. I believe this is one of our most sublime pieces.

12.
"THE ULTIMATE SYMPHONIUS 2000"
AND
"MILLing in the ENNIUM"

What can one say about the Millennium? We all know that it is an artificially constructed number, stemming from the birth of Jesus Christ. It is how we order our days on earth and remember the past history. There are other systems, of course, but this one dominates around the world, and as we annually celebrate the beginning of a new year, we the people feel that a large "celebration" is necessary to kick-start the next thousand years.

What is there to celebrate? Overpopulation and over-consumption—driving thousands of species to the brink of extinction and beyond, massive deforestation, soil erosion, pollution, wars, pain. And just beyond—the stock market collapse, terrorists, the turning of this country into a nervous, fearful watchdog and military aggressor, the decline of the classical arts, university closings, poverty, etc..

I cast around in my mind for an answer. How could we possibly find something positive about this time in history to celebrate? I am not into mass suicide. Whatever mess we humans have gotten ourselves into, we must dig ourselves out. Perhaps a cheerful theme would help.

What is significant about this age? Computers. As I turned on my CD player, it came to me that at our fingertips is a great wealth of recorded music, stretching back to ancient Greek music engraved on columns, and realized by musicians today on the CD I was holding. A celebration is a holding of hands, raising them up to a hopeful new day. What if we celebrated the whole two thousand years of music in one gigantic installation, playing all periods of music simultaneously?

Impossible, of course. I proposed the idea to Bart, who gave me that look ("She's *'over the top again'*"). Well, we could scale it down a little...We would limit it to classical and ethnic music, eliminating the commercial aspect. We needed a sponsor for this, and we approached several colleges about a "round-robin" commission. Five colleges responded favorably, so at the beginning of 1999 we began the huge project. Bart would find and record music from all historical periods, transferring his excerpts to CDs and the computer.

I would find vocal and piano excerpts for live performance stations. I would create two visual arts stations—slowly evolving slides and an hour-long video. The video eventually was entitled *"MILLing in the ENNIUM"*, from pre-recorded excerpts depicting human life and culture around the world–past and present. I decided to use old movie clips, PBS performances, ice skating from the Olympics, my recent footage from Asia, even my contra-dance group and performers from Altamont, New York.

The video took the whole year to create. I made Stravinsky's *"Firebird"* dancer—who has a very short beginning solo in the ballet—which I manipulated, repeating and speeding up/slowing down the dance whirls—the focal point, dancing into and out of other scenes. The fire in our home fireplace became the beginning and ending, along with the bronze antique clock on the mantle. I superimposed, via chroma-keying and luminance keying on our Videonics mixer, London Ballet dancers in the middle of a Dale Chihuly (Tacoma, Washington-based artist) glass sculpture scooped steaming from the oven. I slowed down the motion of a Buddhist celebration in the Himalayas and faded it into a Borneo Iban welcome dance. The firebird came bursting out of a U.S. rocket blasting to outer space. Mozart was composing on his pool table, while the 16th Century Spanish part book page[41] on my piano room wall bled through him. I lined up a Japanese koto player poking through a black jazz pianist superimposed on a harpist—a mass of vibrating strings and fingers. Ballet dancers appeared inside jazz dancers. It was incredible fun!

On October 2, I woke up and realized that I had done nothing about making an hour-long slide show, that the audience would dance into and interact with, using the same theme—also part of the Millenium installation. I jumped out of bed, hurriedly dressed, and without breakfast immediately drove to North Adams, Mass. where the annual harvest parade was just beginning, with a "Y2K" theme. For the next month, I dashed all over the tri-state area (New York, Vermont, Massachusetts), photographing an International Folk Dance Festival in

Albany, old churches and graveyards, an array of folk art from Halloween in people's yards, historic buildings, people walking down the street, etc.

Williams College (Williamstown, Massachusetts), as one of the five commissioners, opened its library for our take-home use for two years. Our home library consisted of about five CDs at the time, so Bart was able to create his excerpts using their vast collection—an incredible boon to us. I hired a professional photographer to make slides from several books and magazines, and tapped into our own large slide collection of past European and Asian tours.

This was a college education all in itself. The end result was immense awe at the glorious outpouring of art through the ages. At last, there was a reason to celebrate the year 2000!

The premiere took place during the days of February 6 and 7, 2000. The principal commissioner, Massachusetts College of Liberal Arts, had arranged the premiere for the Hunter Black Box Theater at Mass MoCA (Massachusetts Museum of Contemporary Art) in North Adams. It was the perfect location. The historic old mill added its own dimension, with its brick walls, towering ceilings, ancient oak floors, snakes of metal piping everywhere. The large staff accented the corners and shapes of the eighty-foot room with blue and yellow lights.

We set up eight stations, our largest installation ever: a giant video screen playing continuously, on the opposite wall the fade-and-dissolve slide show with dancing/gesturing booth and computer manipulation of the participants, electric piano and vocal live performance stations with digital effects, a "Textures and Styles" synthesizer keyboard programmed with forty different musical excerpts on three CDs, from Hildegarde von Bingen to Stravinsky, a "Millennium Mixer"—listening station with CDs containing fourteen tracks of ethnic and classical music to mix and match, a drone station for underpinning the whole musical collage…The combined musics floated out over the eighty-foot space with all the visuals.

Students and friends were appointed guides to help people as they came in the door. Jazz players came. Choirs performed. Over four hundred people attended in this sparsely populated rural area. Even our physician, Dr. John Hearst from Bennington, Vermont, danced in the slides! It was a fantastic celebration, from wild cacophony to ethereal prayer, the expression of the collective creative soul of humankind.

"The Ultimate Symphonius 2000" had three more installations—at Wake Forest University, North Carolina, at Hamilton College in Clinton, NY, and Missouri Western State College—who has loyally supported our concerts for years. The installation was impossibly difficult to transport and stage, requiring a large

room or two. We had hoped for more venues, but in retrospect, more would have been too many. Along with this new piece, we also had our annual tour, performing concerts and the *"Jambori Rimba"* installation as well. Our tour in 2000 began on February 6 and ended on June 6 with a *McLean Mix* final concert at Engine 27, New York City, sponsored by the Electronic Music Foundation.

Later, both video and music coalesced into a set composition for our tours, and the resultant twenty-minute piece–*"MILLing in the ENNIUM"*—became the signature of our new tour, beginning in 2002. The music for this is a harmonious collage of twenty-seven different pieces of music, held together by Bart's original music and improvised violin music by Jonathan Aceto, who has performed with us and commissioned both of us for his midi violin.

The years 1999 and 2000 were almost solely concentrated on creating and performing, a Mozartian life of working frenzy. We knew that the small aperture of opportunity for creating really original works and touring all over the world with them, being able to survive for decades doing so, was closing. We were getting older. The world was getting less friendly. The country was about to implode in its own frenzy of fear and anxiety. At the end I felt a great sense of artistic satisfaction and future apprehension, over a year before the September 11 debacle…

13.
"SYMPHONY OF SEASONS"
AND THE FUTURE…

"Who are you?" said the Caterpillar. Alice replied, rather shyly, "I hardly know, Sir, just at present—at least I knew who I was when I got up this morning, but I think I must have been changed several times since then."
"Alice's Adventures in Wonderland" by Lewis Carroll

When we were children we thought we could do and be anything. Perhaps little girls were more restricted, but at least we felt we could write, sing, dance, draw, and act for our admiring family audience. A few years into school and peer pressures, we began to question what exactly we *could* do, and we began to be channeled into a few accepted disciplines. Out went the "irrelevant" ones, and by high school we had decided—either we could sing *or* dance *or* make art *or* write *or* act (composing wasn't one of the choices). I plunged whole-heartedly into the music activities, which, because I went to a very fine public high school, meant chorus, band, and orchestra, and the one-time opportunity to compose by writing the class song. I gave up all the others (ballet or folk dancing had never been skills of mine). By the end of high school the lines were drawn. Almost everyone had given up the "extra-curricular" activities in favor of mainlining into a career, either via college or out into the unsympathetic world at large.

In America the artistic talents emerge again in folk-like ways, and become a tool for raising and teaching children, decorating the community or one's house, enhancing church life—and with a few skilled people, a side business to supplement the regular income by selling one's handicrafts. America has always been very big on volunteer amateur music and drama groups, which is a wonderful avocation and joy to the volunteer and audience alike.

Those rare students who stand out in high school as specially talented in one of the arts often attend a university for these skills, and delay for a few years the hard truth that there is very little need or desire for professional classical arts in America. These people usually end up teaching in college, the accepted refuge for the arts, and display their own talents as an extra, usually within the university walls or a university publication. The university, as it has developed over the last two hundred years here, has its ancestry in Europe, of course—as, for that matter, do the classical arts.

Bart and I partially broke out of that mold, because our talents could not be constrained to the accepted academic tradition. We were too "dangerous" for full-time work at the university. Pushed out, we redefined ourselves and responded by calling up those lost hidden talents that had atrophied since junior high school. To accomplish what we wanted in our performances, we went back to being children—experimenting with bowing bicycle wheel spokes, singing through cardboard tubes, dancing through Halloween slides of ghosts and smiling pumpkins, videotaping the magical ripples of a river reflecting the blazing colored autumn leaves hanging over its banks, reciting one's own poetry while our voices echoed backwards and forwards, blowing up balloons and squeezing them, with the other "child" skipping around on the violin…We have had thirty years to continue our childhood after being cast out. What a joy this has been!

Who are we? *We are the America that has not allowed itself to be.*

"Symphony of Seasons":
"Jewels of January"

In a frigid dry January day in 1998, I looked out of the dining room window to see our winding mountain stream cascading over stunningly beautiful ice formations, like Roman coliseums. I grabbed our video camera and spent all morning leaning over the stream, taping glinting white sparkles on black rippling water, so close they became abstract moving art, and then bluish ice "teeth"—a variety of shapes and shining formations.

I suddenly realized that I was launched into a new art medium, one that I had vehemently rejected—creating art video. I had been a photographer for our music/slide shows for decades, but the combination of image plus *motion* didn't excite me until that day. A year passed, and the next January I videotaped more ice formations, this time seeking them out. Along the local highway was a granite cliff with huge man-sized icicles…

As I was working on our *"Ultimate Symphonius 2000"* multimedia show, I plotted what would happen after this work was over, as composers do. I was learning how to mix images and handle source material with our simple set-up of camera, two VCRs and a master S-VHS VCR deck, connected through our Videonics Mixer and enhanced by a colorizer and image sharpener (yes, we "poor" musicians who have to struggle to pay *any* income tax were now creating a video studio—connected to our TV in our large old country bedroom). How about a series of short music videos of ten minutes each, depicting the four New England/New York seasons, within the confines, pretty much, of our own backyard?

What I hadn't done yet to any degree was to make good original source tapes, and for this coming project, I would have to do all my own taping. Ah, how much one appreciates the efforts of great filmmakers and video artists working with state-of-the-art equipment! How could I ever come up to those standards—the agony-wail of every beginning video artist. Well, of course one can't. So one must fall back upon what can be created with little resources. However, without commercial restraints, the artist can delve into that creative well inside and realize art not allowed in the money-making world. One is free again. *Imagination* is the key here.

After our long 2000 tour, we decided to take the year off from performing. It was time for me to get back into composing, since I had spent the last two years creating videos and slide shows. It is not good to let a creative art languish for too many years. We must keep ourselves going, ignoring all the little inside voices that whisper incessantly, "Why compose? No one is asking for this music. You've written enough for one lifetime. You'll be forgotten, anyway. The world will blow itself up soon, so why bother? You're too tired/un-exercised/unsocial/negligent of your house and garden/untalented/poor/lazy/etc./etc." It's amazing how long the list of negative thoughts can become! These linger in the background when one is deeply involved in a project or running around the world performing, but they come back loud and stressfully clear when one has a little time to think.

During the autumn of 2000 I finally had enough source video to put together the winter piece, which I called *"Jewels of January"*. With luminance keying and chroma-keying, the two best effects on the Videonics Mixer, I bled through a huge icicle with the glinting lights from the stream, made windows in ice formations and showed other ice sculptures peeking through. I found that the natural winter light gave purple and orange hues to the ice, enhancing the basic black and white. The whole purpose of this was to make people see the beauty around them, to become children again and revel in the jewels of a cold winter's day.

By winter I was creating the music to fit with the video. Video had to come first, because the images were so tricky to photograph, and I had much more experience with making music. I had collected a wonderful sound tape made years before, using an invented instrument by watercolor artist Anne Lindsay–a "bowed chime". She had brought it to our house in the summer—a large heavy sheet of steel hung from a wooden frame, with extended metal rods bowed with a bass viol bow. She, Bart, and I had "entertained" the neighborhood by improvising with it while playing wooden flutes on our deck, resulting in a few coyote howls in the distance…

So I played furiously on it and recorded it one evening in the house. The sounds were long, freezing tones of ice-like beauty. Added to this was piano and chime music created on our sampler, bowed bass strings on the piano harp, and live clarinet samples, ending with "music" from the stream itself–in the spring of 2001. Although the music was created to coincide with the video, it is traditionally thought out, with themes that return, melodies/motives building to a climax, and layering techniques. Tone-painting techniques are employed at the beginning, with the meandering clarinet samples coinciding with the flowing stream, then later with strident xylophone-enhanced piano chord crashes symbolizing the cutting through, in the video, of the huge icicle, and a build-up of musical activity as the icy stream becomes more active. The whole piece gives a feeling of ominous icy bleakness and cold beauty, in a way that traditional music cannot.

The ratios of video and music creating are curious. It takes months or years to film the original video source material, and for me, a month to make a ten-minute artwork from the source. Music takes a day or two to amass the source sounds, and two to six months to create the electronic music, partially because I keep adding and finding new sounds as I go. I "matched" the music to the video by thinking of shapes, movement, color, change of scene, and the overall mood of the season. The finished work became a single unit, a new genre of "music video" or "video/music" quite unlike MTV's version of enhancing the singer and high-lighting the music performance.

Where this is all going, I do not know. What does one do with a new genre, not needing a performer? My job now is just to create the best works I can, and advancing technology will tell me what to do next, in the next few years. If we are all still here, of course...

"Symphony of Seasons": "The Eye of Spring" and "July Dance"

During one hot and sunny June day in 1999 the flowers in my yard exploded—pinksters (wild pink azaleas) and azalea bushes, purple campanula (bellflowers), wild white rose bushes—all blooming at once—a riot of color, which was just the contrast I wanted from the black and white quality of the January piece. I spent an ecstatic morning videotaping, defeating the automatic focus by leaning in too close to the flowers and creating blurry swathes of color, like a watercolor wash. Then I climbed inside the rose bushes and sproinged the flowers with my camera, creating movement. I focused on the sexual center of the pink-ster flower for several minutes, later mixing it with feedback, so the flower "melts". Then I waited a month and recorded giant heads of zinnias, and later by pure accident, a monarch butterfly browsing around in a purple globe thistle. He flew away doing a somersault—is that the way all monarch butterflies take off? I found this out later when I slowed down the playback to a frame at a time.

My idea for the music in this flower orgy centered around spring's fecundity, and I decided to use myself as several singers in sensuous polyphony, murmuring, quasi-pop singing, and moaning bits of melodies and phrases. The words sung and spoken are all Latin names for the perennial flowers in my garden. On video the flowers blur and clear, engulfing the viewer. A section of harp ostinato-like melodies and synth harmonies is accompanied by white wild roses and their reverse negative images in a languid flower dance. Both video and music return to the blurred colors and voices and end with a bouncy flute melody as the butterfly departs in slow motion.

After the initial videotaping of the spring piece, I returned immediately to my ongoing video work for the upcoming Millenium, which took all the rest of the year. During the summer of 2000 I finished the art video (music was finished later) for *"The Eye of Spring"*, and immediately needed to use the remainder of the precious short New York summer season to film source video for the *"July Dance"* piece. This kind of nature filming is so time-restricted, that the loss of one day can mean a wait of another whole year to complete the source shooting!

Now came the dilemma of a July video…When one has used up all the flowers in a spring piece, what does one do for summer? How could I compete with the great images of the first two videos, and also with the fourth, which already had been recorded? For a few years, I had wandered around asking these questions, filming aborted attempts. The colors of deep summer are green green green. Not too exciting.

What makes summer unique here in the Northeast? People outside. Children playing, parties. My first action was to lay out a bunch of resonant cut logs from our woodpile and sound them out, striking them with rubber mallets. Soon I had a weird "xylophone", also using croquet posts for the highest pitches. I found that large empty plastic trash cans create good resonators, and covered them with long foam pads and a black curtain used in our slide shows. Then I laid the logs on top in order of pitch.

We drove to the house of old friends on Hill Hollow Road, Ray and Gene(vieve) Bogucki, who were temporarily absent. They have a large backyard meadow facing 200 acres of wilderness. There we laid out the "xylophone" and Bart recorded me performing, dancing, and clowning around. A stiff wind blew the cloth around, making it "dance"—a wonderful effect! Next, I filmed a string of birch trees in the Adirondacks, and gyrating wind-blown black leaf shadows on a large white granite rock. At home, I went to a local daycare center with two large bags of balloons, and filmed the small children running and playing with them in the backyard. I recorded the balloons alone, filling up the whole frame. This took the whole summer of video recording.

Bart and I had received a commission/residency from the i/EAR studios of RPI to work in their studios with the latest computer video equipment and create a composite video/music piece. In the fall of 2001, while working on the music for the spring video, I worked with Joseph Reinsel on computer effects for both "July Dance" and the last video, for autumn. Bart began learning MAX MSP software, which would eventually allow him to create a whole synthesizer and all the effects on the computer, thus revolutionizing our home studio and concert performance.

In the summer of 2003 I completed "July Dance", which is reminiscent (but only slightly) of MTV. Everything dances to recorded wild drumming from log xylophone, wobbling pizza pan, balloon squeals and children laughing, my improvising on the violin, and a drunken saxophone-like melody created by twisting a rubber microphone cord while the mic is on (plus other sounds): birch trees boogie, children jump through a giant balloon that trails multi-colored fire, like a comet, I gyrate among the logs while the whole image twists into a ball and rolls away…Isn't summer supposed to feel this way?

"Symphony of Seasons": *"Autumn Requiem"*

The autumn video came about during a mountain climbing trip to Mt. Katahdin in Baxter State Park, northern Maine, in September of 2000. We regularly mountain climb/hike from ten to fourteen mountains each summer—whole summers of 1987,'92, and '98 were spent in the Canadian Rockies and Columbian Range. The day after our Mt. Katahdin climb I was overwhelmed by the vivid autumn reds and yellows of the surrounding woods, especially reflected in the stream running by our campsite. I spent four hours hunched over the stream (causing neck tendonitis for a year afterwards), recording the most amazing moving colors I had ever seen! Fall colors back home had been muted the last few years, with the summer droughts and destructive results of the maple leaf cutter worms, but here in Maine all was still unspoiled.

More videotaping was accomplished later in Petersburgh, and in November of 2000 I had a flash of insight—what if I started and ended the piece with a lone naked tree on a hill, backed by cold sky, a reminder of what comes after the autumn color orgy? Just outside of Troy was a bleak, fat, black tree on a hill by a farmer's field, and I videotaped this with the bonus of a lean sunset just beyond. This death image I used later to punctuate sections during the piece.

I was painting the ceiling of the laundry/Jacuzzi room the day of September 11, 2001. I remember the brilliant white of the paint and the blaring sunny morning, as Bart ran into the room and yelled, *"They've blown up the World Trade Center!"* I felt darkness crash into all our lives. I wept and painted that afternoon, listening to a CD of Benjamin Britten's *"War Requiem"*, knowing that a fundamental feeling of safety and good will had disappeared, perhaps forever, from our consciousness, along with the pain of all those New Yorkers involved, in and out of the rubble.

As with all Americans, this horrific event haunted me that fall (it still does). The whole nation went into deep mourning, for the dead and their loved ones and for our lost innocence. I was at the point of picking out the text excerpts for the autumn piece, and decided to mold it as an elegy, not just for fall turning to winter, but for those who died and the rest of us who live now precariously. The piece became *"Autumn Requiem"*.

This work had to be longer, more significant than the other pieces of the set, and was to be performed live for the RPI commission. I created a twenty-five minute video, and Bart worked on the music. In January of 2002 we sat down in the studio together, and for the next month chiseled out the live performance. Whenever the tree image is seen, I sing in an operatic voice *"Requiem Aeternam"* from the Roman Catholic mass, and later while also plucking and bowing *"Dias Irae"* on the violin. Each return of the tree image, which builds in length and complexity, has a return and expansion of the melodic/harmonic ideas, until the penultimate tree sequence creates a tension and mood akin to the end of the world…

Throughout the piece, I recite from Thoreau's journals about the passing of the seasons, plus other quotations, and sing in, alternately, heavy cabaret and light youthful style excerpts from the classic pop song *"Autumn Leaves"*. Each of us has invented his/her own music: Bart for his bicycle wheel, clariflute, recorder, and computer sequences, and I with my violin playing, squeezing balloons, which produce waves of high-pitched whining melodies, and both of us using myriad small found instruments, all with new audio processor effects Bart has conjured from his MAX software. The contrast of the gorgeous autumn colors and the stark black tree mixed with the plaintive, cataclysmic music creates a rending of the soul. It may be the most profound, disturbing piece we have ever created.

We premiered *"Jewels of January"* and *"Autumn Requiem"* on March 22, 2002, at Missouri Western State College, who had also been one of the commissioners of the Millennium work we had performed there two years earlier. Also on the concert was our new concert version of *"MILLing in the ENNIUM"*, a distillation of the *"Ultimate Symphonius 2000"* installation, using my video collage, and Bart's assembling/composing the music. This concert tour was the debut of all my own videos, and I was terribly apprehensive of the audience response. As we traveled around performing the concert, our performance improved, and by the University of Louisville, many in the audience were lining up to congratulate us. They loved it! They were disturbed, elated, and fascinated with the mixture of music and video. Just as Bart and I had felt creating the pieces.

The Fragile Future—

As with most of our tours, disaster stalked continuously. On our second day on the road in Dayton, Ohio, as we left our motel to go to dinner, the rear wheel of our wonderfully reliable 17-year-old Honda Wagon decided to disconnect itself from the strut (we suffer from terminal rust here in the Northeast), and roll in a different direction from where we were going…That night we combed the newspaper, and in the two-hour slot we had available the next morning before our drive to St. Louis, we bought a new Toyota Matrix. In the typical style of the

McLeans, we were throwing the huge pile of equipment and baggage into the car as the attendants were frantically scrubbing off the "for sale" decals and the manager was drawing up the contract. But we drove in style to St. Louis!

Four weeks later, after an intense but very successful tour, along with laboring under a continuous head cold and fiery red facial fungal rash, late the last night on the way home through Syracuse, NY, I was outracing a would-be car thief who had seen the dealer's plates and decided that this was the model for him…In James Bond-fashion, we veered off the road onto an exit, turned off our lights and snuck through the gas station's rear truck entrance and back onto the highway, just as the villain was entering the front of the same station! I was shaking all over, but the thief had been deflected.

Returning from that very intensive 2002 tour, Bart became quite ill from an intestinal bleed, and almost died on the way to the hospital! He had ignored the bleeding and had been digging up hemlock trees and replanting them around our house, and then calmly driving to the doctor's, even gassing up the car on the way! Right after he called me to announce that he would be placed in the hospital, he passed out in the doctor's arms, with no pulse. He had lost a quart of blood, and Dr. Hearst carried him over to the hospital (in a wheel chair), just next door to the office. It is amazing how kind people can be if you have no health insurance (at least at first). But Dr. Hearst is a living Dr. Marcus Welby, always kind.

Bart lay in the hospital for the next four days, while I rescued the garden and wondered about how close *"Autumn Requiem"* had come to resembling our own demise…We are such fragile creatures, filled with a river of blood and mysterious "underground" life forces that can go at any time, and we are so complacent about it. I know that Bart's life is so entwined with mine, that his death would destroy large parts of me, perhaps forever. Perhaps the well of creativity itself would be drained. Over the summer, Bart completely recovered. A blood vessel had broken in his colon. He has the benign sacs of diverticulosis, as does 50% of the American population after the age of 65. Somehow, the blood vessel had gotten squeezed or twisted among the sacs, probably from falling during skiing or hiking, as Bart had had pain since January. We must always be mindful that the cliff edge is near and threatening…

I completed the video work to *"July Dance"* just before we left for Rocky Mountain National Park in Estes Park, northern Colorado in August, where I was Artist-in-Residence for two weeks. For the first time in my life, I was selected to create a new piece (music video) as a video artist! So the life of an artist goes on. We live from piece to piece, creating and performing and trying to honor our mortality before all is lost. Some of us are lucky (and frugal) enough to not have to work at jobs not involving our art. But even performance is a full-time job, with selling oneself and lining up engagements. We try to keep in touch with our life source of nature as best we can. I have mostly accepted my place in the world, which is to be the wanderer, following my own special light, never in tune with the world at large. In summers, alone on a mountain top I feel the interconnectedness of all beings, and know that if my voice is a small one and hardly heard, it is still filling in the web which holds us all together. And faintly, when I feel happiest, I sense the large "I" that our inner selves are, and spread my hands and arms to embrace the sky, the world, the mountains, the many people who are One—*the very being of life itself!*

4

Dangling Thoughts

"There is no use trying," said Alice, "I cannot believe impossible things." "I dare say you haven't had much practice,"said the Queen."When I was your age, I always did it, for half an hour a day. Why, sometimes I've believed as many as six impossible things before breakfast."

— *"Through the Looking-Glass" by Lewis Carroll*

Creating is all about manifesting the impossible from the trackless void, and bringing it to life. Nowhere is this more evident than in composing, and even then, the sounds floating in the air are still magically not visible. It takes a huge leap of faith to pull something together from nothing, and the blank piece of paper or the blank computer screen can be very intimidating indeed.

Over the years in my private journals I have gathered thoughts and memories that float like flotsam, but may help to flesh out the image of an artist's life. For what they are worth, I add some of them here—some serious and profound, and others humorous, silly, and perhaps for all that, even more profound! For those patient readers who have gotten this far, I say, Enjoy, and think kindly on us, the slightly askew dreamers in this world, walking not only to different drummers, but inventing the rhythms as we go...

1.

INSIDE THE MIND OF A (WOMAN) COMPOSER

from August 2, 1989 Journal: "...My *Kingdom* for an idea...The piece *("The Dance of Shiva")* began with a wonderful sample of a live Buddhist chant, then glissandos I had performed on the unfettered autoharp (no chord bars) rose in cascading waves, added to by a sitar (performed for me by a member of the Indonesian gamelan ensemble at the University of Hawaii during my semester there as

223

visiting Professor of Music in 1985), processed through the sometimes-working analog Eventide Harmonizer. This rose to a glorious climax, and died out to a fake "didgeridoo"—me on a kazoo lowered two octaves–and a "bass viol" sound on the TX 81Z (digital synthesizer), plus bumblebee.

"Then phrases whispered by me—text from an old unfinished choral piece about mountains, specifically Mt. Everest, and native American philosophy along with Buddhist philosophy. These sampled on different keys sound like a choir of voices, including men's. Then drums—again from the Hawaiian gamelan ensemble played by myself...

"The title 'Dance of Shiva' or 'The Dance of Shiva' comes to mind. But—is it too high rolling? Will the Hindu world be after me with knives, like the Moslem world is pursuing Salman Rushdie?! Am I 'taking the Lord's name in vain'? Will the Buddhists be after me for using their chants as a tribute to a Hindu God, written by a Christian? Am I a hypocrite?

"Wow—what a weight. Think I'll stick with *'Pris: New Piece '89'* for now!"

◆   ◆   ◆

August 3, 1989: "It's really frustrating. I am very advanced creatively, and a technical dunce. Out of the first two hours in the studio this morning, 1:45 were taken up with flubbing technically, and :15 with some mildly creative work. I have a burning idea—I can barely wait to 'get it down on paper'...several hours of numbers, patches, and disks later my idea has almost completely vanished. I should call this piece *'The Vanishing Hands of Shiva'!*

◆   ◆   ◆

August 21, 1989: "Vagabonds. People think of us as vagabonds. Their opinion: 'Look at the two of them! Holing up on a God-forsaken dirt road in an ancient rental farmhouse, where to get to it one has to dodge sixty-seven potholes and one attack goose, ambling deer, mulling wild turkeys and any old thing that might jump out into the road! The woman—forty-seven years old, can be seen swimming with beavers in the tea-colored mucky farm pond, in the middle of a field of goldenrod. Any time of day you can drive by and see one or both of them sitting on the front porch by the peeling painted porch columns—don't they ever go to work? And the man—white beard, bare of chest, he spends his day picking raspberries in the viney overgrown fields near the house, or hiking up the nearby hills.'

"People drive by, heads shaking. 'What a way to spend one's life! They hide out in the large ex-bedroom in the front of the house, converted to a giant electronic playpen, and every day for several hours one of them creates music that nobody is even slightly interested in. No insurance—health, house, or goods—no sense of adult responsibility—how dare they defy American standards of the work ethic: children, retirement policies, paid vacations, burial plots, accident insurance, life insurance, health insurance, equipment insurance, insurance to ensure continued success? Disgusting vagabonds.'"

◆   ◆   ◆

July 11, 1989: "Ah, the studio. Curse of my life, yet a blessing. Simon Legree, yet emancipator. Pain and misery, frustration, anger—yet, joy. Since 1976 I've worked in my own studio, creating electronic music. My first tape piece was created in 1970, in a summer course on electronic music at Indiana University, made in a 12-hour blaze of inspiration, and I named it *'Experimental Landscapes'*. It was an amazingly good 'beginner's luck' piece, but of course raw, thin, and naive. But I knew. Sitting with our two-channel Sony tape recorder in our graduate student summer apartment, feeling the first joy and thrilling wonder fill my head and body—I knew—this was it. Like marriage, it was Love.

"John Cage had written *'Imaginary Landscapes'*, but I was unaware of it. Pretty much unaware of him, also. From a boiling coffeepot, a microphone, mayonnaise jar, Moog (synthesizer) cascading bubbles in 1970—to 1989, almost twenty years later. How, progress?

"No more Moog. We never did own one—got into Arps by 1971, our first electronic purchase, the Arp 2600. Good old Arp. How I loved Thee—let me count the ways! What electronic piece did I create, except *'Dance of Dawn'*, that didn't use at least *one* sound from the Arp? *'Invisible Chariots'*, *'Night Images'*, *'The Inner Universe'*, *'Ah-Syn!'*—Arp 2600 and autoharp processed through it—I toured with that piece from 1975 to 1979, *'A Magic Dwells'*, and even the siren sound in *'O Beautiful Suburbia!'* in the Wilderness set, plus the pedal tone in *'Invocation'*.

"But with our new digital stuff, we needed the room. Arp was old and drifting, scratchy. Bart put it in the attic. I snuck it to the corner wall of the studio, to use ostensibly for 'test tones', but really for moral spirit. A foil against all those bright, blinking new digital eyes and numbers. Alas, Bart put it back in the attic. I must go it alone, facing the revolution without Arpie, facing the torrent of cold, metallic eyes that have no mercy.

"Back to the original question—how have I progressed from 1970 to 1989? Well, today I worked with the Prophet 2000 and 2002 (sampling digital synthesizers), with spiraling masses of an autoharp pluck and double glissando, a kazoo sounding like a didgeridoo, a bumblebee inside a (you guessed it) mayonnaise jar! You can take the *musique concrete* away from the old electronic composer, but you can't take the composer…We've turned full circle with the new sampling equipment…"

◆   ◆   ◆

August 25, 1989: "A stretch of four workdays in the studio:

"*1ˢᵗ day:* Waking at 8 a.m., you dawdle over breakfast, pushing the awful moment of confrontation away as long as possible. Maybe the piece is horrible. What was it I created last week? Bart is doing *fantastic* things on *his* days in the studio—*much* better than my ideas…maybe I am 'all used up' ('she peaked early').

"Do dishes. Make beds. Put mail away. Straighten up couch. Stare at dust…no, that goes too far. Finally, one has to face the Mirror of Truth.

"But—the studio is an alien place; all the equipment has been set to accommodate Bart's music. Another hour is lost resetting the computers and processors, unpacking tapes, getting out sketches, loading the disks. You ponder over an idea for a new section—should I listen now to the piece up to where it stops?—not yet, not yet. I'll set up this new sound, to be ready to play on the Prophet as the end of the tape comes, so I'll see if it is suitable for the next part…

"Amnesia has happened in the three day's absence. Now why won't the Prophet sound? Synchronizer work? TX 81Z receive the program? Etc. etc.. The new sound takes until 1 p.m. to set up.

"Lunch time—out into the blazing sun on the picnic table, reading Joseph Campbell's *'The Hero of a Thousand Faces'*, a wonderful book on mythology through our use of heroes. The catbird thinks it owns the backyard, and meows angrily. The petunias are climbing up the birdbath and rollicking with the mums and blue flowers. Crickets hum. Lord, it is too pleasant here. You lose all ambition, head bangs indolently on table in an impromptu nap. But—duty calls. You enter the dark, cold house with heavy heart…

"Back in the studio, you march to the recorders, flick them on, and resolutely listen to the whole piece. The beginning goes well. You mess up the levels in the middle, and forget to play the new sound at the end point (it doesn't fit, anyway).

The whole piece rolls along—how can it just utterly grind to a halt like that—like a cliff yawning after the last note?

"So the day goes. The re-acquaintance of the first day is hard, hard.

"*2nd day:* A sound or group of sounds is carefully constructed, shaped, tried out successfully against the completed tape. A long day of dials, numbers, levels, disks, sliding pots…tedious and nerve-wracking. By six p.m. your nerves are shot and ears are haggard. A dip in the icy pond is too much to bear, so you stagger out of the house and visit the peeper tadpoles with new little legs in the watery ditch up the road.

"*3rd day:* You awake at 7:30 a.m. with a clear head and ravenous desire to compose. By 9:30 you are in the studio, efficiently starting everything up. Today you record—first playing each new sound on the sequencer, playing the sequencer again with the tape, moving the sequence to the time desired in alignment with the tape, improvising the next sound in synchrony with the tape, playing it back, eliminating or modifying some of the notes, becoming a whirling dervish of frenzy playing the parts—not human anymore but the *Goddess of Music*, creating your universe, unaware of time, place, Bart, hunger, cold—anything but the molten *Sounds* being shaped into music.

"Then you stand by the recorders and listen to the whole piece so far unfold. No, you don't stand. You writhe, squirm, grimace, hold breath, pound the table, raise fists to the ceiling, jot down ideas, boil. It works! It works—it *works—IT WORKS!!!!!*…so far…

"*4th day:* 8:30 a.m. you slither out of bed, eyes like slits. Breakfast takes too long. You are tired to the marrow. Does Bart want to use the studio today? No? It's my day? Oh. You mean I have to equal that boiling maniac of yesterday? Maybe more coffee will help…

"The studio sends out warm messages of friendliness. You discover (with relief) that you didn't have time to write down the patches and settings used yesterday. This takes hours, again delaying the crucial and feared listening until after lunch. But your spirit is buoyant and confident. By afternoon you are diagramming a new section, and beginning to make new sounds, perhaps recording live and sampling. This is fun—the best part of composing. Other potential pieces burst into your mind with the new samples, which you mentally note for later.

"By 5 p.m. you stop, changing into hiking clothes, and head up a nearby small mountain, barely aware of being outside for the first half of the time. Bart has gone into the studio to use the word processor in your absence—he's always using Mac when you leave the studio, but like the catbird, you meow softly while keeping a safe distance.

"The woods are lovely, dark, and deep. Bear turds. Deer tracks. Here at the end of August many birds have left already, and only the crickets fill the void. At the top of Poplar Hill, you sit on the moss, looking down into tiny Petersburgh, and feel fulfilled. The piece is good so far. Maybe only you care and Bart cares. It will never win a Pulitzer Prize, play on TV, be a household word, be heard by a large number of people who would love it, be considered as important as a Brahms Symphony, but it is cognizant of your spirit's creative expression and it satisfies...You."

◆   ◆   ◆

Sept. 13, 1989: "A Composer's Unsung Patrons"

"Everyone knows about the major 'patrons': the National Endowment for the Arts, the state arts foundations, the performer or organization who commissions the composer, the Meet the Composer funding organizations, and many others. But, as great as these are, an artist or composer would have a hard time surviving on just these few and sporadic philanthropists, without the others.

"What others, you say? The ones I call 'unsung'—the 'little' patrons that help an artist at just the right time, or give him/her that little necessary boost—the ones who pull a composer through this rough, uncaring world.

"Here are a few I can think of that are angels-in-disguise for us. Our landlady, for one. Two-story farmhouse with livable basement and attic on 300 acres of land, pond, nearly deserted road, and quiet neighbors, all for $450 a month. And the 200-year old house is so soundproof that we can both compose simultaneously in rooms at opposite ends, and not hear each other. This is a *rare* house! Mathilda (Congdon) likes us, and she respects our choice to be independent artists, so she holds the lid on the rent.

"Another patron I encountered yesterday at the office supply store in Bennington, Vermont (Business World) where I do most of our score copying. I had worked all afternoon unaided, copying over 500 pages of legal-sized scores. She, the clerk who has seen me there very often and who admires our work, dropped the charge from ten cents a page–the advertised price–to three cents, saving me over $40. I gasped when she asked for $17.63, and she blushed and said, 'Well, you work so hard, and we don't have to help you on the machines!'

"Then there is the neighbor who buys all your records and goes to your concerts. The neighbor/friends who threw a party for us after our McLean Mix debut with the Albany Symphony in the premiere of *'Voices of the Wild'*. Moral support—so important, and overlooked.

"Then last year there was the local political reporter who felt that a music premiere should be reviewed, and since the newspaper couldn't afford a music reviewer, he would do it, even though he knew little about music and nothing about new music. This was an important event, and shouldn't be overlooked! So the Bennington Choral Society got its first-ever review, and my *'In Celebration'* (for six-part chorus, piano, conga drum player and recorded tape) got a genuine Yankee New England all-time unlettered enthusiastic review that was so naive in its optimism and delight that I was blushing, but so charming that it helped me through the endless rejections the choral piece later received from somnolent conductors. That review was soul-food.

"Then there are all of the dear people who put up wandering performer/composers for the night during our tours, who save us so much money that we would otherwise spend on lodging and meals–like more traditional performers–that we may have had to give up touring. The overly busy wife who has a family and full-time job, who leaves us a casserole to slip in the microwave; the teachers who have to get up at dawn, but who have everything laid out for you when you 'fly' in from your concert at 1 a.m., or who are often waiting up for you or who have even helped you pack up after the concert. The loyal friends at universities and other venues who hire you over and over, sometimes seven or eight times, because they believe in your music and what you are doing, and help you stay afloat year after year. Where would we be without these patrons, the ones who really make you feel that it *is* worthwhile."

2.
STUDIO AND TOURING AXIOMS

From July and August 1989 Journal entries:

1. Musique concrete was mysterious for an audience in past years. One could alter familiar sounds via the tape recorder or analog synthesizer, and come up with a disguised sound, which fascinated people. Nowadays, people are not stirred by mysterious sounds created through the computer. The computer is capable of doing anything, so why be excited? Now, if one uses a sampled sound, people want to know if it is the "real", original sound, which will

allow them to get excited again—as long as it's not made or altered by a computer!

2. If you have 167 pieces of equipment, and you need to use only three, one of the three will malfunction. Add to this Larry's Law:[42] "If you can demonstrate how it works, it won't!"

3. Watching the back of an organist performing in a church is similar to watching loudspeakers during a tape composition, which is very like watching a composer perform on digital equipment during a "live" electronic piece (This was discussed with William Albright, nationally famous composer and organist, who laughingly agreed with this picture)!

4. The difficulty of the artistic endeavor is inversely proportional to the amount of money involved. I.e., an orchestral commission for me recently was $2,000 (from the Womens Philharmonic in San Francisco). *"Rainforest"*, our McLean Mix installation, will eventually net us $100,000 or more.

5. Famous Last Words: "This set-up is going so easily, we'll have *plenty* of extra time (to go to dinner, relax, warm up, etc.)!"

6. The larger the hall, the smaller the audience (quote from host: "I don't understand it—we put up posters all over the place!").

7. The larger the media audience-potential, the more botched up the interview. Example: In 1982 I had a telephone interview with NPR's "All Things Considered" because of receiving a large NEA composer grant. Broadcast all over the country was an excerpt of my *"Beneath the Horizon III"* for tuba solo and taped whale ensemble—played *backwards*.

8. *Written on Feb. 15, 1990:* Some circumstances can be intensely disappointing or golden opportunities. Example: Our computer has been down for a month. So instead I wrote six very satisfying songs for voice and piano, and am designing two brochures/posters for new McLean Mix ventures. One can fuss and brood over lost or ailing equipment/time/body parts, or use it as a springboard for learning or doing something different, or meditation and renewal...

9. Humankind feels its own stupendous importance, but the *real* super-animal is the virus...cockroaches are second.

10. No matter how much oat bran you eat, you are still (eventually) going to die.

11. One comes naked into the world, spends decades amassing giant quantities of everything, ensuring immortality, and then exits life—naked.

12. How many songs can we hum that are 2,000 years old? The human being has been here for seven million years...

A Few On the Road Thoughts with The McLean Mix (1985)—

"March 3, 1985, Midwest tour: Six days from home. Typical questions at receptions—'Petersburgh? Where's that?' 'Near Williamstown, Mass.—beautiful country, accessible to colleges, dirt road, farmhouse, mountains...inexpensive living...technical help...coyotes—really ideal!' 'Oh. Well...I kind of like living near Columbus and enjoying the plains...dirt road, eh?'

'This piece has music by...whales? I read about a whale once in the *National Geographic.* Oh yes, that's a picture of the ocean, isn't it? I read about the ocean once in the *National Geographic*...'"

Five days from home: "Bart—isn't it improper to stretch our suitcase out in the middle of the highway to find my hair curlers? Isn't that your suit coat blowing down the road in this 80 mph wind at 32 degrees with my hair rollers...and this car three inches from my hip honking, and my wet hair trying to blow away with the rollers? Bart? Where are you? Honda??"

Famous McLean Mix Tour Meals—

"*Breakfast:* an orange, turning greenish white on top (three days at bottom of food bag in hotel room), tortilla chips (from last night's 'celebration' with a bottle of beer, watching the eleven o'clock news in hotel room, Bart asleep on the bed and all our hosts gone home after waiting 45 minutes for us to break down and pack up all our gear, losing hope), industrial-strength granola loaded with Drano bran and dried milk plus spoiling evaporated milk, instant coffee flecked with said rotting milk.

"*Lunch:* If with hosts—*huge:* reubens, salad, brownie ala mode, coffee...If alone—peanut butter and sliced apple sandwiches made in hotel room, tortilla chips, coffee and rotting milk, buns filched from reception the night before (note: reception for the university percussion ensemble, not *The McLean Mix*), chocolate from pocketbook.

"*Dinner while rehearsing:* Takeout varies: horrible Greek spicy souvlakies on soggy pita bread, frozen yogurt (and stuffy nose from milk intolerance), cold

French fries, chocolate milkshake (and stuffy nose), or: cold baked potato with congealed "beef stroganoff" (instant gravy, three mushrooms, and one canned piece of pot roast beef), milkshake (and nose…) or: cold vegetables on soggy pita, milkshake, etc. etc. plus mashed linty chocolate from aromatic pocketbook, and vitamins.

"Reception after Concert: Varies—98% of time: 1 bottle of beer from Seven/ Eleven store, tortilla chips (in front of TV), Bart asleep…1.5% of time: red fruit punch with one ice cube, stale cookies and iced cakes (for McLean Mix reception, on loan from last night's percussion ensemble reception, the buns having gone), 50 eager students, 1-2 yawning professors…1/2% of time: one dark beer in pub with falling-asleep host who bravely survived our equipment breakdown. This is the best, although it only lasts a half hour, as said host passes out…"

Famous McLean Mix Subtle Moments On-stage

Bart talking to audience: "Paul Winter has a real cute way of introducing his latest recording during his concerts." Arm raises, clutching McLean Mix CDs: "However, I have no cute way."

Me, after a possibly jarring avant-garde piece: "Please don't leave! Our concerts are varied, and the next piece is quite different—you might even like it!"

Bart, preparing the audience for *"The Last Ten Minutes",* an electronic piece describing the last ten minutes of human existence before the Holocaust: "Before I perform this piece, I usually warn the audience about having small children stay through this piece, as it may prove frightening. However, this audience is so sophisticated, that I do not even have to mention such a problem!"

Me, during question and answer session afterwards: "Was I in England when I wrote *"Wilderness"*? Because it sounds European? (even the wolf howls?) Is that because it doesn't sound like jazz or pop style? And would our music sell well for a science fiction film? *Is that a stupid question?* No, *many* people ask that question, and I don't mind answering it again and again and again…"

3.
DROPPING (FAMOUS) NAMES

1. John Cage

John Cage has become one of the best known American composers, a guru of modern music, and someone who experimented and created in just about every medium invented up to the time he died, influencing most composers, regardless of their style. He was not accepted in academic circles until later in his life, probably because he made his reputation outside of any university, in the world of dance and performance. My first encounter with John Cage was as a graduate student in 1969 at Indiana University, when he came as a guest lecturer for the Composition Seminar, a weekly meeting of all composers and faculty on the fourth (top) floor of the circular music building. The week before that event we had heard Pierre Boulez[43] speak, a very urbane and intellectual performance that created a worshipful respect in the young listeners.

This afternoon Mr. Cage appeared, a bit "tipsy" (this was before his giving up of liquor and adhering to the macro-biotic diet for which he later became famous)—and proceeded to weave toward the brand new Busendorfer grand piano, waving a lighted cigarette with a long ash over the magnificent glistening black ebony piano lid. As he lectured on his chance technique of composition, all of the students leaned forward with great anticipation to see if the ash would fall on the sacrosanct piano lid, and unfortunately, were too engrossed with a gleeful dread to hear anything Mr. Cage actually said. Finally, when it seemed that the ash could not possibly grow any longer before succumbing to gravity, Dean Wilfred T. Bain (sophisticated and erudite head of the School of Music) came dashing forward with an ashtray to barely catch the errant ash, while Cage muttered, "Oh, yes, my cigarette…thanks!" and continued on lecturing as if a busboy had just run up, while we all suppressed our joyous pent-up giggles. I think that act of Cage's endeared him to every student in the hall for many years afterwards!

The next time I encountered John Cage was when I was a contributing reporter for *"Musical America"* Magazine, at the 1981 International Computer Music Conference held at the University of North Texas, where I roamed around from November 5-8 attending and reviewing concerts and events. To celebrate the Conference, the university sponsored a mega-event—an enactment of *"HPSCHD"*, the collaboration of Lejaren Hiller and John Cage in a giant multimedia spectacle, held for four hours in the University Courtyard. This was perhaps the most elaborate mega-event inspired by a computer up until that time, with seven harpsichordists on three balcony levels performing in overlapping cycles, backed by a mix of fifty-one electronic sound tapes using insistent repetitious bleeps, and the projection of over five thousand slides on at least seven screens, and several films. I wandered around, interviewing both Mr. Hiller and Mr. Cage amid the boisterous, noisy, milling crowd. It occurred to me then, while watching Cage discussing his macro-biotic diet surrounded by avid students, how truly humble and serene he had become since I had seen him last.

Two years later the McLean Mix performed on the 1983 North American New Music Festival at the State University of New York at Buffalo, which turned out to be one of the most interesting American festivals of new music in which I have ever participated, with a potpourri of well-known composers of new and electronic music—Morton Subotnick, Joan LaBarbara, Henry Brant, Lejaren Hiller, Morton Feldman, Larry Austin, Ben Johnston, Canadian Murray Schafer, and many others—and John Cage, who had a concert of his works two nights after our concert. (Later we learned that when the concert committee had planned to include five hours of his music on Cage's concert, he had said wistfully, "Isn't that too much music? Why would anyone want to sit through *five hours* of my music? *(sigh)*". At Hiller's home party for the guests, Cage sat quietly by himself. I timidly circled around him, but only said hello. The day after our concert, Cage came up to us and said, "You're the McLeans, am I right? Hello. I am John Cage, and I really enjoyed your music last night." I felt ashamed that he had had to break the ice, because he was so famous we were afraid of him! So were others, and he was alone much of the time.

There has been much written about John Cage, his music and philosophy, which I won't duplicate here. I write only to give a few personal glimpses from my contacts with him (and others forthcoming). In 1984 I was to spend a week at the Charles Ives Center for new music in New Milford, Connecticut, from August 12-19. The Pittsburgh New Music Ensemble conducted by David Stock was the performing group, and a piece I had written entitled *"Elan! A Dance to all Rising Things From the Earth"*, for flute, violin, 'cello, piano, and two percussion was my featured work. Each invited composer would hear two rehearsals and a performance of her(his) work while attending the performances of everyone else's music. John Cage had been invited as "master composer" to give lectures and a premiere of a new work.

Since this is the last time I ever saw him, and I talked many times with him over the course of a week, and near to the end of his life, I will quote from my diary at the time: (During one of his morning lectures) "John Cage said he never could hear harmonies, so he turned to rhythm as his main interest. Arnold Schoenberg (his teacher at University of Southern California) told him that without a tonal sense, he would come against a wall, and never go beyond it. Cage replied, 'Then I shall beat my head against the wall.' He says he has decided to write pieces that can be performed—to live on after him because he 'is getting nearer the end' and wants to leave something behind.' Very wise man—he never insults, backbites, criticizes—you cannot trap him into saying something negative...He always floats above, looks beyond, converts it into a positive, helpful thought. If trapped, he says nothing. Never wastes words. Never repeats himself. He floats above people, too. Seems to be aloof-friendly. Comes from being so famous, I guess." He made us all smile when he complained, smiling, about his refrigerator. "I wish I could do something about the noise it makes. It echoes through my whole apartment, and no matter how I try to meditate the sound away, it is still there!"

His premiered piece, *"Music for Six"* (Bb clarinet, flute, violin, 'cello, piano, and percussion, all spread around the hall) fascinated me, because the pianist was leaning into the piano harp and bowing the strings with fishlines, and because of the hot, muggy evening, the tones came out fuzzy and hauntingly strange, in contrast to the other instruments. I complimented him afterwards on the beautiful piano color, and he said he had been completely shocked by the gumminess of the rosined nylon lines, not at all expecting those sounds. After *"Music for Six"* had played for a half-hour, an irate elderly man in the audience stood up and loudly shouted, (just before the piece was to end), "It's ten after ten (p.m.)!" which added a great Cagean spirit to the ending. John Cage was not amused. He may have been a composer of "chance" music, but he expected the performance to be as perfect a rendition of the score as possible, minus verbal outbursts.

The last words to us composers informally were that Cage wished his life were not so frenetic. He had too many commissions and no time to reflect, a position that seems so enviable to most of us, yet I understand too well that the spirit needs time to ponder and just be, without all the notes floating by...

2. Henry Brant

Henry Brant is a true American composer. He is an original, an individual voice following his own Muse, going where no one else can follow. He has created dozens of works for very large mono-ensembles, such as a piece for 90 trombones, or *"Rosewood"* for 100+ guitars, along with varied ensembles, but always unusual combinations. I had known him only from the contemporary music history books when one day I opened my front door in Austin, Texas, where we were living in 1982, and he was standing there with a friend we knew, who introduced us. My first surprise was to discover that this man with the giant conceptual mind was only slightly taller than myself, (5 feet 4 inches tall), and wearing a railroad conductor's cap.

Then followed a fascinating hour and a half of conversation. He had heard of us and wanted to meet us. It was pure serendipity, because we had decided to move from Austin to the Northeast the following year, but had not yet pinned down a location. We were going to try touring for a while, so were free to live wherever we cared. Henry was teaching at Bennington College in Vermont, which had an incredible avant-garde music department at the time, with many well-known composers and performers living in the area and commuting from New York City. He enthusiastically raved about Bennington and the whole region, and worked on persuading us to move there as soon as we could. In retrospect, he had the most influence of anyone in convincing us to choose our home where we have been now for the last twenty two years, which is two towns away from Bennington and the college he loved so much (Ironically, as he persuaded us to move there, he retired and moved to California with a new young wife who could hit the highest notes I have ever heard).

Henry was not so interested in talking about himself and his famous music as he was about drilling us (and he wrote down the answers!). Why had we chosen electronic music? He disliked any medium that would constrict the area of the sounds, choosing for himself vast spaces to spread out his giant ensembles, which he said could never be realized in one's living room coming from loudspeakers—which of course in the end he had to settle for, since carrying around ninety trombones can grow old very quickly...Was our music spiritually influenced (yes)? And on and on...I had never been around any composer who was more interested in me than in himself! But I have noticed that the more well known the composers, the more humble and modest they are when met in person. I liked him instantly.

Just a year later we shared a festival with him in Buffalo, which brought together John Cage, Morton Feldman, et al in the North American Music Festival. At the party hosted by Lejaren (Jerry) Hiller, Henry Brant lectured Bart and me nose-to-nose in a rousing description of the perfect acoustical concert hall, and how to create a portable one for our touring. As he stood there wildly gesturing, his eyes flaming, I was reminded of a pixie Harpo Marx (without the wig), and marveled at the immense energy of this septuagenarian. Three nights later, at one of the most exciting concerts I have ever heard—a 50-year retrospective of his music—as I saw him dueling at the piano with the great concert pianist of contemporary music Yvar Mikhashoff, in *"Hand Organ Music"* from 1933, I realized that his energy came from his great love of life and music. Wonderful!

Two concerts, back-to-back, of John Cage and Henry Brant—it was almost too much to bear! Henry ran around the hall in his conductor's hat and jacket, now playing the piano, now conducting different ensembles scattered all throughout the hall, with his new wife Amy standing in the balcony adding a piccilino voice line to much of the varied musical offerings.

·Here is a paragraph from the review by Andrew Stiller (*Buffalo Evening News*) the day after the concert: "*'Inside Track'* is a much more substantial work. Here there is a circus band (with pixillated valkyrie) in the organ loft, string assertions on the left, woodwind ditto on the right, and manic, virtuoso piano (Yvar Mikhashoff) with chimes, xylophone, and abstract slide projections (from eight carousels): front and center. Just when you think you have it figured out, the winds and strings switch to playing palm-court music, then a final rhythmic unison for the whole group. A vastly entertaining piece, hugely applauded."

I have never heard again a concert like that one. And I doubt if I ever will again. Brant is too original for this world, too impractical (can the spirit be contained in a music box?). Henry moved to San Jose, California soon after this concert. We saw him once again in a commissioned premiere of *"Bones"*, using space, choirs and many unusual instruments at a church associated with Skidmore College in Saratoga Springs, New York several years later. It again was a fascinating piece, probably never performed again. Henry talked to us at length, now in his eighties, just as lively, with another new young wife by his side. Go, Henry—for all of the music world less courageous than you and your sprite-like child-spirit!

3. Henry Cowell

Henry Cowell was another great inventor, another American original, who lived slightly earlier than the two just mentioned. He had been brought up on the West Coast, and the Asian influence is heard in much of his music. He was also a child-like pixie who was endlessly fascinated by all kinds of music, and wrote over a thousand works. Not believing in revising, he would sit down and write another piece instead. He taught summers at Eastman School of Music, Rochester, New York, and my husband Barton McLean studied and worked with him. Here are some of Bart's personal observations:

"He did not teach composition in the traditional sense, although he did go through the motions of examining each student's work in a small composition class. Even so, his presence made a tremendous impression on me, because of what he was and did, not what he taught. We (some of the other composers and I) were fortunate to have many dinners with him and his charming wife Sidney at the Eastman dorm, where we and they resided during the summers. Hearing him talk about the early days when the composers' organizations were forming, his work with Cage, Edgar Varese, Charles Ives, and a host of other pioneers, and his encyclopedic knowledge of composers' techniques and strategies made a lasting impression. After the dinners, I would go back to my room and try to imprint and absorb his topics of the evening. Also, unlike the other teachers at Eastman, he and his students would get together and play works for each other during evenings at a resident's house. In these sessions, all were equal, including Henry. The final impression I have is of a consummate mentor who had only encouragement and kind words for his students."

Bart also relates how Henry Cowell loved to perform his famous little piece *"The Banshee"*: "When asked by anyone how it sounded, he would enthusiastically approach the first grand piano he was near to, and draping himself over the harp (strings), practically climbing inside, as he was a short man, he would hold the sustaining pedal down while scraping his fingernails along the bass strings the length of the string, usually one at a time. Out would bellow frightening shrieks and moans, startling everyone within earshot, and Henry would laugh, thoroughly enjoying himself." Henry Cowell wrote in all styles and genres, and was a pioneer of "electronic" sounds before there were any.

4. Pauline Oliveros

"Singing is a natural human impulse. Making sounds with objects as extensions of the body is next. Though not everyone will develop to a high level, it certainly should be possible to try and to find encouragement and support for creative activity in music."

—*Pauline Oliveros, from "To Make a Universe of Sound: Four Visions", Paid My Dues Magazine, Summer 1978*

Pauline Oliveros is probably the best-known woman composer in the U.S. if not the world, and has developed a new style of music which involves "deep listening" and "sonic meditation" (names she uses). She engages not only well-trained musicians, but anyone willing to listen to their inner voices and dare to bring music forth, joining others in music meditations. Pauline has written a large body of music of all kinds, is a virtuoso performer of the accordion, and took early retirement from University of California at San Diego to move to New York and become a freelance composer/performer. Since then she travels the world, setting up "deep listening" performances in cisterns in Germany, writing an opera about a black African queen entitled *"Njinga the Queen King"*, premiered at the BAM (Brooklyn Academy of Music) Festival, December of 1993, organizing the New Music America many-day festivals from 1981 to 1987 in major cities around the country, founding the Oliveros Foundation in Kingston, New York where she lives, which sponsors dozens of concerts featuring young composers, and eventually taking her deep listening message back to the university—teaching it as a course at RPI (Rensselaer Polytechnic University), Troy, New York. Which brings her right into our neighborhood.

The first contact I had on a personal level with Pauline was obliquely—she and I both had articles about the "universe of sound" in *Paid My Dues* Magazine, a very short-lived woman's lib magazine that I believe had only the one issue devoted to women musicians. But everyone who read new music books knew Pauline—from her famous picture atop an elephant at the San Diego Zoo. The rest of us wished we had thought up that pose. In fact, many of us continued wishing we had thought up many other very successful ideas of Pauline's. But Oliveros is singular, not to be copied!

She remained a picture in a textbook until 1982, when to our good fortune, she came to Austin, Texas to work on a dance piece with Deborah Hay, who had left Merce Cunningham's Dance Ensemble a few years earlier to freelance in Austin. Bart immediately engaged Pauline and Deborah in premiering their joint venture under the auspices of the University of Texas Electronic Music Center he directed. He found willing top student performers, and they became co-conspirators in a deceptively simple work involving seven notes and six commands, as "merge, listen, soar", etc.

So *"The Well"* was born. After the premiere on Sept. 24, I wrote in my log, "They created a fascinating piece! The dance group was interesting, also, emerging with the sound until all ended in a happy jam session. Lots of fun." The university turned a cold eye to all this, and refused to subsidize in any way Oliveros or the performers. Deborah Hay, the choreographer, already had a Guggenheim grant.

At our house for dinner, Pauline discovered that we were contemplating leaving the academic world for that of touring, and she urged us to dare—she was doing the same, living temporarily in a Buddhist meditation retreat in Mt. Tremper, New York. She was probably the single strongest influence in our decision, having left a comfortable academic position at a very prestigious school at the age of fifty, to step into the abyss...Pauline has always amazed me. A small, round woman who is very spare with her words, she gives the impression of inactivity. But her list of involvements and accomplishments is very, very long, and her list of admirers even longer. She also has struggled with the cold world of rejection, being of that dubious group who are true innovators and also women. In her youthful days she had been angry and blatant, until she embraced Zen Buddhism, and like John Cage, called upon inner resources to change her outlook. When I am around Pauline, I feel an ancient strength and power that is very reassuring.

5. Vladimir Ussachevsky

What person who has even a brief acquaintance with electronic music history in the U.S. has not heard of Vladimir Ussachevsky? He founded the whole classical electronic music scene here in 1951, with a concert of his and Otto Luening's music at Columbia University, dragging their giant Ampex reel-to-reel tape recorder on stage (and, as Vladimir told me many times, permanently injuring his back), and performing the strangest music anyone in New York had ever heard...Mr. Ussachevsky founded the Columbia/Princeton Electronic Music Center, and by the time I got to know him, was also directing the University of Utah Electronic Music Center, flying across country constantly.

His collaborative compositions with Otto Luening earned them world fame, and were a great inspiration to us, as proof that two composers could work together on one piece and not claw each other's eyes out! I had heard of him for decades before our paths ever crossed, but in 1976 during a rare trip to New York before moving to Texas, we visited the Columbia/Princeton Electronic Music Center. Vladimir was warmly cordial, and we ended up having lunch with him at a small Chinese restaurant nearby.

Ussachevsky, we learned later, had grown up in China as the son of missionary parents. When the Communists invaded his small village when he was seventeen, his parents fled, but he stayed to watch over the mission. He ended up spending three days hiding in the large wood stove in the kitchen. The electronic music world can be glad that no one felt the necessity to build a fire! After that, he left China and emigrated to New York, becoming involved in vaudeville to survive...

It is hard to imagine Ussachevsky crammed in a wood stove, because he was a very large Russian, with a strong athletic build. He always had an infectious enthusiasm for everything, and a paternal feeling towards all the new electronic studios springing up around the country. With tremendous energy he flew around the country constantly, visiting studios, encouraging composers, teaching and hearing his works performed. He is the only U.S. composer I know who has had a commission from Iran (and lost it when the Shah was overthrown in the late '70s). During our lunch he laughed and suggested we not try to contact him for a year, because he was about to leave for a residency in Outer Mongolia!

In 1977 I wrote an article for Music Library Association *"Notes"* Magazine in which I described and reviewed a new recording featuring his and Otto Luening's first compositions written in 1952, but it wasn't until the next year that we really became acquainted with him and his lovely poet-wife, Betty. Around that time we were visiting the University of Utah, and I recall matching successive glasses of wine with Vladimir in a small restaurant, while we laughed at everything—the over-serious Mormons, the western American accent, his Russian accent—the plight of electronic music in general—our own over-seriousness!

The next year we drove from Austin to the University of Florida in Miami to attend the ASUC[44] convention, and arrived at the Holiday Inn to have lunch with Vladimir and Betty. He greeted us in his bathing suit, having just swum several laps in the motel pool, and I was taken aback with his handsome physical frame. We kissed hello, and a spark happened that completely surprised both of us. I was reeling—one doesn't feel this way towards a textbook icon and man almost as old as one's father...These feelings we both immediately buried deep inside, never to re-emerge until one day a year later when Vladimir had called about our upcoming concert at Columbia, and murmured wistfully into the phone, "Oh, and are you still beautiful?"

In October 1978, Ussachevsky came to the University of Texas as invited guest composer of Bart's *"Electric Sinfonia"* concert series. This was the second lecture he had ever given here at the university, the first being in 1952, shortly after his revolutionary concert at Columbia. He hovered over Bart's patched-together studio with fatherly interest. As we showed him our own growing home studio, I played my latest piece, *"Invisible Chariots"*, and waited eagerly for his comments, as I felt it was the best work I had ever created up to that time. The first comment he made after it was over was (paraphrased), "Oh, I think Mario Davidovsky is the greatest living electronic music composer, don't you?!" I may have liked Davidovsky's music previously, but at that moment, I despised him and Vladimir both! My self-image dropped to the size of a gnat...I had been involved in the field only a few years, after all, and Ussachevsky wanted to remind me of that, I guess.

The McLean Mix performed on May 2, 1979 at Columbia University's Mac-Millan Hall, the same hall that featured that premiere 1951 electronic music concert. Ussachevsky had been running around putting up posters, having just arrived from his residency in China. It was near the end of a long countrywide flying tour for us, and I was very tired, but felt great pleasure in seeing so many friends in the audience and being part of the history of this place. Afterwards, Vladimir and Betty threw a big reception for us at their spacious family apartment, with the living room Steinway grand piano adorned with a Persian rug (to muffle the sound when he composed), and had wonderful special snacks and wine, while we met and mingled with our friends and the many students from the Electronic Music Center.

I found time the next day to interview Vladimir and Otto Luening for our ASUC Radio Series. As I announced Ussachevsky's last name, I kept mispronouncing it, and we would have to start over. Otto chuckled, "Mic fright." Otto Luening, when asked how it felt to be famous, said (paraphrased), "Fame is a funny thing in this business. One day you wake up famous, and everyone wants to perform your music. Then one day you wake up, totally forgotten, and your music sits in the drawer. Later you wake up famous again, with people doing retrospectives of your music. Soon it will be forgotten again. The important thing is, not to take any of it too seriously." Whenever I was around either man, I could feel the excitement they always had of being the pioneers of a brand new kind of music, the exploration into a world of creativity never dreamt before.

6. Morton Subotnick

During the lowest depths of my public school teaching experience, in 1970, after dragging myself home from a day attempting to teach reluctant fourteen-year-olds how to sing choral music, I would try to reclaim some of my graduate school enthusiasm by listening to classical contemporary music. One evening Bart handed me an album entitled *"Silver Apples of the Moon"*, an actual commissioned Nonesuch record encompassing one long electronic piece by Morton Subotnick. This was before I had had any exposure to electronic music, except for a few student pieces I had heard in Bloomington, and our student soirees where I had heard Edgar Varese's *"Poeme Electronique"*.

I thought that I didn't like this kind of music: I had all the musician's prejudice against "machine sounds", but here was a music that created its own fascinating world. This was not imitation-instrumental, but a new genre altogether. The sounds slid around, swooped up, pinged, bounced, and morphed into a conglomerate unthinkable to my ears! I remember playing this album over and over, alternating with Iannis Xenakis' *"Orient-Occident"*, which also creates its own sound world, but differently. These two albums directly influenced my decision to try this music myself later.

By the time we moved to Austin, Texas in 1976, I was very familiar with Subotnick's next two albums, *"Wild Bull"* and *"Touch"*, the latter my favorite of the three. Bart's first impulse as a new director of the UT studio was to expose his students to professional concerts of electronic music, with the invited guest composer in attendance, talking with the students. On these *"Electric Sinfonia"* concerts, he also included the best of the student compositions—a great learning experience for everyone.

Bart arranged a Symposium of Music and Electronics for a whole week, sponsored by the Texas Union Musical Events Committee, and Morton Subotnick was the featured guest composer from April 3-7, 1978. I was extremely excited—all these years admiring his music, and I was picking him up at the airport!

He brought his pianist, Ralph Greerson, who would perform one of Subotnick's *"Ghost pieces"*—a set of works for amplified acoustic instrument, which when played triggered electronic controls that altered the resultant sounds—along with a new all-electronic work, *"Butterflies"* (I have always admired his imaginative titles, spurring me on to create my own). My first impression of the two men was that they were terribly exhausted. They asked to be driven straight to their motel room to take a nap. While they slept, I waited in the car, and then it was off to the concert hall for rehearsal. After the very successful concert that night, which began with *"Clouds of Sulfur"*, a piano improvisation electronically altered by Subotnick, to a packed auditorium, we gave a big reception for Subotnick, Greerson, and invited guests at our home in the Austin hills. In my Journal I wrote a few impressions of Mort:

"Short, chubby, bearded, with black hair around a large bald spot, with ruddy jovial face and sensitive eyes, about 45 years old, dressed always in a jeans suit...I found him very amiable, very human. He again has that incredible intensity, that pierced-arrow mind (discovered in all composers of high caliber). He bursts with new compositional schemes, radiates a tremendous energy and vitality. He is fascinated with improvisation. Mort described an opera, which is in the conceptual stages. One of the characters is a bird-woman, who cannot fly and cannot communicate, and goes around throughout the whole opera squawking (Note: this was *before* Subotnick married Joan LaBarbara, a virtuoso soprano of avant-garde music). Another character is Death. It sounds very allegorical. I wonder if he will actually write it..."

I was intrigued to find Mort carrying around a small bag of wheat bran, "sprinkling it on everything edible, almost in desperation. He says our (American) diet is too unhealthy, and this helps" (from *Journal*). It is curious how little we creators actually invent just from ourselves...I note here in this journal that in Subotnick's *"Ghost Piece"*, the pianist strokes a superball along the bass strings, and bounces it on the strings—this is also a technique I heard used in Lukas Foss' *"Ni Bruit Ni Vitesse"*, a piece for piano, piano harp, and percussion written in the '60s. Many influences I had forgotten about for my "The Inner Universe", composed in the '80s...

The next morning Morton Subotnick had a discussion with Bart's electronic music class. He stated that a serious composer had to do away with the idea that as soon as (s)he graduated, the money would start flowing in. Instead (s)he had to be prepared to continue living like a graduate student indefinitely, that composing/performing was very, very difficult in this country and liable to pay very little. This shocked the students, but I took it to heart. Those words had a direct effect on our attitude when we gave up the comforts of university artistic life and "hit the road" in '83.

When it was time for Subotnick and his pianist to leave, Bart drove them to the airport. As they were unpacking the car, Bart's key broke off in the trunk, thus locking in our car the famous Buchla Box[45] Subotnick had used for all those wonderful electronic pieces! Mort was frantic. Bart ran into the airport, borrowed a crowbar from the flight staff, and broke open our poor trunk to rescue the Buchla. Ah, what we do for famous composers!

We have, of course, run into and performed alongside Morton Subotnick on several occasions since, even sharing panels and public discussions. When he married Joan LaBarbara, the two performed together for a couple of seasons, and we felt less alone in our touring. Both have been a great inspiration to us over the years, and Mort is a very rare electronic music composer who, beginning in the '60s, had a major record company, Nonesuch Records, commission several albums of his music, as an orchestra would do—thus giving musical legitimacy to a new medium desperately in need of some image. Thank you, Mort, for being there for us all.

7. Vivian Fine

There are very few woman classical composers, a situation drastically changing in this new millennium in Asia, but still very true in the unsupportive U.S.. The field of electronic music has only a handful, most of the women being very young, newly graduated from university. The women I have chosen to write about have influenced me strongly, and I have chosen older women than myself, who have been models for my own life.

I was a member for several years of the American Women Composers, Inc., a U.S. organization that sponsored a magazine and yearly concerts, founded by Tommie Ewert Carl. Vivian Fine was also a member, and so I knew her obliquely. Once, when visiting the American Music Center in New York City in 1976, I was introduced to her in the office (she was there, browsing the library stacks, as was I). "Hello," I said, immediately putting my foot in my mouth, "You must be the wife of (composer) Irving Fine." "No," she glared, "I am just Vivian Fine, all on my own!"

When Bart and I moved to Petersburgh, New York in 1983, we discovered that Vivian lived in the next town from ours–Hoosick Falls, with her artist-husband Ben Karp. She was one of the fireball music faculty at nearby Bennington College whom Henry Brant had praised, where he had previously taught. Every Friday the faculty composer/performers would gather for lunch in Shaftsbury, Vermont, at a restaurant that featured the best New England Clam Chowder on Earth, and we would often join them. When I taught at the University of Hawaii in 1985, while browsing a contemporary music magazine, I noted that of all the orchestras in the country that commissioned new music (and many women composers), The Sage City Symphony of Bennington, Vermont was #1 in numbers of commissioned premieres! Bennington has a population of slightly over 9,000 enlightened hardy souls. At that time, the Sage City Symphony was conducted by Louis Calabro, a dynamic composer/percussionist who taught at the college and was a regular at the luncheons (he tried to commission us, also, but I was in the middle of writing two other orchestral pieces, and had my hands full).

I remember being astounded at the talent who showed up for these luncheons. Joel Chadabe, who later founded the Electronic Music Foundation and was the director of both the SUNY (State University of New York) and Bennington College Electronic Music Studios—who often brought a guest composer from Europe with him, Allen Shawn, active Manhattan composer and his famous novelist African-American wife–Jamaica Kincaid, Lou Calabro, Vivian Fine and husband Ben Karp, among others. Here we ate at a large country table, surrounded by farmers, loggers, tourists, and housewives, while we vehemently discussed, with violent hand gestures, the latest avant-garde technique of composing or performance group, or staff firing at the volatile college...In Vermont, anything is possible, and people took no notice of us. Vivian and Ben were always there, and we renewed our acquaintance in much more pleasant mood than my earlier foot-in-mouth disease at the American Music Center.

Contemporary music was (and mainly still is) everywhere in the small corner area of the three states (Vermont, New York, Massachusetts). Besides the Sage City Symphony, The Vermont Symphony premieres new works regularly, especially Vivian's; the Bennington Choral Society commissioned and performed my "In Celebration[46]etc.." in 1988; there were (and are) new music concerts regularly at Bennington College, along with the several-week Bennington Composers Conference in summers, with festivals of new music spilling out to the high school auditorium. And besides Vermont, there is now Mass MoCA (Mass. Museum of Contemporary Art) in North Adams, several playhouses, Tanglewood, Jacob's Pillow Dance Theatre in Becket, Mass., Williams College, Williamstown Theater, the Clark Art Museum–also in Williamstown, Rensselaer Polytechnic Institute in Troy, NY, Hubbard Hall concert series and La Ensemble professional musicians in Cambridge, NY. All of these places feature new music, art, and dance regularly, plus there are several summer opera companies, all within an hour's drive.

Back to Vivian Fine. I loved her audacity. She had a completely unique background. Born in Chicago of Lithuanian Jewish immigrant parents, she was studying private piano with Ruth Crawford Seeger[47] by the eighth grade in school. After graduating from high school, Vivian did not wait to go to college, but fled to Manhattan where she became a pianist with several dance ensembles, working with Aaron Copland and the Martha Graham Dance Ensemble. When she was twenty she married Ben Karp, an aspiring artist. When Bennington College began in the '30s, they both were hired with a group of other active composers and artists (that included Otto Luening before he moved to Columbia University) to form a dynamic hands-on faculty to inspire great creativity among the carefully chosen students.

Vivian was bold. In her seventies, she marched into the executive office of American Composers Orchestra in Manhattan and convinced Francis Thorne, the director, to commission her to write and perform a piano concerto with the orchestra, which was premiered a year later in 1986. She was married to Ben for over sixty years, with two children, and yet continued to actively compose and to regularly receive performances nationwide—one of the very few women who could juggle marriage, children, composing, a full-time job of piano teaching, and make a name for herself, all with a charming Old World grace and dignity she always had. A true inspiration!

When I was grieving over my mother's entrance into a nursing home, and whether life was worth living for someone old and ill, Vivian, who was only a few years younger than my mother, said thoughtfully, "Sometimes life is worth living if you can still enjoy just a good cup of coffee". She was hard-driven, but incredibly kind to Ben, her husband, and their marriage was one long romance, to the very end.[48] I celebrated her seventy-ninth birthday with her at one of the Bennington composers' luncheons at a new Chinese restaurant in town, and wrote this poem which I gave to her:

> Two Limericks for Your Birthday

> (written for Vivian Fine on her birthday, 1992)

> There is a good friend of mine
> Who has just turned seventy-nine.
> She's made (beautiful) music and song,
> Has a (beloved) husband life-long,
> And her life has turned out so Fine.

> Now I have just turned fifty,
> And my life has been pretty nifty.
> But compared to Vivian
> I haven't begun livian!
> So here's a toast to Women, Song, & Wine!!

8. Carter Harman

Back before computers, CDs, digital tape or videos of any kind, the music phonograph recording industry was very lively. After Morton Subotnick's spectacular success (classically speaking) with his first three electronic music records, the industry looked toward more music of this genre to record. Just before Subotnick's breakthrough came *"Switched-on Bach"* by Walter (now Wendy) Carlos, which crossed the lines and enraptured listeners from pop and classical interests both. Artists from both fields began to look toward electronics in music, which was just about the time we became involved. After I had finished *"Dance of*

Dawn", a twenty-two minute electronic work I had taken over a year and a half to create, Bart had also concluded a twenty-minute piece, "Spirals". We wanted more than the occasional concert performance, so we began sending out copies to several record companies. Columbia Records liked "Dance of Dawn", but wanted me to shave it to eleven minutes total (!), which would have destroyed the whole flow of the piece. I believe they wanted to put out an anthology, with my piece being one of several.

We decided to look into Composers Recordings, Inc. CRI was a small but very active self-help record company founded by Aaron Copland and others to produce music usually overlooked by commercial corporations. It had grown to be a very respectable company with international distribution and an excellent reputation. They accepted our music, and the director, Carter Harman, wrote an enthusiastic note, saying that they planned to make this recording in "quadra-phonic sound", i.e. for four loudspeakers, each in a corner of the room—the lat-est style in the mid-70s. We had created the pieces this way, along with the traditional stereo version, and all our early concerts featured the four-channel sound. Unfortunately, this proved too costly for CRI to do, and the idea evapo-rated, but for several years all our concerts were performed in quad, which was very thrilling to the audience (and composers).

This "golden time" of records featured several idealistic, eccentric, super-charged "pioneer" directors, and I am profiling two with whom we worked. Carter Harman was the first director we came to know, and in September 1975 he wrote to say that our record CRI SD 335, "The McLean Mix: Electro-Surrealis-tic Landscapes" had just been released. This seems unbelievable today, but shortly after its release, we received *ten* reviews from all over the country, from *The Buf-falo Evening News* to *The Greensboro* (North Carolina) *Sun* to *New World Records*, and *Audio Magazine*–national publications. And these were thoughtful, long reviews by intelligent reporters. And this is for two unknown composers living in the Midwest, on a self-help record label...But CRI Records had a strong and loyal following.

Carter Harman developed a novel idea about "Dance of Dawn", that it used musical climaxes in a peculiarly feminine way, and he wrote an article about this. Although (thankfully!) it was never published, he did include it in his press release for our record. Here is one paragraph he wrote: "CRI's recent release of Priscilla McLean's "Dance of Dawn" is a dramatic example of the high quality woman's music has achieved. Not only is it a fascinating composition but it is easily one of the finest electronic works to appear on record in the last few years...Listeners have suggested that her music has an unmistakably feminine character of expression. The piece does not follow the most obvious of subsequent release. McLean's piece is a theater of many smaller musical events, which accumulate excitement and tension in a manner that has been described as distinctly female. Perhaps it is in the electronic medium, unfettered by 'great' historical models, that a woman can best achieve music that is distinctly her own."

I was flattered and honored by his attention, but had never believed that women wrote much differently than men, and I still do not believe it. Often Bart's music seems much more "feminine" than mine, and mine is often hard-driving. But Carter was convinced he was onto something, and a composer never discourages an avid record producer!

We were happy with the recording, all decked in an artistic rainbow of pink and blue. The size of a phonograph record made for extravagant program notes on the outside of the album, the back cover, while the front could have elaborate "cover art". Little CDs cannot match these portable artworks. The next spring, 1976, we traveled to Manhattan to visit CRI, its sister publisher, ACA Publications, and the two performance rights organizations—ASCAP, of which we were both members, and BMI. So we finally met Carter Harman.

From my 1976 Journal: "Carter—a delightful fifty-nine year old kid, full of ideas and enthusiasm—an old face, long white hair, watery eyes under a cap, corduroy tan jacket housing a sleek body, and a gait of a jogger. All energy!" He took us to my first Szechaun Chinese restaurant, and I proceeded to eat a very hot pepper, and spent the rest of the meal drinking quarts of water and dabbing at my streaming eyes.

Carter Harman loved all kinds of music, as a good record producer should, and was a composer himself. Summers he spent creating his own electronic music at the Bregman Studio at Dartmouth College, New Hampshire, working with Jon Appleton, the director and fine composer himself. In those heady days, all of the record producers were active composers who had a deep love of music. The "music biz" was only a secondary thought, at least for a few more years. Today, CRI has ceased to exist. It quietly succumbed in 2003, after 49 years, turning its collection over to New World Records, who is now issuing the converted record-cum-CDs on a single order basis. But for those happy years in the '70s and '80s, it was Saint George (slaying the commercial dragon) to hundreds of composers and university libraries nationwide.

9. Oliver Daniel

Performance rights organizations in the U.S. were formed in the 1930s to protect the creators of music and words against unbridled use of their creations in public places—concert halls, on jukeboxes, radios, or on TV. Without these licensing organizations, a composer's work could be performed at will, providing the performer with his(her) fee or the jukebox provider with the given money, but the creator would receive nothing. Soon the composers and writers would give up this profession for work that paid their bills, because no one can live on nothing...This is especially true of song writers who do not receive commissions. Before these organizations were formed, a work such as Aaron Copland's "Appalachian Spring" would net a modern dance company or record company thousands of dollars' fees for its performance, and zero for Copland!

This was, of course, not the way for a vital music/art scene to survive, so three main performance rights groups were formed—ASCAP (American Society of Composers, Authors, and Publishers), BMI (Broadcast Music, Inc.), and SESAC (The Society of European Stage Authors and Composers). After many legal battles, rules were set up so that each venue playing music by living composers pays a yearly license fee, which enables the different licensing companies to pay performance royalties to composers, writers, and their publishers. Each organization is different in how it treats the classical composer, and first we both joined ASCAP, the largest of the three. ASCAP gives annual "awards" to those members whose music has appeared on large surveys ASCAP uses to sample the myriad performances around the country. This can be a nice supplemental income for a composer who garners a lot of performances, some of which appear on their surveys. Our problem was that we had joined too early, when we were still students, and we had thrown away our music almost as fast as we had written it, after a few non-paying student performances.

I had not received a dime from ASCAP for seven years, even after I began to receive paid performances, when I decided to switch to BMI, a smaller organization which had, I felt, a kinder outlook toward the more esoteric classical music composer, and didn't work with surveys. The composers sent in their cards listing performances, with all the details, and were given "guarantees" based upon the actual paid performances. In 1976, the same time we visited CRI and Carter Harman, we met with the head of the classical music division of Broadcast Music, Inc., Oliver Daniel. We had tried to meet with the head of the classical division of ASCAP, and had spent a frustrated afternoon running around their giant skyscraper office—ASCAP owns the whole building at 1 ASCAP Plaza (not *too* important)—without ever discovering who the classical head was. No one there seemed to know! They shuffled us from office to office. And their surveying system was just as vague. No one could explain how that worked, either. Amazing, for such a large and prosperous organization...

We had heard many tales about the mercurial Oliver Daniel—there was no guesswork on who ran the classical music division at BMI! I had heard he was an evil genie who only supported his favorites, that he was difficult and irascible, that he hated certain composers, and was hardly ever sober, etc. etc.. We were to have lunch with him, and were sitting in his office feeling very intimidated and fearful...

The minute Oliver Daniel walked in, I knew BMI was for me. Here was a *human being*, not a machine full of off-putting secretaries! He greeted us warmly, and ended up treating us to lunch at an expensive restaurant, then upon returning to his office, regaling us with the inner workings of BMI that verged on tales of Scherazade for their bizarre qualities. Daniel said about the composers joining the different organizations, that George Crumb had joined ASCAP about the same time that David Reck had chosen BMI, causing everyone in the business to remark wryly that "the Crumbs go to ASCAP, while the Recks join BMI!"

He also told us about BMI's orchestral catalog. In order to prevent plagiarism, BMI invents composers, complete with full name, orchestral work, number of parts, price, etc.. If these then appear in any other catalog, BMI has a case for suit. So Oliver Daniel listed an "Egyptian" composer with the name M. Tekel Upharson with a piece called the *"Agyptische Symphonie"* for seven strings, twenty-three percussion, and various other weird combinations of instruments, for a piece that was *three* minutes long. The name M. Tekel Upharson is from the book of Daniel in the Bible—the handwriting on the wall, which means "You have been judged and found wanting, and your kingdom will fall"!

Soon, George Szell, conductor of the Cleveland Orchestra, wrote to BMI, asking for this orchestral piece—he wanted to examine it for performance. So the (fictitious) composer wrote back—in Egyptian. Szell answered—and we read his letter in Oliver Daniel's office—"Dear Mr. Upharson: Thank you so much for answering. However, I cannot read Egyptian. Could you please rewrite the letter in either English, French, German, or Italian? Sincerely, George Szell". Another fake name was the counterpart of Italian composer Luigi Nono—Pierre Oui-Oui. And still another has the name of a New York restaurant, and his pieces are listed as: "Suite Gastronomic", etc. Daniel told us that the restaurant has had letters from conductors asking for the music.

So I joined BMI in 1977. By then, the fascinating, eccentric Oliver Daniel had died, and James Roy accepted me into the organization. I have never regretted this, as BMI has paid me many tens of thousands of dollars since, enabling us to continue our commitment to touring. Bart also switched to BMI in 1982, with similar results. Three cheers for these brave organizations that help out the classical composer!

10. Moses Asch

Perhaps the most colorful of all the musicians who started up the independent record companies in the '40s was Moses Asch. Mr. Asch, when a young man, carried his recording equipment all over the world to tribal communities, collecting on tape the precious folk songs and rituals before these groups died out or were changed by the encroachment of "civilization". He came back to New York loaded with tapes, masks, spears, artworks galore, and Folkways Records was born. We met him in 1978, on another of our trips to Manhattan, seeking a willing record producer for our latest electronic music, Bart's *"Song of the Nahuatl"* and my *"Invisible Chariots"*.

First we met with Ilhan Mimaroglu, who headed the Finnidar Records section of the parent company, Atlantic Records. Ilhan is also an electronic music composer, and as we walked in his office door, he sat us down and videotaped us—cold—for a documentary he wanted to make on composers such as ourselves. To this day, I do not know if anything ever came of it, but it was a pleasant surprise to be considered important enough to be videotaped, and we both love talking about ourselves—anytime!

Over lunch together, Ilhan said that all the record companies in 1978 had grown disillusioned with electronic music, because it was not a "hot seller" (did they think it would be?), and even Finnidar, the more adventurous branch of Atlantic Records, would not record any more of this music. All the big companies–Vox, Columbia, Nonesuch, Atlantic–were beginning the long attrition that has now forced all of us to seek small, independent labels or create our own. John Cage about this time issued his own Tomato Records.

Just when we felt the worst, Mimaroglu dropped the other shoe. There was one company still interested. No, more than interested—Folkways Records was actively seeking new electronic music to record, and Mimaroglu had told Moses Asch that we had the "best electronic music in America". In fact, Mr. Asch was waiting for us right now...!

So our next stop was Folkways Records, on the top floor of an old brownstone. Walking into the main office was like a trip to a museum, but it was mild compared to Mr. Asch's private office, where every inch of wall space was covered with spears, masks, weavings, etc., and behind a huge desk, smoking a stogy, looking just like an old Hollywood producer, sat Mr. Asch, puffing the air blue. A large, round man close to eighty, he looked as if he could fire Elizabeth Taylor and not blink an eye. Flanked by all those surreal other-world masks and spears, Moses Asch was truly imposing. What kind of man is this, anyway, we were wondering?

After brief introductions, unlike the unctuous Oliver Daniel who needed hours to relax and get to know his composers, Moses Asch, launched immediately into his pitch, saying (paraphrased), "As Mr. Mimaroglu told you, I want to put out some records of American electronic music, which I consider to be the new "folk music" of America (this seemed a stretch, but I wasn't going to argue). Besides the pieces recommended by Ilhan, I want to commission you to create a teaching album, using your own works and describing the way you go about creating them. We need to preserve this new music here in America while it is still fresh and interesting."

I thought I would drop dead. *Pay us? For making an album on the kind of music we loved the most?* It was too good to be true. Especially when all the other companies were cutting back and canceling. But that was Moses Asch. He had no interest in making loads of money. He wanted to preserve the neglected music of the world, and if all the companies were cutting it out, Folkways would step in and save this music, just as it had done for decades. Their catalog boasted more than 17,000 recordings of world music at that time. We talked a little further, but only slightly about his own exploits. He was too busy to talk about himself, and too old to engage in comfortable lunches and small talk. There was too much worthy music left unrecorded! It would be impossible not to fall madly in love with Moses Asch, the saint with the thick New York Jewish accent and the cigar, surrounded by his African masks.

We made three albums with Folkways, the last featuring the new computer music[49], and then Mr. Asch died. The huge Folkways collection went to the Smithsonian Institute, who now sells converted CDs by special order. Within a few years, all these remarkable men who had pioneered these recording and performance rights companies died, and the industry changed forever.

4.
TO BORNEO, WITH LOVE

This section is an excerpt from two years of monthly articles I wrote which were published in our independent local newspaper, "The Eastwick Press", concerning an opportunity never given to new music composers, unless they are very, very lucky...

Entry in diary, Nov. 1, 1996: "Oh, God, what have we gotten ourselves into?" As already written, we were hired to go to Malaysian Borneo and record nature and tribal music, adding our own composed music to join it all together in a celebration of the oldest rainforest in the world. The apex of this experience was to have been a several-days' visit to the Kenyah tribe in the middle of Sarawak, as these tribal people are renowned for their beautiful music. A student at the university was from the tribe, and offered to be our guide. Hasnul Jamal Saidon and Mohammed Fadzil Abdul Rahman, the video artist and fellow composer had set it up, and were very excited, as we would all go together.

Unfortunately, unknown to us, plans were afoot to creat a gigantic dam in the interior Kenyah lands, and the government was in the process of clear-cutting the primary rainforest there in order to pay for the building of the dam, to be one of the largest hydroelectric projects in the world and to supply all of Malaysia with electricity. An American had snuck into the affected area, photographed it, and had notified the environmental organizations, such as World Wildlife Fund. As a result, Malaysia was on the "black list", damaging its reputation and funding, and besmirching its name around the world.

The government then declared, "No Caucasian foreigners (i.e. Americans) will be allowed in the project area." This happened just as we were there, so the doors closed on our plans. Our two Malaysian artist friends went into a deep depression, and refused to find an alternate trip to another tribal region. This was the crux of our project, and left us on our own to find something, not knowing where or how, and without any way to find out. Back at the university we discussed our dilemma with Sabina Teuterberg, the Swiss ceramics teacher, who was supplying our new installation with artistic student-painted ceramic drainpipes cut to short lengths for drumming upon. Sabina immediately solved our problem, as she had just taken a similar expedition with "the best native guides in Malaysia", but to native Iban country instead—much closer and a river people rather than upland plains.

The Malays, who are the original settlers and who rule the country, are Muslim and "civilized" and very wary of the Ibans, the ex-"wild men of Borneo" who used to entertain guests, lead them to the river and cut their heads off for enjoyment…Now the Iban tribes have all been converted to Christianity, but it does not take long to see this as a thin veneer on a much older, deeper way of life, the wildness vibrating slightly under their surface restraint and glinting in their eyes. The Iban people originally came from Cambodia and Indonesia, and, unlike our native Americans, are the "newcomers" to the island, living here about four hundred years.

So a four-day expedition was organized, to begin on November 1st with a six-hour drive over increasingly rutted and dangerous dirt roads, ending at a huge deserted dammed up lake (Sarawak's first hydro-project) and a tiny dock and marina canteen (cafe), where we sat and nervously waited for the guides to arrive in a longboat, leading to one of the most profound experiences of our lives.

The steep banks of the River Ai were covered with towering jungle or swaths of rice plantings, Ibans tending the crops wearing giant Chinese triangular cone bamboo hats. After two hours we came to a group of ramshackle buildings on the right bank, and a wooden footbridge leading to the left bank, where a guest "lodge" sat. Several nearly naked children were running eagerly across the bridge to the dock, and my diary reads: "Oh, God—what have we gotten ourselves into?! Will the children be mobbing us for money or candy, will they be in our rooms stealing our stuff, do we have to stay right next to this woebegone series of unpainted shacks with several noisy roosters crowing, pigs running around the lodge grunting (and growling at you), children yelling, a guitar strumming, and all those dark weird people?" (Bart was thinking the same thing).

My fear lasted five minutes. The guest lodge was beautiful, if spartan. A towering dipterocarp tree was "inside", surrounded by roofed bare rooms that contained a raised wooden platform, mattresses and mosquito netting. Nails and a shelf completed the private accommodations. The floors were slatted, and windows were open holes. We threw our packs on the mattresses, and grabbing our video camera, headed for the *real* action across the bridge, where the Ibans lived.

Diary: "It is now 2,000 BC (give or take the T-shirts and a radio playing Iban pop music, a languid melodious near-Eastern style with guitars) and we pass naked boys frolicking in the river. We climb up the wooden extremely small and narrow hand-hewn steps notched from one vertical long tree and enter what feels like a tree-house! High up on stilts, the longhouse extends for hundreds of feet along a spongy bamboo walkway. To the left are a series of closed private family rooms, but ahead and on the right is a huge open social area where people sit on bamboo mats and swing their babies from hammocks, chat, and sort rice. One very old woman is weaving an intricate colorful tapestry on a long loom. Open doorways to the right lead to a terrace where the boys and men are cleaning fish, chopping wood, drying clothes on lines.

Hardly anyone looks up as we enter, except to say "hello" in the Iban language. An old man sits writing on a pad by the doorway, and James our Iban guide introduces us to this man, his father. Suddenly it all becomes real—this actually exists—a beautiful, clean, quiet, peaceful and loving group of people living all together for over four hundred years, we learn later, never moving their home from this river!" I still become choked up when I think about this, the native life we will never know in our own country, having systematically destroyed or changed it all a century ago.

The "Borneo" book[50] we had read earlier warned us about residing with the wild Ibans, about their "welcoming" ceremony of drinking into a stupor, forcing everyone to dance all night, not sleeping, etc.. My vision was, of course, of an imaginary ancient Apache tribe wearing its visitors out in an outside wild orgy, ala old "Tarzan" movies, and this must have mirrored the fear of our Muslim friends, as they brought their own food, and stayed in their room until we bodily dragged Hasnul out to attend dinner and videotape the ceremony—he was terrified!

Dinner in the dining room was one of the best we had in Asia: little succulent eggplants, tiny okra, chicken cooked in bamboo, fried just-caught fish, ferns and hot/sweet spices, beef, green beans, tiny fresh bananas, all from their gardens. Afterwards, marching single-file (as to a guillotine) we climbed up to the longhouse and on through to the rear, where the ceremony was staged. As soon as the dance began, all my previous images evaporated, for this was straight out of Bali or Java...

First, we were served their homemade "twak", or rice wine—a cloudy evil yellow concoction, tasting fizzy and bitter, and then we sat against the wall facing the thirty or so babies-to-teenagers gathered by the other wall, the adults sitting further down, and the gamelan music ensemble on the right—eight metal tuned round gongs laid flat, and a large skin drum, played by a great-grandmother and a young boy.

Journal: "Then out of the (gas lit) gloom came a supernatural vision: a man dressed in bright red and black loincloth with long bird-like tail. One of the elders, perhaps in his 60's, he did an incredibly graceful dance, his legs shapely as a woman's and very lithe, his arms gyrating outwards in what we think of as ancient Egyptian movements. At times he would stamp and shriek..." His wife performed next, dressed in bright beaded and metallic coined headdress, like a peacock, and glittering metallic and beaded dress, her face turned to the ceiling like an ancient Buddhist painting[51]. All danced with bare feet, and when her very beautiful daughter swayed and spun, a small boy called out, "Mommy!", reminding me that I was watching a *family at home* after dinner dishes had been cleared! About ten families live here, each alternating the performing for new guests. Our video friend Hasnul finally caught on artistic fire with the photographic possibilities, and from then on, until his batteries went dead (no electricity here) he spent every waking moment at the longhouse shooting everything that occurred."

Nov. 3, 1996: "I am lying on my mattress at 6 a.m. in a small hunting lodge on stilts. Hearing something, I remove my earplugs, and—deafening screeches assault my senses, literally hurling me out of my net and through the cooking area and almost falling down the ladder-like stairs. I am hardly awake, but a bugle in my brain is blaring, 'You're missing the recording of your life!' With one bare foot and one boot I stagger wildly down the river's edge to see Bart calmly crouching by the already recording tape deck. Another reason that marriage between two composers works...The morning cicadas "sing" for twenty minutes and then stop, never to sing in our earshot again. Ah, the opportunities come and go so quickly here in Borneo!"

Nov. 7: After four more incredible days with the Iban tribe, photographing and recording, we returned to our guest house at the University of Sarawak for a day of washing—ourselves and clothes, and resting. The very next day, early in the morning, began our next adventure—to Kubah National Park, a primary mountain rainforest with thousand-year-old, two hundred foot high dipterocarp trees, directly outside the growing city of Kuching. While Hasnul Saidon videotaped the surrounding jungle, Bart, Gila Rayberg (American, visiting music faculty), and I took this as an opportunity not only to record nature sounds, but to do some much longed-for hiking in these incredible majestic woods, with five foot ferns and snaky vines among the giant trees and mist-shrouded mountains. This is from my log, during a long arduous hike to a waterfall we never saw, after a day of almost fainting from the heat, losing our way several times and fighting off leeches:

"Leeches! Falling from the trees, like cold spaghetti onto your arm, and bouncing to your leg, then your hand, while you desperately resemble a corkscrew gone mad. Or one crawling up your boot. You try to pull it off. It wiggles under the eyelet of the boot. You try to crush it in there. It hides. You pull it out while blubbering, and try to dissect it with your fingernail. It doesn't break. It *is*

Indestructible Rubber! and bent on sucking you. It is a Straw using You as its Coke…

"Finally you fling it away, and after thirteen falling leeches, amid piercing continuous jungle insect screams and soaking sweat running into your eyes and gluing your clothes to you, you get an attack of the *Heebie Jeebies*. Are those giant vine-encrusted trees getting closer and closer together? Is the trail a running slippery mud sore? As you hurl yourself back to the lodge, have the ever-deafening cicadas suddenly gotten ear-splittingly louder? Does the (vague) trail go this way or that? What ever happened to the 'waterfall' you never saw after hiking five hours? As you slide dangerously down the rock and mud path you reach out for a handhold to keep from stumbling (and falling on the ground with all those…black…leeches waiting there for you) and impale yourself on a huge rattan tree with spikes up and down its bark. A giant red ant crawls up your arm to see what's going on. The temperature, hovering at 90 degrees, has just shot up five degrees, and you realize that if you start hysterically screaming, you will just sound like every other sound here!! (here in this writhing pit of Hell…*Oh God*—What happened to my 'i-love-nature' philosophy?) Welcome to the Primary Borneo Rainforest!"

The first night there, just before the next day's hike just described, we were strolling in the jungle not too far from the guest houses, where there were several giant virgin dipterocarp trees, and many birds singing. It was turning to dusk, and just as we were wrapping up our recording of the birds and getting ready to pick up our equipment before total darkness, an incredible, totally unexpected event occurred.

From far in the jungle, marching towards us, was a sound like a heavenly choir singing. We stood in the now total darkness mesmerized as the voices came closer and closer. The nearer the sounds, the more strident they became, but all were simultaneously singing the same phrase, on the same pitch, as if with a conductor! Within a few minutes, the mysterious voices were on every tree throughout the forest, and the sound was overwhelming, the jungle singing as if its heart would break (did it know how rare these virgin stands of giant trees are anymore?). I could hardly keep from weeping myself, being completely emotionally overwhelmed.

After a while another group of voices entered with different "music", and another, until a symphony of rich singers, singing in harmony, filled the fetid night air. It was the single-most profound nature music experience of my life, and we recorded it as best we could, in the vast amphitheater that is the jungle. Later when we returned to our lodgings, we were told that these singers were special black mountain cicadas, only found in the highland virgin dipterocarp jungle. When we were back at the university, I read that the tribal people greatly fear these voices, which they believe are the calls of their dead ancestors who are on the prowl to snatch living souls to carry to the (dreaded) afterworld, and the tribes-people will run away terrified from these sounds. However, times have changed since this book was written…

When we finally presented our finished composition to the university, a Kayan tribal woman, Dianne, who was a graduate student, came up and thanked us for a "wonderful experience" with the cicadas, reminding her of coming home from playing in the rice fields near her working parents, when the tribe walked through the twilight to the cicadas' music. The old fears are now only ancient pre-Christian myths, but I wonder, remembering that incredible spiritual power I felt in that jungle that very special evening in 1996…

Nature has been a very important companion in my music and art. I gave up decades ago trying to deny it and compose only "pure" music. I realized that the voices of the natural world and ours are in harmony, and we need to stop shutting out the rest of ourselves, who live outside of our little human abodes. When we finally accept who we are, we will become whole, and our music and all our arts will be immeasurably richer.

5.
CONCLUSION: ON BEING A WOMAN COMPOSER

Two roads diverge
　　in a yellow wood,
　　　　A branch stems from
　　　　　　the lesser-traveled one…
　　　　　A "twig" snakes out
　　　　　　from the tiny branch,
　　　　　　　And hanging off the edge
　　　　　　　Dangle….I—

(apologies to Robert Frost)

When I attended my first college, I wondered why anyone today would be a classical music composer. It seemed so out of touch with our society, and antiquated. Even when I was enthralled with the music, I still could not imagine such a profession in light of today's world…But the music won out. Running from this kind of life but yet composing in after-hours, there came a time when I could avoid it no longer, when the main path in the "yellow wood" was not for me to follow. I saw that either I had to continue irrevocably on with the traditional role of all-subjects school teaching for which I had been training, or turn now to the "twig" of composing serious art music that probably wouldn't sustain me very long, and which I believed no one in my family wanted for me. I agonized for years, and finally, when I could bear the pain of smothering my inner spirit no longer, I leapt out and chose the insecure way.

There was always the undertow of being a woman, of not belonging in the profession I chose. Rarely did anyone say anything, and even more rarely did I acknowledge this feeling, but it was there. There was Dr. Edward Gilday, head of the Music Department at Lowell State College, who spent a whole class period explaining why it was a waste of time for women to compose. I can remember the burning anger I felt, the intense setting of my decision to show him how wrong he (and others) were.

There was the male Norwegian undergraduate student composer who tried to discourage me from majoring in music composition at Indiana University, because "women composers are no good, and all the professors here are against them." This was a blatant lie, and I laughed in his face, but my memory still can hear his words. I played the game at times, baiting directors of ensembles with never having chosen music written by women, and abashed, they looked at my music and sometimes chose it. I turned to women's' groups, also.

Eventually my touring life with Bart insulated me against most of these problems. We tour together, write and perform together, and Bart has always been more egalitarian than I ever have been. He doesn't see any excuse for not being able to figure out manuals or technical diagrams, or applying for grants, or boldly going up to conductors, etc.. With him by my side, I have accomplished more than I ever would have alone. He is *always* there for me, and we go through life together as equals.

I am ending this book on a lighter tone than I have just taken. One last serious statement: I see little progress in this country for equal sharing of the classical composing spotlight. As I have written, in much of Asia the situation, which was more dire than ours in decades past, has turned so much around that there are more women than men pursuing this occupation, and coming over here as honored guest composers!

In 2003 at a national festival of electro-acoustic music in Arizona, I was saddened to see hundreds of men and less than a handful of women—even worse than twenty years ago. The world for new music has gotten more expensive, and women cannot afford to go to festivals, or buy the latest tech equipment, generally.

Now for the lighter side. I remember being at a Midwestern composers' conference 25 years ago, and seeing only one or two other women there. After a day of all-male company, I stopped in the Ladies' Room. As I was in the stall, another woman came in, and I panicked. I was in the wrong rest room! Then the shock came—I had so identified with the men that I forgot what sex I was! This is a true story.

There is a protocol of dressing and acting that a woman learns rather quickly in a business world of men. I was not to overplay my feminine side, so my clothes became more and more unisex. I did not flirt or play up to any of them, or go to after hours drinking parties alone, or go by myself to conventions, if I could help it. This way, I could be considered a "sister", and everyone was more relaxed. Fortunately, I was happily married, and not a threat. Even so, I remember sitting in the dark during an afternoon concert, and felt someone slipping his hand around mine as I sat there—next to Bart! I can easily imagine the loneliness and vulnerability a single woman must feel at these times, and opening one's creative soul to music affects one's whole life, making a woman extremely sensitive and easy prey.

The funniest situation happened once when I stepped out of the role as composer. I had come alone to Cleveland to perform as soprano soloist with the Cleveland Chamber Symphony in a version of *"Wilderness"* for soprano, chamber ensemble and stereo tape. Because I was now a featured performer, and a soprano at that, I decided to "dress to the nines", and wore a floor length dress and styled hair, very chic.

When the concert was over, several men and I were riding down the elevator to the parking garage below the hall—Edwin London, the conductor, Rudolph Bubalo, the director of the Cleveland State University Electronic Music Center, Virko Baley, guest composer from Nevada, and two other gentlemen. As the elevator door closed, I caught Rudy staring at me. He then blurted out, "Priscilla—you are a very beautiful woman!" There was dead tense silence. Uhoh. I knew I had to say something quick to put the others at ease...So I laughed, eyed Rudy and said, smiling, "We are in a closed elevator with all men and me, and you are telling me I am a beautiful woman?" Immediately, everyone burst out laughing, relieved (but still a little tense). Everyone relaxed at the restaurant afterwards except Rudy, who had "stepped over the line". He accidentally poured water over himself twice and was generally nervous the whole meal. I do not mean to pick on Rudy, as he was a very decent, sweet person, but just to show how fragile these situations are.

We are all human animals, after all, and emotions will surface. There have been really very few times as I have been describing, in the forty or so years I have been involved in the business (some of the worst experiences I have left out, for propriety's sake). I can think of many men who have suffered far worse sexploitation problems, from other men in the business, than I ever have as a woman.

Generally, over the years I have found the composers to be some of the best people on the planet. They are in touch with their inner selves, they exude a child-like joy and enthusiasm, they hate violence and mostly would never hurt anyone, they generally are not consumed with greed or power, but with a great love of music—to give it to others, to teach others, to deny themselves recreation time and money in order to reach for the ineffable world beyond others' imagination and use their gifts to enlighten the darkness we all walk through in this hard world. I love the world of composers, and feel so privileged to have shared my life with them for so long. And especially with my favorite of all of them, my alternate soul, my ever-creative and fiery, volatile, hard-driven and lovable husband!

I had a vision on one of our U.S. tours several years ago, just as we were starting to perform our music involving wilderness sounds. We had just finished rehearsing on stage, and I heard Beethoven's *"Ninth Symphony"* being performed in another room by the university orchestra. Suddenly I pictured the whole world in a giant circle holding hands—people, wolves, birds, whales, bees, all beings on this planet raising their individual songs to God in a glorious hymn of praise for life and the beautiful world with all of us together in it. And it was the most powerful music on Earth, the Music of Life. And the pain and struggle were part of the music, also.

Listed Works of Priscilla McLean

Composition Date	Title and Instrumentation
1959	*"Men and Angels Share"*, S.A.T.B., Piano
1960	*"In Old Wachusett's Shadow"*, S.A.T.B., Piano
1963-67	*"Four Songs in Season"*, S.A.T.B., Piano
1964	*"Trumpet and Piano Sonata"*, Bb Trumpet, Piano
1965	*"Holiday for Youth"*, Symphonic Winds
1965	*"In the Spring the Mountains Sing"*, S.A., Piano
1965-67	*"Rainer Maria Poems: Three Songs"*, Soprano Voice and Violin
1967	*"Three Children's Night Songs"*, S.S.A., Piano
1967-75	*"Variations & Mozaics on a Theme of Stravinsky"*, Symphony Orchestra
1968	*"Lighting Me as a Match"*, Tenor Voice, Violin, F Horn, Piano, Percussion
1969	*"Quartet for Strings"*, String Quartet
1970	*"There Must Be a Time"*, S.A.B., Flute, Piano
1970-71	*"Interplanes"*, Two Pianos
1970-71	*"Silver Echoes"*, S.A.T.B., Piano
1970-71	*"Snow Whispering Down"*, S.A.T.B., Piano
1971	*"On the Laughter in Our Faces"*, S.A., Piano, Two Guitars, Flute
1971-72	*"Spectra I"*, Five Percussion, Synthesizer, Prepared Piano
1972-73	*"Spectra II"*, Prepared Piano and 5 Percussion

Composition Date	Title and Instrumentation
1973	*"Night Images"*, Electronic Music on Tape
1973-74	*"Dance of Dawn"*, Electronic Music on Tape
1973-75	*"Messages"*, Chorus, 4 Soloists, Chamber Ensemble
1974-76	*"Ah-Syn!"*, Processed Autoharp & Synthesizer
1975-77	*"Invisible Chariots"*, Electronic Music on Tape
1977	*"Fire & Ice"*, Tenor/Bass Trombone & Prepared Piano
1977-78	*"Beneath the Horizon I"*, Tuba Quartet & Stereo Tape
1978-79	*"Beneath the Horizon III"*, Tuba Solo & Stereo Tape, DVD
1979-80	*"Fantasies for Adults and Other Children"*, Sop. Voice, Piano: two performers
1979-82	*"The Inner Universe"*, Prepared Piano and Stereo Tape
1982	*"Beneath the Horizon"*, Stereo Tape, Fade and dissolve Slides, now DVD
1983-84	*"O Beautiful Suburbia!"*, Soprano, Autoharp, Narrator, Bicycle Wheel, Stereo Tp.
1983-86	*"A Magic Dwells"*, Symphony Orchestra and Stereo Tape
1984	*"Elan! A Dance to all Rising Things from the Earth"*, Fl, Vln, 'Cello, Piano, Perc.
1984-85	*"Invocation"*, Clariflute, S.A.T.B. Chorus, Percussion, Bicycle Wheel, Stereo Tape
1985	*"On Wings of Song"*, Soprano Voice, Bicycle Wheel, Stereo Tape
1985-88	*"Wilderness"*, Soprano Voice, Ten Instruments, Stereo Tape
1988	*"In Celebration"*, S.A.T.B. Chorus, Piano, Percussion, Stereo Tape
1988-89	***"Rainforest"*** (installation)*, Two Synthesizers, Two Microphones, Bicycle Wheel, Table containing small instruments, Digital Processers, F& D Slides/Video
1988-89	*"Voices of the Wild"*, Electronic Music Soloist and Symphony Orchestra
1989-90	*"The Dance of Shiva"*, Electronic Tape, F& D Slides/Video

Composition Date	Title and Instrumentation
1989-90	*"Wilderness"*, Soprano Voice, Flexatone, Stereo Tape
1990	*"Flight Beyond"*, Electronic Music on Tape
1991-92	*"Everything Awakening Alert and Joyful!"*, Narrator and Symphony Orchestra
1992	*"Sage Songs About Life! (and Thyme...)"*, Soprano Voice and Piano
1992-93	*"Rainforest Images"**, Electro-Acoustic Music on Tape
1993-94	*"Where the Wild Geese Go"*, Bb Clarinet & Stereo Tape
1994	*"Rainforest Images I"**, Electro-Acoustic Music and Video (video by Hasnul Jamal Saidon)
1994	*"Rainforest Images II"**, Electro-Acoustic Music and Video (video by Hasnul Jamal Saidon)
1995	*"Earth Song"**, Digitally Processed Chamber Ensemble, F& D Slides
1995	*"In the Beginning"*, Soprano Voice, Digital Processors, Stereo Tape, Video (video by A.J. Jannone)
1996-00	*"Jambori Rimba"**, Soprano Voice, Digital Processors, Soprano Recorder, Percussion, Stereo Tape, Video (video by Hasnul Jamal Saidon)
1996-97	*"Jambori Rimba"** (Installation), Electro-Acoustic Ensemble, Stereo Tape, Video, Slides, Dance Station with Digital Processing
1997	*"Amazon"**, Sop. Voice, Electro-Acous. Chamber Ens., Digital Proc., F&D Slides
1997	*"Desert Spring"** (installation), Elec-Acous. Ensemble, Stereo Tape, F&D Slides
1999	*"Desert Voices"*, Midi Violin, Digital Processors, Stereo Tape
1999	*"The Ultimate Symphonius 2000"**, Electro-Acoustic Ensemble, Stereo Tape, Video**, F&D Slides, Dance Station with Digital Processing
2000-01	*"Angels of Delirium"*, Electronic Music on Tape

Composition Date	Title and Instrumentation
2000-01	"Symphony of Seasons: "Jewels of January", Electronic Music and Video**
2001	"MILLing in the ENNIUM"*, Electronic Music and Video**
2001	"Symphony of Seasons: "The Eye of Spring", Electronic Music and Video**
2001-2	"Symphony of Seasons: "Autumn Requiem"*, Elec-Acous Music Ens and Video**
2001-3	"Symphony of Seasons: "July Dance", Electronic Music and Video**
2003-04	"Xaakalawe" (Flowing), Electronic Music and Video**
2002-4	"Sunburst Songs", [Four Haiku for Winter], Soprano Voice and Piano
2005	"Cyber-lament", Electro-Acoustic Music on Tape

*Collaboration with Barton McLean   **Video by Priscilla McLean

Recordings and Music Publishers

CD Recordings (Discography):

Capstone Records CPS-8617 CD: *"Rainforest Images"*, *"On Wings of Song"*.

Capstone Records CPS-8622 CD: *"Gods, Demons, and the Earth"*: *"Wilderness"*, *"Dance of Shiva"*.

Capstone Records CPS-8637 CD: *"The Electric Performer"*: *"The Inner Universe"*, *"Where the Wild Geese Go"*.

Capstone Records CPS-8663 CD: *"Fantasies for Adults and Other Children—Vocal Music of Priscilla McLean"*: *"Fantasies for Adults and Other Children"*, *"In the Beginning"*, *"Wilderness"*, *"Sage Songs of Life and Thyme"*.

Composers Recordings, Inc., CRI CD 764 (now available under New World Records): *"The McLean Mix and the Golden Age of Electronic Music"*: *"Invisible Chariots"*, *"Dance of Dawn"*, *"Night Images"*.

Vinyl Recordings (Discography)–Some Still Available:

Composers Recordings, Inc. CRI SD 335: *"Dance of Dawn"*.

Advance Recordings FGR 19S: *"Interplanes"*.

Folkways Recordings, FTS 33450: *"Invisible Chariots"*

Folkways Recordings, FPX 60503: *"Electronic Music from the Outside In"*, Mvt.1 of *"Invisible Chariots, "Night Images"*.

Louisville Orchestra First Edition Records LS 762: *"Variations & Mozaics on a Theme of Stravinsky"*.

Opus One Records #96: *"Beneath the Horizon III"*, *"The Inner Universe: Salt Canyons"*.

Cassette–MLC Publications, *"In Wilderness is the Preservation of the World"*: *"On Wings of Song", "Invocation", "O Beautiful Suburbia!"*

Principal Music Publisher: MLC Publications, 55 Coon Brook Rd., Petersburgh, NY 12138.

Others: Bourne Co., NY, NY: *"Holiday for Youth", "In the Spring the Mountains Sing"*.

Elkan Vogel Co. Inc., Philadelphia, PA.: *"Men and Angels Share"*

Major Articles, Books, and Biographical Descriptions:

Books as Reference, aka Priscilla McLean

The Art of Electronic Music, Tom Darter, Ed., Quill/A Keyboard Book, NY, 1984: "Artists of Electronic Music: Barton and Priscilla McLean", pp. 231-235.

Bakers Biographical Dictionary, 1989, 1996.

Electric Sound by Joel Chadabe, under *"Where Are We Going?"* pp. 330-331, Prentice-Hall International, Inc. 1997.

International Encylopaedia of Women Composers, A.J. Cohen, Editor. New York, NY, 1981, 1985.

International Who's Who in Music and Musicians' Directory: 10th-14th Ed., International Biographical Centre, Cambridge, England, 1984, '87, '94, '98, '00, '02, '04.

Introduction to Contemporary Music by Joseph Machlis, Third Ed. W.W. Norton & Co., New York, NY. 1984.

On the Wires of Our Nerves: The Art of Electronic Music by Robin J. Heifetz, 1990: Reprint of *"Fire and Ice: A Query"* by Priscilla McLean, pp. 148-154.

The Electronic Arts of Sound and Light by Ronald Pellegrino, Van Nostrand Reinhold Co. New York, Cincinnati, Toronto, London, Melbourne, 1983.

The New Grove Dictionary of Music, Ed. by Barbara Petersen, Lesley A. Wright, 1994, 1999.

Who's Who in American Music, Carol Borland, Ed. Jacques Cattell Press, Tempe, AZ 1983.

Women Composers, Conductors, and Musicians of the Twentieth Century: Selected Biographies, Vol. III by Jane Weiner LePage, The Scarecrow Press, Inc., Metuchen, NJ & London, 1988: "Priscilla McLean", pp. 128-146.

Unsung by Christine Ammer, Amadeus Press, Milwaukee, WI, 2001.

Articles by Priscilla McLean*

"At North Texas State: Computer Music", Musical America Magazine, Mar.1982, pp. 34, 40.

"Fire & Ice: A Query", Perspectives of New Music, Seattle, WA, Fall/Winter 1977, Vol. 16/1, pp. 205-11.

"Planting the Seeds of Music Technology in Borneo", Journal SEAMUS, Vol. XIII#1, Apr. 1998, pp. 4-7.

"Reflections on 'Finale' and My Last Orchestral Piece", Journal SEAMUS, Vol. 8#2, 10/93, pp. 8-11.

"The Albany Symphony's Daring Path", Musical America Magazine, New York, NY, April 1985, pp. 28-29.

"Thoughts As a (Woman) Composer", Perspectives of New Music, Fall '81/Spring/ '82, Vol. 20, #1&2.

"Tod Machover's New 'Brain Opera', A Review", Journal SEAMUS, Vol. XI, #2, Nov. 1996, pp. 14-16.

"To Make a Universe of Sound, Vision 3", Paid My Dues, Vol. 11#4, Summer 1978, pp. 10-11, 39.

"Tunugan '97, Asian Composers League Festival: A Report", SCI Newsletter, June/ July 1997, Vol. 27 #6, pp. 4-5.

"Vladimir Ussachevsky and Otto Luening: 1952 Electronic Tape Music; the First Compositions–an Historic Edition", Music Library "Notes", Mar. 1978, pp. 716-717.

"Zagreb's Music Biennale No. 11", Musical America Magazine, Oct. 1981, pp. 33-34.

Articles by Priscilla and Barton McLean*

"Composing with Sounds of the Wilderness", ADIRONDAC Magazine, Feb./Mar. 1988, pp.17-18.

"The McLean Mix: Inner Tension of the Surrealistic", AWC (American Women Composers) NEWS, Vol. III #3, Jan. 1982, pp. 8-13.

"The McLean Mix Muses Upon the Ultimate Musical Instrument", Experimental Musical Instruments, Vol. 10#1 Sept. 1994, pp. 20-23.

"The McLean Mix Tours Australia: First Impressions", Sounds Australian, (Journal of Australian Music), No.28, Summer '90, pp. 32-33.

*Major articles can be read on the McLean website at:
http://members.cisbec.net/mclmix/articlesreviews.html

Priscilla and Barton McLean, Composers, Home Page Website:
http://members.cisbec.net/mclmix/index.html

McLean Email Address: mclmix@cisbec.net

Musical excerpts of the compositions described in Section THREE can be heard by accessing the American Music Center's "New Music Jukebox" web-site as follows—http://www.newmusicjukebox.org/composers/ Register and click on McLean, Priscilla. List of works with icons will appear. Click on Sound-file icon for the piece you intend to hear. Excerpts are from two to seven minutes in length.

To obtain a high quality CD of the excerpted musical pieces of Section THREE, the reader is asked to send a check or institutional purchase order for $15.00 to: Priscilla McLean, MLC Publications, 55 Coon Brook Rd., Peters-burgh, NY 12138. Make check out to "Priscilla McLean", and include a paper with your name and address and request for "CD for Section THREE".

Endnotes

1. Cedric Wright, "Words of the Earth", ed. Nancy Newhall, Sierra Club Books, San Francisco, CA, 1960, p.38.

2. Carl Sandburg, "Isle of Patmos" from "Harvest Poems 1910-1960", Harvest Books, Harcourt, Brace & World, Inc., New York 1960, pp. 31-32.

3. "Through the Looking-Glass" by Lewis Carroll, Random House, NY, 1946, p.18.

4. All programming and processing redone in 2004 by Barton McLean, using the MAX/MSP Program.

5. Small high-bouncing hard rubber balls

6. The use of real, not synthesized sounds, as in musical instruments or sounds from the world, usually electronically altered afterwards.

7. Composed folk music of the genre of the 1960's

8. The birth control pill, newly available at this time, was only given to married women in Massachusetts.

9. "Pictures at an Exhibition" was orchestrated by Maurice Ravel.

10. All published music by Priscilla and Barton McLean is currently available through MLC Publications, 55 Coon Brook Rd., Petersburgh, NY 12138.

11. Prominent composer, living in New York City, who founded the Group for Contemporary Music

12. Famous German 20th Century composer

13. Eminent international cellist

14. A clearly defined melodic phrase, repeated persistently

15. Short early 20th Century orchestral piece

16. Indiana University at South Bend

17. "Father" of electronic music in America

18. "On the Wires of Our Nerves: The Art of Electroacoustic Music", ed. by Robin Julian Heifetz, Bucknell University Press, Lewisburg/London/Toronto, 1989, pp.148-154.

    "Fire & Ice: A Query". along with McLean's other published articles, can be read on the Web at: http://www.members.cisbec. net/mclmix/articlesreviews.html

19. CRI SD 335, re-mastered to a CRI CD 764 and now available through New World Records.

20. "The McLean Mix & The Golden Age of Electronic Music", CRI CD 764, available through New World Records.

21. Both "Dance of Dawn" and "Invisible Chariots" are on CRI CD 764.

22. Premiere colony in the U.S. for creative artists of all disciplines.

23. December 2002

24. International Society for Contemporary Music

25. Inspired, I am sure, by Henry Cowell's piano piece "Banshee"

26. Capstone Records CPS-8637 CD, "Music of Priscilla & Barton McLean—The Electric Performer".

27. This is the same quotation as "In Wildness is the Preservation of the World". Books vary on the actual quotation from Thoreau's essay.

28. "Alaskan Eskimo Songs and Stories", Lorraine Koranda, Ed., Alaskan Festival of Music, 1972

29. Prominent, innovative American composer

30. Jimmy Killigivuk from Point Hope, Alaska: Alaskan Festival of Music recording, 1972

31. Doubleday, Page, & Co., Garden City, NY, 1911, pp. 107-108.

32. Ewan Clarkson, "Wolf Country", E.P. Dutton & Co., Inc., NY 1975, p.123.

33. "The breath of life" from Lao Tsu, "The Way of Life" (Tau), China, 604 B.C. and King James version: "Holy Bible", Genesis. "The tree of life" from King James version: "Holy Bible", New Testament, and is a sacred creation symbol for most cultures of the world. "Mirror of Creation" from the Ankh, from Egyptian religion. "Ye are the branches" from Holy Bible,

New Testament. "All colors of the world" from Creation myth of the American Wintu Indians. "It was not born; it sees not and is not seen" from Lao Tsu: "The Way of Life (Tau)". "A magic dwells at each beginning" from Hermann Hesse: "poem from "Magister Ludi".

34. Lao Tsu, China, 604 B.C.

35. The structure of the work involves progressive extension of the rhythmic and melodic ostinati in the orchestra (the "life"), reaching a climax when the tape proclaims: "All colors of the world" and sustaining a solo orchestra section afterwards, gradually dying down as the last phrases are heard. Harmonically, the tape provides a dense chord against which the other sounds on tape and in the orchestra progress from simple to complex and back to simple chordal structures at the end.

36. "Dance of Shiva" is available on Capstone Records—"Gods, Demons, and the Earth", CPS-8622 CD.

37. "Rainforest Images" divides loosely into five movements, although the work is continuous. Mvt. One (sections 1,2,3) introduces the rainforest ambiance through taped Peruvian and Australian bird calls over a steady drone, with string tremolos performed by Barton McLean on the violin. Sections 2-3 introduce the myth, chanted by Priscilla McLean, mixed with music by Australians Kerrie Ryan and Ivana Troselj, voices, and Brendan Dickie on the didgeridoo, a large hollowed-out log with beeswax mouthpiece, made by the Aborigines. Mvt. Two (sections 4-5) is primal and rawly rhythmic, after a meditative bird and violin transition section, improvised by Barton McLean on the soprano recorder with sampled percussion.

Mvt. Three (sections 6-7) begins with a soliloquy played by a hybrid instrument used often in McLean Mix performances, a clariflute (clarinet mouthpiece on a recorder body), improvised by Barton McLean. Section 7 is the longest and most rhythmic and wild vocal/didgeridoo section, by the three Australians, and contains the other chanted message of the piece, created by Ivana Troselj, spun in and out of focus: "Talk, words, sounds. Words, sounds, talk, movement. Words, words from afar, sounds that reach your ears…input from those who don't necessarily want to hear, they say words all the time. People don't want to know what is happening to them, to the earth. They want to listen only to themselves. But sometimes they must listen to others. They can't remain isolated in their towers of glass and steel, and push their pencils across the table...They have to change their words..." Mvt. Four (sections 8-9) begins with a medley of ethereal bird songs, continuing with an interlude of plaintive and poignant calls performed by Priscilla McLean on the recorder, and Barton McLean on the clariflute. Mvt. Five brings back the Wintu myth and closes with singing by Priscilla McLean and chants by Panaiotis, vocalist and sound technician, whose voice has been heard throughout the piece in disguised drones.

38. "In the beginning there was no sun, no moon, no stars. All was dark, and everywhere there was only water." (ancient Maidu belief) Basically the form of the piece is very simple. Beginning with the birth-cry described, fragments of creation myths are heard enmeshed in bubbly sounds and nonsense syllables. As the music unfolds, the phrases are clearer and longer, and the music builds to a large climax, which explodes and disintegrates into word fragments, cries, and wild sounds. The voice becomes a choir of ethereal chords, and the piece ends with a plaintive scream-call, which evokes the cry of whales deep in the ocean.

39. "Olelbus, the Creator, built a great and awesome sweat-house..." from North American Wintu Indian creation myth.

40. Our performance was outside, in the music department courtyard. A typhoon had just grazed the islands, and several students were kept busy holding together the blowing video screen during "Rainforest Images". I sang "Wilderness" to a wild, dark roiling sky, complete with full moon.

41. Music for one singing part of a chorus, one large score being held by the group

42. Larry Austin–prominent U.S. composer, often with electro-acoustic music, and kindred spirit

43. Eminent international composer and conductor

44. American Society of University Composers, now called Society of Composers.

45. Designed by Donald Buchla, it was a custom-made analog synthesizer and effects processor.

46. "In Celebration...of the Historic Alaskan Wilderness Act and of All Consciousnesses of Our Bond with Nature", for SATB Chorus, Piano, Stereo Tape, and Solo Percussionist by Priscilla McLean.

47. One of America's most famous women composers, and also the mother of Pete Seeger, famous composer/folksinger.

48. Vivian Fine died in an automobile accident in 1999.

49. "Electronic Music from the Outside In" and "Computer Music from the Outside In", now available as CDs from Smithsonian Records.

50. "Fielding's Borneo" by Robert Young Pelton, Fielding Worldwide, Inc. Redondo Beach, CA, 1995.

51. This dance was filmed and is used in our "Jambori Rimba" video for our touring.

978-0-595-37548-6
0-595-37548-0